Theorizing Pedagogic

M000275166

Pedagogical interaction can be observed through many different landscapes, such as the graduate seminar, the writing skills center, the after-school literacy program, adult English-as-a-second-language (ESL) classrooms, and post-observation conferences. By viewing these settings through the lens of conversation analysis, this volume lays the groundwork for three principles of pedagogical interaction: competence, complexity, and contingency. The author explores these principles and how they inform what makes a good teacher, how people learn, and why certain pedagogical encounters are more enlightening than others. Drawn from the author's original research in various pedagogical settings, this volume collects empirical insights from conversation analysis and contributes to theory building.

Theorizing Pedagogical Interaction will appeal to students and scholars in applied linguistics, educational linguistics, and communication studies who are interested in the discourse of teaching and learning.

Hansun Zhang Waring is associate professor of applied linguistics and TESOL (Teaching English to Speakers of Other Languages) at Teachers College, Columbia University, United States.

Routledge Research in Education

Theorizing Pedagogical Interaction

Insights from Conversation Analysis

Hansun Zhang Waring

Routledge
Taylor & Francis Group

LONDON AND NEW YORK

First published 2016
by Routledge

2 Park Square, Milton Park, Abingdon, Oxon OX14 4RN
711 Third Avenue, New York, NY 10017, USA

Routledge is an imprint of the Taylor & Francis Group, an informa business

First issued in paperback 2017

Copyright © 2016 Taylor & Francis

Library of Congress Cataloging-in-Publication Data
A catalog record for this title has been requested.

ISBN: 978-1-138-80695-5 (hbk)
ISBN: 978-1-138-08610-4 (pbk)

Typeset in Sabon
by Apex CoVantage, LLC

For Baba

Contents

Acknowledgments

In the spring of 2013, I was going through my third-year review as a tenure-track assistant professor at Teachers College, Columbia University. My department chair at the time was Ruth Vinz, a professor of English education who taught middle and high school for 23 years before coming to Teachers College. I had heard brilliant tales of "the amazing Ms. Vinz" before ever meeting her in person. It turned out that Ruth was as brilliant with teenagers as with us junior faculty. During the review meeting, Ruth enumerated my department colleagues' many generous compliments on my work. At the same time, there were clearly some questions of how the close analyses I did contributed to theory building. I no longer remember how the conversation ran off precisely, but it was sheer magic that Ruth was able to make me listen with an utterly open mind to an otherwise devastating critique. I think that was because, throughout that conversation, she was able to make me feel, with great certainty, that my work was respected and that I was taken seriously. While carefully nudging me to envision the meaning of my meticulous findings on a larger canvas, at one point, Ruth slightly leaned forward, and in a most unassuming, perceptive voice, wondered, "Do you mean principles (of teaching/classroom interaction)?" That was an insight I would never have arrived at on my own. It was by no coincidence then, when the time came for me to articulate the big messages of my scholarship, those messages emerged as the *principles* of competence, complexity, and contingency (CCC). In numerous ways, Ruth embodies the CCC of this book.

Around the same time, upon Kristen di Gennaro recommendation, I was invited to deliver a plenary address at the Pace University Faculty Institute in New York City. Because of my work as a classroom discourse analyst, I was expected to say something useful about teaching, and my audience would be a group of college professors of a variety of subjects. I had never spoken to colleagues outside applied linguistics and outside the field of language and social interaction before. It was a petrifying experience. For the first time as an academic, I was forced to think about how to explain, in nontechnical language, to a somewhat general audience what I did and why that mattered. I was forced to convey the big picture in a way that was entirely unfamiliar to me. Miraculously and to my great relief, as I took a step back to reach for the possibility of a big picture, the bits and pieces that populated the kaleidoscope of my work started to self-organize and coalesce into a few recurring themes. In the end, in the introduction to my talk, I promised to say something potentially useful about the *language* of teaching, and that was where the CCC made its very first, and only, public appearance to date. It clearly struck a chord, and one professor said to me after the talk that she would love to read my Deborah Tannen book for teachers. Had my talk at Pace been received with any less interest and resonance, I would not have pursued this book project with the same faith and passion as I have. Although my understandings of CCC have evolved in many ways since then, my public engagement with the colleagues at Pace was unquestionably the genesis of this book.

I owe much of my training as a conversation analyst to the 2004 Conversation Analysis Advanced Studies Institute (CA ASI) at UCLA, led by Manny Schegloff and Gene Lerner, as well as the 2005 Rutgers Conversation Analysis Summer Workshop, led by Manny Schegloff, John Heritage, Anita Pomerantz, and Gene Lerner. Over the years, I also have learned a great deal from my fellow analysts at our monthly meetings of the Language and Social Interaction Working Group (LANSI) data session on the campus of Teachers College, Columbia University in New York City. The final version of this book makes infinitely more sense because of the many suggestions offered by friends, colleagues, and students as well as the two anonymous reviewers at Routledge. For their generosity and insights, I would like to thank Nancy Boblett, Catherine Box, Ignasi Clemente, Sarah Creider, Donna Delprete, Joan Kelly Hall, Rong Rong Le, Heidi Liu, Carol Lo, Hugh Mehan, Saerhim Oh, Elizabeth Reddington, Gahye Song, Nadja Tadic, Junko Takahasho, Santoi Wagner, Jean Wong, and Di Yu.

My husband Michael is the only person in the world who is able to laugh at what I write and make me laugh along, and my six-year-old daughter Zoe reminds me every day that even though I'm the mommy, I don't know everything. Because of them, I know not to take myself too seriously.

This book is a tribute to the amazing teachers I have had, observed, and studied. Baba (dad) was the first person who made me realize what a difference a good teacher could make. He taught me violin with liberating clarity, and I could always count on him to explain complex ideas with simple elegance. Diagnosed with liver cancer in March 2014 around the same time I signed this book contract, Baba passed away only four months later soon after his 74th birthday. This book is dedicated to him.

1   Introduction

As a language teacher, a writing center tutor, a teacher educator, an applied linguistics professor, as well as a student of many years, I have experienced firsthand the myriad tensions and nuances of pedagogical encounters. These experiences are the emotional core of my research as I traverse the terrains of the pedagogical landscape. Equipped with the powerful lens of conversation analysis (CA; see Chapter 3), I have been gifted with the vision of "a world in a grain of sand" (William Blake, *Auguries of Innocence*). Every direction I look, I learn just a little bit more about what it means to navigate the intricacies of teaching and learning. The journey is sometimes frustrating with the unknowns that lie ahead but endlessly riveting. I have had no reason to pause and survey the larger landscape—to theorize. After all, the data speak for themselves, and making incremental discoveries has been all-consuming. I have, in other words, been an obsessive explorer—until recently, when a set of big messages started to flash across my mental screen repeatedly and relentlessly. It occurred to me that they have been latent in my empirical work over the years but remained unarticulated and that perhaps, they are the organic outcomes of such accumulative gains. They are the forest of my trees, and my forest demands to be heard, not just in my private sphere but on a public platform. I find that platform in this book.

CA AND THEORY

Despite the mounting momentum of CA work on a wide range of ordinary and institutional encounters (e.g., Antaki, 2011; Drew & Heritage, 1992; Sidnell & Stivers, 2013), conversation analysts have generally shied away from theories or theorizing. This is not surprising given CA's trademark adherence to disciplined empirical work. The concept of "unmotivated looking" (Psathas, 1995, p. 45) perhaps best captures this "atheoretical" stance. That is, free from any preformulated theorizing, the analyst can proceed with an open mind as s/he examines any naturally occurring data gathered from any source, without treating any aspect of that data as more or less significant a priori.

It is crucial, however, to register that the relationship between CA and theory is not a clear-cut one, and CA itself is not an atheoretical enterprise. Insofar as a theory is a view of how things work (Shoemaker, Tankard, & Lasorsam, 2004), CA is not free from such a view, especially when it comes to social interaction. Psathas (1995) refers to CA as a "theoretical and methodological approach" (p. 3). Kasper and Wagner (2011) also speak of the "theoretical principles" of CA (p. 116). "Although perhaps theoretically uncommitted," as Larsen-Freeman (2004) observes, "CA surely is committed to a social view of language, and by extension here, to a social view of language acquisition" (p. 605). Indeed, there are certain epistemological assumptions that drive CA inquiries (Heritage, 2008).

Drawn from Harold Garfinkel's (1967) ethnomethodology and Erving Goffman's (1967) interaction order, CA as a theoretical framework comprises the following set of assumptions that prioritize analytic induction (ten Have, 2007) and participant orientations (Schegloff & Sacks, 1973): (1) social interaction is orderly at all points—that is, no detail can be dismissed a priori; (2) participants orient to that order themselves—that is, order is not a result of the analyst's conceptions or any preformulated theoretical categories; (3) such order can be discovered and described by examining the details of interaction. By engaging in analytic induction (Pomerantz, 1990) or abductive reasoning (Svennevig, 2001), CA analysts discover in each case a theory that underpins the practices of social interaction. In addition, CA offers a range of theoretical tools for analyzing social interaction. Earlier findings such as turn-constructional unit (TCU), transition-relevance place (TRP), adjacency pair (AP), and preference became conceptual tools for later discoveries. Notably, such theoretical tools are not conceived in the abstract but grounded in careful descriptions of interactional data. As Clayman and Gill (2004) remind us, the empirical findings of past research form "a well-developed conceptual foundation" that guides CA research (p. 590), which has undoubtedly been making sustained contributions to a theory of social interaction. After all, "[th]ere is a delicate form of the empirical which identifies itself so intimately with its object that it thereby becomes theory" (Johann Wolfgan von Goethe, 1829 in Schegloff, 2007). Still, conversation analysts are not in the habit of articulating theories. In this book, I venture that articulation vis-à-vis a domain very close to my heart. This project, therefore, embodies a modest step toward pushing that boundary between the empirical and the theoretical in the domain of pedagogical interaction.

Within applied linguistics, the issue of CA and theory has been taken up in discussions of whether or how it can contribute to describing and explaining second-language acquisition (SLA), that is, to building a theory of SLA (e.g., Gass, 2004; Hall, 2004; He, 2004; Hellermann, 2008; Kasper, 1997; Larsen-Freeman, 2004; Liddicoat, 1997; Markee, 1994). Wong (1994) was among the first to argue for the relevance of CA in applied linguistics and SLA. As she writes, "a CA methodological framework may provide a sounder foundation for the study of interactive SLA than SLA approaches that are only focused on linguistic form" (Wong, 2000, p. 264). In their introduction to the special issue of *The Modern Language Journal*, Markee and Kasper (2004) provide a broad spectrum of viewpoints with regard to CA's viability as an approach to SLA. While objections to such viability emphasize the cognitive nature of learning, CA's identity as a behavioral science, and language acquisition as a separate process from language use, proponents view language learning as a social activity accomplished in and through interaction, where socially shared cognition may be located, thereby learning observed. Markee and Kasper (2004), for example, maintain that CA has much to offer of theoretical interest about the nature of language, language learning, and learner identities in SLA. For conversation analysts, language is a local and collaborative achievement, learning is a process accomplished in and through talk, and learner identities are permeable categories deployed in situ as resources for learning. Hall (2004) boldly explores CA as a theoretical approach to studying language acquisition (p. 610) as such:

> If what we know as language knowledge is really a dynamic, constantly evolving set of recurring regularities, the shapes of which emerge from their frequent and predictable use, and if use is fundamentally interactional, then in order to understand how language develops and the outcomes that arise in terms of acquired language knowledge, we need to begin our examinations with the interactional practices that learners are involved in.

Kasper (2009) builds her argument around the notion of socially shared cognition (cf. Goodwin, 1994), noting that if learning is participation, CA illuminates what exactly participation means and how learning happens during that participation (pp. 31–32):

> The understandings that emerge through the co-participants' orientation to sequence organization and turn progression are also what enable the participating L2 speakers to notice and understand new pragmatic meanings and forms, and to register how the co-participant understands the L2 speaker's contributions. In this way, L2 development is located in socially shared cognition as a practical accomplishment.

In perhaps one of the most exciting recent developments in connecting CA and learning, Hall, Hellermann, and Pekarek Doehler's (2011) edited volume showcases how CA can be fruitfully utilized to examine the nature and development of second language (L2) interactional competence. A useful review of how both longitudinal and cross-sectional CA studies illuminate the learning process also can be found in Seedhouse (2011). In short, the applied linguistic engagement with CA and its connection to theory to date has revolved around questions of learning. This book launches a related, and perhaps somewhat overlapping, engagement. Rather than exploring CA's role in elucidating learning (e.g., what gets learned, when it gets learned, and how it gets learned), I show how CA findings can contribute to building a theory of teaching—by explicating how teacher conduct can shape opportunities of learning, or put simply, what lies at the heart and soul of good teaching beyond technical aspects such as lesson planning and classroom management.

THEORIZING EDUCATIONAL DISCOURSE

The intellectual giants of education, sociology, psychology, and applied linguistics over the past four decades have installed major advancement in our thinking about teaching and learning in the classroom. Their theorizing rests firmly on the stories and evidence drawn from data in the classrooms they are intimately familiar with as teachers and researchers. Resonating throughout their pursuits are questions such as how classroom interaction in general, or teacher talk in particular, shapes who gets to learn, what gets learned, and how it gets learned. From each of them, we have inherited a particular view or theory of how educational discourse works. This book continues the long tradition of theorizing educational discourse from a deeply empirical landscape.

As a British school teacher and researcher, Douglas Barnes (1976/1992) was perhaps the first to argue for the centrality of language in the classroom, where language is considered not only the communication system of the classroom but also a means of learning. For Barnes, there is no such a thing as curriculum on the one hand and the communication used to deliver that curriculum on the other. The communication ultimately determines what is learned. Communication *is* curriculum. Teachers, for example, play an important role in creating interaction that is either explorative or *final draft*, which in turn leads to different types of learning: while explorative talk promotes learner responsibility in the learning process, *final drafts* treat learners as receptacles of authoritative knowledge; the former prioritizes understanding and the latter judging.

In *Classroom Discourse: The Language of Teaching and Learning*, Cazden (2001) also posits that communication is central to educational institutions and that classroom discourse is a communication system of its own: "[d]ifferences in how something is said, and even when, can be matters of only temporary adjustment, or they can seriously impair effective teaching and accurate evaluation" (p. 3). Drawing from a broad range of research examples in K–12 settings in the United States as well as her background as a primary grade teacher and a university researcher, Cazden offers a framework for understanding the classroom communication system as one that varies by speaking rights and listening responsibilities, teacher questions, pace and sequence, and routines and tests. Understanding that such varia-tions engender differential learning opportunities, according to Cazden, can help teachers develop a repertoire of lesson structures and teaching styles to best support student learning.

Edwards and Mercer (1987) offer the most unsettling visions of how teacher talk can negatively affect student learning. Beginning with the premise that all education is about the development of common knowl-edge or shared understanding, Edwards and Mercer (1987) analyze video-recorded school lessons with groups of 8- and 10-year-olds in Great Britain and show how knowledge is presented, received, shared, controlled, nego-tiated, understood, and misunderstood by teachers and children during classroom interaction. Their inquiries yield a set of stunning insights that challenge the progressive ideology at the time (and that is still prevalent in American education today), which posits that the child is best left to be making discoveries on his or her own through a learning-by-doing model. One of their most poignant arguments, in my view, is that developing com-mon knowledge in part hinges upon sharing a set of educational ground rules, but against the backdrop of child-centered ideology, such rules are typically left implicit, which hampers the development of common knowl-edge. In a desert island activity, for example, a main goal for the teacher is to help children build knowledge, through their own experience, of how a society should work and use concepts such as division of labor, coopera-tion, and interdependence to manage the island. When asked what they learned after the activity, one child said, "I would never go on a boat trip again." As Edwards and Mercer (1987) point out, the children were left on their own to infer the lessons of the activity, and there was no evidence that they ever did:

> When teachers go out of their way to avoid offering pupils overt help in making sense of their experiences, the consequences may be that the usefulness of those experiences is lost . . . For many pupils, learning from teachers must appear to be a mysterious and arbitrarily difficult process, the solution to which may be to concentrate on trying to do and say what appears to be expected—a basically "ritual" solution.
>
> (Edwards & Mercer, 1987, p. 169)

In the end, "the teacher's role as authoritative bearer of the ready-made knowledge simply finds alternative, more subtle means of realizing itself than the crudities of brute 'transmission'" (p. 163).

Tharp and Gallimore's (1988) *Rousing Minds to Life: Teaching, Learning, and Schooling in Social Context* is perhaps the most explicit in articulating a theory of teaching within the Vygotskyan sociocultural framework. As the authors so perceptively proclaim, despite recurrent national conversations on impoverished teaching in the United States, efforts of reform rarely went beyond policy arguments such as attracting stronger teachers with better pay or increasing the content-to-method course ratios in teacher education programs. None addressed the teaching practice itself. This absence of attention to the act of teaching itself is dramatized in the following remarks:

> In American classrooms, now and since the 19th century, teachers generally act as if students are supposed to learn on their own. Teachers are not taught to teach, and most often they do not teach.
>
> (Tharp & Gallimore, 1988, p. 3)

Drawing examples from a small elementary school they designed and built, the authors demonstrate how teaching must be redefined as assisting performance, what responsive assistance looks like, and what such assistance entails.

Working from within the school systems in the UK and the United States, these scholars are concerned about the quality of classroom interaction, the teacher's role in controlling that quality, and the relationship between that quality and student learning. Each has persuasively argued for the absolute centrality of communication in educational discourse, whether that communication is fashioned to obstruct learning, facilitate learning, or produce different kinds of learning. Each has offered us a theory of educational discourse that has become foundational in our thinking, research, and practice.

The current book continues this tradition of building empirically based theories but does so from a CA perspective (see Chapter 3). In particular, proceeding from the assumption that exalts the primacy of communication in classroom interaction, I offer a set of proposals addressed to three particular aspects of this communication—those that revolve around what teachers do. Given my interest in building a theory of teaching, I believe these proposals encapsulate the defining features of what it means to do teaching, not just inside the walls of the classroom but across a broad range of pedagogical contexts including second-language classrooms, graduate seminars, tutoring sessions with children and adults, and post-observation conferences in teacher education programs. I have come to call these proposals principles given the robustness of evidence both within and across contexts that lends credence to their reality:

1. Competence: achieving competence entails assuming competence.
2. Complexity: teacher talk is multivocalic (i.e., imbued with multiple voices).
3. Contingency: teaching requires being responsive to the moment.

Although individual chapters are devoted to each principle, the CCC will be briefly explicated in the next section to provide an initial sampling. For the purpose of this book, I use *teacher* and *teaching* as umbrella terms for myriad roles and activities in pedagogical encounters that may be variously referred to as, for example, *tutor* and *tutoring* or *supervisor* and *supervising*.

PRINCIPLES OF PEDAGOGICAL INTERACTION

The principles of CCC each highlight a distinct aspect of pedagogical inter-action that is of some relevance to student learning. Given their messy habi-tats in the lived world of pedagogical encounters, they do not necessarily cohere into an elegant framework that features symmetry or parallelism. They do not, for example, uniformly constitute features of optimal teacher conduct. Nor do they uniformly specify the conditions for developing learner competence. Still, let me entertain at least one way of conceptualizing their relationships. While *competence* emphasizes an overall ethos of teaching that takes seriously learners' competence concerns, both *complexity* and *contingency* address the nature of teacher conduct, with *complexity* under-scoring its challenges, and *contingency* its ideal quality, with some inevitable overlap between the two. In what follows, I offer an initial glimpse into the empirical bases for each principle.

Competence

Before proceeding, it merits clarifying that I use *competence* to refer to learner competence in the most commonplace sense of being able to do X. As will be demonstrated in greater detail in Chapter 4, regardless of age and setting, learners take every opportunity to assert, maintain, and defend their competence, and expert teachers know how to nurture that delicate concern. Paradoxically, then, it seems that assuming competence is a pre-condition for or an integral component of achieving competence. Such a paradox is perhaps best captured in this Bakurst remark: "treating children as if they had abilities they do not yet possess is a necessary condition of the development of those abilities" (cited in van Lier, 2004, p. 153). In fact, being treated as competent appears to be essential for many learners. In the following Excerpt 1 from graduate writing center interaction, Heidi the tutor has just advised Lena the tutee with regard to some organization issues of her paper (see appendix for transcript notations):

1. I agree

```
01 Heidi:  ((reading the list of headings)) I was ↑wondering,=
02 Lena:   =Okay?
03 Heidi:  if you ↑could (.) for the general organization
04         I wanna make the 'rejecting' part (.) part of your
05         intro to the chapter
06         [∘I don't th]ink that's your focus.∘
07 Lena:   [>Okay?< ]
08         >I agree.<
09 Heidi:  Yeah [that's like a back]ground ()
10 Lena:        [I totally agree.   ]
11         I didn't even know if I should just cut it.
```

12   [You kn]ow I mean,
13 Heidi: [Yeah.]

A more detailed analysis will be provided in Chapter 4, but notice for now that Lena's acceptance of Heidi's advice is packaged in such a way that highlights like-mindedness (*I totally agree*.). By overshooting Heidi's suggestion (*I don't even know if I should just cut it*.), Lena also manages to substantiate her stance as an independently arrived-at matter. In other words, she is not simply acquiescing to Heidi or offering any pro forma endorsement. As a competent participant in this interaction, she values Heidi's advice on her own terms (Waring, 2007).

My data are replete with cases where the less-than-competent parties in the pedagogical encounter orient to their competence as a central concern. Such concerns can seem superfluous to a bystander or even the more competent parties involved. In Chapter 4, I will show how expert teachers can manage to remain sensitive to these concerns in the midst of the unfolding choreography of teaching, and how such sensitivity reaps important pay-offs.

Complexity

Teacher talk is complex in that it is routinely imbued with multiple voices, with the same turns or turn components accomplishing multiple actions, and such multivocality can be either an impediment to or a resource for promoting learning. When the multiple voices conflict, outcomes unfavorable to learning can ensue. When the multiple voices are carefully tuned to balance multiple demands, however, the opposite transpires. Routine classroom language such as *very good* or *any questions*, for example, can yield unintended outcomes, where the voice of supporting learner development clashes with that of inhibiting such development, and awareness of such complexities is foundational to the competencies of teaching. In the following example from an adult English-as-a-second-language (ESL) classroom, the class is going over a grammar exercise with items such as the following (a more detailed transcript and analysis can be found in Chapter 5):

> *Wow, I didn't know you were married.*
> *How long* _____?

2. very good

    01 T: Nu::mber three::::: ((*points*))-Kevin.
    02   (1.0)
    03 Kevin: Wow. I didn't know (.) you were married.
    04   (0.8)

```
05              "Ho:::w lo:ng have you:::::::::(.) b:een married."=
06 T:           =$ Very good=how long have you been married.$
07              =Very good. Nu:mber four. Mai,
```

As shown, the teacher receives Kevin's response with two explicit positive assessments (*very good*), and she moves on. The case is clearly closed, and to everyone's satisfaction, or so it seems, until 66 lines later, when Miyuki asks a question:

3. I have a question

```
01 Miyuki:  I have one [ques]tion,
02 T:                  [Yes. ]
03 Miyuki:  Number three is if without "be:" °is not good?°
04 T:       How lo:ng (1.0) you've been marrie[d?
05 Miyuki:                                    [Have you
06          married. °have you married.°
07 T:       °Oka::y?° >Let's write this d↑own.<
```

This sequence goes on for two and a half minutes and becomes the most complicated error correction sequence in the entire two-hour class. Briefly, Miyuki wonders whether "How long have you married?" as opposed to "How long have you *been* married?" (line 03) would qualify as an acceptable answer. Since the mere form of *married* may be either a verb or an adjective, Miyuki's confusion is not surprising, but the earlier *very good* closing may have made it difficult for her or others to attend to potential understanding problems such as this. Thus, the multivocality of *very good* lies in its expression of positive assessment along with its pronouncement of "case closed" (Waring, 2008). While positive assessment extends support, "case closed" precludes necessary exploration. As will be shown in Chapter 5, the complexity of teacher talk goes beyond such simple utterances as *very good*, and its defining feature of multivocality can constitute a resource as well.

Contingency

Of the three principles, *contingency* resonates most strongly with existing theories of learning and teaching, especially those in the Vygotskyan framework that place great emphasis on offering assistance tailored to the learners' *zone of proximal development* (ZPD). Teaching requires being responsive. One might observe the absence of such responsiveness in the example here taken from an after-school literacy program (Waring & Hruska, 2011, 2012). Mindy the tutor is helping Nora the six-year-old first grader spell the word *manatee*. Nora has written down the first five letters so far and is having difficulty figuring out the ending *ee*. Mindy tries to help by getting Nora to notice the *ee* endings in *tree* and *bee*, and Nora is supposed to underline the *ee* in both *tree* and *bee* to demonstrate such proper noticing:

4. underline it

> 01 Mindy: Okay so underline the similarities.
> 02   What's the same in the word "tree" and "bee."
> 03   (0.2)
> 04 Mindy: Un[derline it.
> 05 Nora: [((*draws one long line under everything she wrote*))-
> 06   (°the le::tters? °)
> 07 Mindy: What letters. What letters are the same in each word.
> 08 Nora: u:h
> 09   t:, t:, ((*points to t in 'manatee' and then in 'tree' with pen*))
> 10   (1.0) e:, e:,-((*points to e in 'bee' and then 'tree'*))

A more detailed transcript and analysis will be given in Chapter 6, but for now, simply note that despite Nora's difficulties throughout the sequence, Mindy's successive moves are largely repetitive without being carefully calibrated to address those difficulties. As will be shown in Chapter 6, such lack of responsiveness may become manifest in a range of ways, while responsiveness in managing learner resistance, attending to learner initiatives, and working with problematic learner responses may be demonstrated with great ingenuity.

It bears repeating that these three principles necessarily offer a partial view of pedagogical interaction grounded in the specific data I work with. Just as my predecessors who each share a unique perspective on classroom communication through their particular viewfinders, the CCC is a product of my own viewfinder that is distinctively CA. After all, teaching is too complex an act to be explicated from any single perspective. I can only hope that my particular vision contributes a useful piece to the larger jigsaw puzzle of teaching and learning. In addition, much of what I write will sound familiar to very experienced teachers, and the three Cs will resonate to varying extent with some existing literature in the field. I do not proclaim, in other words, to have discovered a new world. What I aim to offer is a depiction of the existing world we all experience intuitively or engage with empirically. In reflecting upon his work on classroom interaction, Mehan (1979) observes that such work

> may reveal patterns of interaction that surprise participants or scientists, but surprise is not the criterion of value. . . . The members' yawned "of course" is not to be taken as criticism; it is a compliment. It affirms that the researcher has depicted a segment of a people's cultural knowledge in a way that is consistent with their practice.
>
> (p. 173)

My hope, in part, is that (1) my own depiction of what expert teachers do is done with sufficient accuracy and texture to render that world replicable and that (2) the CCC offers some useful elucidation of what pedagogical interaction is, or more specifically, what it means to do teaching.

PLAN OF THE BOOK

Chapter 2 reviews classic and current scholarship on classroom discourse. By considering various approaches such as (applied) linguistics, sociolinguistics, language socialization, sociocultural theory, and critical discourse analysis, I synthesize and highlight the major findings on the discourse of teaching and learning so far and thereby situate the CA approach to be explicated next within a broader landscape of intellectual standpoints and empirical endeavors.

Chapter 3 introduces CA as both a theory of and an approach to analyzing social interaction. The readers will be familiarized with the various technical aspects of CA as well as certain controversial issues with regard to the validity, reliability, and generalizability of CA findings and the relationship between CA and context. The chapter also offers a review of existing CA work on classroom discourse and ends with a discussion on how CA insights might contribute to building a theory of teaching.

Chapters 4 through 6 introduce the reader to the three principles of pedagogical interaction: competence, complexity, and contingency. Transcripts and analyses of interaction from a variety of pedagogical contexts are offered as evidence for the relevance of these principles.

Chapter 7 situates the three principles of pedagogical interaction within a broader discussion of theory building. It highlights how issues of CCC (as made evident in the details of interaction) can advance our current understandings and what they may mean for the practicing teacher. It also underscores an affinity between these CA-grounded principles and sociocultural theory, as well as complexity theory, and proposes, in the final analysis, that such affinity strengthens an integrated understanding of the profoundly social and dynamic nature of teaching and learning.

REFERENCES

Antaki, C. (Ed.). (2011). *Applied conversation analysis: Intervention and change in institutional talk*. Basingstoke: Palgrave MacMillan.

Barnes, D. (1992). *From communication to curriculum* (2nd ed.). Harmondsworth: Penguin.

Blake, W. (1994). *Blake: Poems*. New York: Everyone's Library.

Cazden, C. (2001). *Classroom discourse: The language of teaching and learning* (2nd ed.). Portsmouth, NH: Heinemann.

Clayman, S., & Gill, V. (2004). Conversation analysis. In M. Hardy & A. Bryman (Eds.), *Handbook of data analysis* (pp. 589–606). Thousand Oaks, CA: Sage Publications.

Drew, P., & Heritage, J. (Eds.). (1992). *Talk at work: Interaction in institutional settings*. Cambridge: Cambridge University Press.

Edwards, D., & Mercer, N. (1987). *Common knowledge: The development of understanding in the classroom*. London: Methuen.

Garfinkel, H. (1967). *Studies in ethnomethodology*. Englewood Cliffs, NJ: Prentice-Hall.

Gass, S. (2004). Conversation analysis and input-interaction. *The Modern Language Journal, 88*(4), 597–616.

Goodwin, C. (1994). Professional vision. *American Anthropologist, 96*(3), 606–633.

Hall, J. K. (2004). Language learning as an interactional achievement. *The Modern Language Journal, 88*(4), 607–612.

Hall, J. K., Hellermann, J., & Pekarek Doehler, S. (Eds.). (2011). *L2 interactional competence and development.* Clevedon, UK: Multilingual Matters.

He, A. W. (2004). CA for SLA: Arguments from the Chinese language classroom. *The Modern Language Journal, 88*(4), 568–582.

Hellermann, J. (2008). *Social actions for classroom language learning.* Clevedon, UK: Multilingual Matters.

Heritage, J. (2008). Conversation analysis as social theory. In B. Turner (Ed.), *The new Blackwell companion to social theory* (pp. 300–320). Oxford: Blackwell.

Larsen-Freeman, D. (2004). CA for SLA? It all depends. . . . *The Modern Language Journal, 88*(4), 603–607.

Liddicoat, A. (1997). Interaction, social structure, and second language use: A response to Firth and Wagner. *The Modern Language Journal, 81*(3), 313–317.

Markee, N. (1994). Toward an ethnomethodological respecification of SLA studies. In A. Cohen, S. Gass, & E. Tarone (Eds.), *Research methodology in second language acquisition* (pp. 89–116). Hillsdale, NJ: Lawrence Erlbaum.

Markee, N., & Kasper, G. (2004). Classroom talks: An introduction. *The Modern Language Journal, 88*(4), 491–500.

Mehan, H. (1979). *Learning lessons: Social organization in the classroom.* Cambridge, MA: Harvard University Press.

Kasper, G. (1997). 'A' stands for acquisition: A response to Firth and Wagner. *The Modern Language Journal, 81*(3), 307–312.

Kasper, G. (2009). Locating cognition in second language interaction and learning: Inside the skull or in public view? *IRAL, 47*(1), 11–36.

Kasper, G., & Wagner, J. (2011). A conversation analytic approach to second language acquisition. In D. Atkinson (Ed.), *Alternative approaches to second language acquisition* (pp. 117–142). New York: Routledge.

Pomerantz, A. (1990). On the validity and generalizability of conversation analytic methods: Conversation analytic claims. *Communication Monographs, 57*(3), 231–235.

Psathas, G. (1995). *Conversation analysis: The study of talk-in-interaction.* Thousand Oaks, CA: Sage Publications.

Schegloff, E. A. (2007). *Sequence organization.* Cambridge: Cambridge University Press.

Schegloff, E. A., & Sacks, H. (1973). Opening up closings. *Semiotica, 7,* 289–327.

Seedhouse, P. (2011). Conversation analytic research into language teaching and learning. In E. Hinkel (Ed.), *Handbook of research in second language teaching and learning* (Vol. 2) (pp. 345–363). New York: Routledge.

Shoemaker, P. J., Tankard, J. W., & Lasorsa, D. L. (2004). *How to build social science theories.* Thousand Oaks, CA: Sage Publications.

Sidnell, J., & Stivers, T. (Eds.). (2013). *The handbook of conversation analysis.* Chichester, UK: Wiley-Blackwell.

Svennevig, J. (2001). Abduction as a methodological approach to the study of spoken interaction. *Norskrift, 103,* 1–22.

ten Have, P. (2007). *Doing conversation analysis* (2nd ed.). Thousand Oaks, CA: Sage Publications.

Tharp, R. G., & Gallimore, R. (1988). *Rousing minds to life: Teaching, learning, and schooling in social context.* New York: Cambridge University Press.

van Lier, L. (2004). *The ecology and semiotics of language learning: A sociocultural perspective.* Norwell, MA: Kluwer Academic Publishers.

Waring, H. Z. (2007). Complex advice acceptance as a resource for managing asymmetries. *Text and Talk, 27*(1), 107–137.

Waring, H. Z. (2008). Using explicit positive assessment in the language classroom: IRF, feedback, and learning opportunities. *The Modern Language Journal, 92*(4), 577–594.

Waring, H. Z., & Hruska, B. (2011). Getting and keeping Nora on board: A novice elementary ESOL student teacher's practices for lesson engagement. *Linguistics and Education, 22,* 441–455.

Waring, H. Z., & Hruska, B. (2012). Problematic directives in pedagogical interaction. *Linguistics and Education, 23,* 289–300.

Wong, J. (1994). *A conversation analytic approach to the study of repair in native-nonnative speaker English conversation: The element 'yeah' in same-turn repair and delayed next turn repair initiation.* Unpublished doctoral dissertation, University of California, Los Angeles.

Wong, J. (2000). Delayed next turn repair initiation in native/non-native speaker English conversation. *Applied Linguistics, 21*(1), 244–226.

2 Issues in Classroom Discourse

Life is an enormous collage populated with a succession of nonstop snapshots of teaching and learning. We witness teaching and learning when a father helps his two-year-old daughter get on her skis for the first time, when a child shows her aging grandmother how to navigate her new Kindle, when an aspiring photographer inquires about what camera to buy, when tutees seek advice and clients seek consultation, and when apprentices are socialized into the norms and practices of various professional institutions. Despite this wide array of scenes, what dominates our imagination is perhaps those of the classroom, where teaching and learning preside as the official business of the day. Not surprisingly, much scholarly attention has been devoted to illuminating the discourse of the classroom. In this chapter, I review the classics in classroom discourse as well as the various approaches that have yielded critical insights into the nature of classroom discourse. My own thinking and exploration of pedagogical interaction owe much to this intellectual foundation of classic and current scholarship.

CLASSICS IN CLASSROOM DISCOURSE

I begin with the classics that have inspired subsequent work and shaped our understanding of what makes classroom discourse unique, how such uniqueness may present challenges for children with diverging home practices, how such discourse may foster or inhibit learning, and finally, the sociocultural foundations of teaching and learning.

Structure of Classroom Discourse

The concept most evocative of classroom discourse is perhaps initiation–response–feedback (IRF), a feature identified by the British linguists John Sinclair and Malcolm Coulthard as integral to the infrastructure of classroom discourse (cf. Bellack, Kliebard, Hyman, & Smith, 1966). That IRF departs from ordinary conversation is now no longer news. The classic example is that an ordinary exchange of asking for and offering the time can be effectively turned into classroom discourse if it is followed by "Very good!" (e.g., *A: What time is it? B: It's 5:30. A: Very good!*). As Sinclair and Coulthard (1975) searched for linguistic descriptions of verbal interaction in the classroom, it became obvious that such descriptions could not be handled within the framework of traditional grammar, with sentence occupying the highest rank. Beginning from the assumption that analytic units can be arranged on a rank scale (e.g., a sentence consists of one or more clauses, which in turn consist of one or more phrases, etc.), they proposed *discourse* as a new level with five ranks capturing the structure of classroom instruction: lesson, transaction, exchange, move, and act: a lesson consists of one or more transactions, which consist of one or more exchanges, and so on. What we now know as IRF is what makes up an exchange, which can implement various instructional tasks such as directing, eliciting, and informing. An eliciting exchange, for example, consists of an IRF implemented via the acts of elicitation (I), reply (R), and evaluation (F).

Although Mehan (1979) is often cited alongside Sinclair and Coulthard (1975) for the tripartite structure in classroom course (IRF/ initiation–response–evaluation [IRE]), he comes from a very different intellectual background (also see Mehan in Chapter 3). Hugh Mehan is a sociologist with an interest in the sociology of education. His findings on the structure of classroom discourse bear some resemblance to those of Sinclair and Coulthard's—at least at first glance. Like Sinclair and Coulthard, Mehan also views classroom discourse as hierarchically organized, with the event (lesson) subsuming phases (opening, instructional, and closing), which are in turn realized by sequences (directive, informative, and elicit) that consist of IREs. Aside from the rank-scale hierarchical organization, however, Mehan also highlights a sequential organization that divides a lesson into an opening phase, an instructional phase, and a closing phase. In addition, he writes extensively on turn allocation in the classroom (also see McHoul, 1985), showing that unlike turn allocation in ordinary conversation that features a combination of current-selects-next, next-speaker-self-selects, and current-speaker-continues (Sacks, Schegloff, & Jefferson, 1974), classroom turn allocation places a great deal of power in the hands of the teacher, who exercises control over basic procedures such as individual nomination, invitation to bid (e.g., *Who knows the answer to X?*), and invitation to reply (e.g., *What's the capital of China?*). Although most of Mehan's data were accounted for by the three basic turn allocation procedures, there remained a total of 29 unaccounted-for cases. Mehan looked further and found that these "exceptions" occurred under certain circumstances, where the teacher exercised improvisational strategies such as *the work of doing nothing, getting through, opening the floor,* and *accepting the unexpected.* In the end, a total of four cases remained unaccounted for. Rather than resorting to speculations such as the history of or relationships between the participants, Mehan left them, remaining open to the possibility of further specifying the system. An important feature of Mehan's (1979) model is reflexive tying:

Each observed behavior between teacher and student is a function of the interconnected behaviors that retrospectively precede it in time and those that are prospectively possible. An interactional model recognizes, secondly, that behavior between participants is not unidirectional, it is reciprocal. Students not only are influenced by the teacher, they influence the teacher in turn.

(p. 77)

In other words, everything one says influences both what comes next and what comes before. There is a constant if–then relationship (or what is often referred to as contingency in discourse) that goes in both directions, and such contingencies are negotiated by the participants on a turn-by-turn basis. A specific elicitation projects a specific response. If a response fits an elicitation, we get a third turn that evaluates this successful fit and ends with a three-part sequence. If the response does not fit the elicitation, we get an extended sequence, where the teacher pursues the fitted response in various ways.

What also distinguishes Mehan (1979) from Sinclair and Coulthard (1975) is his strict adherence to participant orientations in his approach to data:

A goal of this research was to ensure that these procedures were oriented to by the participants, and were not just a researcher's analytic device. Therefore, I examined the actions of teachers and students themselves for the purpose of seeing whether the machinery I described actually organized the behavior of the participants during the course of their interaction.

(Mehan, 1979, p. 96)

Mehan does not, for example, present the turn-taking procedures as prescriptive, top-down categories imposed on the interactional data. Rather, he shows how these procedures are oriented to by the participants themselves: when a "rule" is broken (e.g., individual nomination responded to by the group), repair work kicks in, manifesting the participants' understanding that an individual nomination is normatively responded to by an individual. A product elicitation requires a product response not just because we as researchers think it makes sense but because the product response is what the participants themselves pursue when they don't get it.

Like Sinclair and Coulthard as well as Mehan, the theoretical physicist turned science educator Jay Lemke also was interested in how lessons in the classrooms (science classrooms in his case) were structured. For Lemke (1990), classroom discourse consists of a series of activity types. Some of the activity types are purely structural, some have functions attached to them, and some are more clearly functional. He identifies a great variety of activity types but chooses to highlight a few in his 1990 book in the form of a continuum, which indicates decreasing teacher control from *triadic dialog* to *teacher–student debate*. Some of the activity types are fairly self-explanatory, but four warrant some explication. *External text dialog* is a variation of *triadic dialog*, where a textbook item, for example, plays the role of initiation. *Teacher–student duolog* refers to sustained talk between the teacher and an individual student. *True dialog* occurs when the teacher asks a genuine, rather than a known-answer, question. *Cross-discussion* takes place among the students without any teacher intervention. *True dialog* and *cross-discussion*, as Lemke observes, are rare in the science classroom.

These activity types are what Lemke refers to as the unwritten rules of classroom discourse. The success of a lesson hinges upon playing these games smoothly (e.g., a triadic dialog runs off smoothly as a triadic dialog). And for that to happen, teachers use a range of control tactics that are often implicit as opposed to explicit (e.g., admonition sequence). Teachers exercise control of the activity structures via structural tactics such as *shift signals, interrupt students,* and *control the pacing.* Control of how the subject matter is presented, on the other hand, is maintained via thematic tactics such as *assert irrelevance, mark importance, mark new/old information, regulate difficulty, be funny and get personal.*

As Lemke points out, teacher control tactics are deployed to serve the teachers' interests (e.g., divide and conquer), which are not always in line with the students' interests (e.g., seek safety in the collective). Students resort to their own tactics for their own interests such as *call-out answers, chorus answers, questioning answers, override obligations, nonverbal disattending,* and *side-talk.* The most frequently used tactics used by students in the science classroom, according to Lemke, are *call-out answers* and *side-talk. Side-talk,* for example, serves the students' interests in building a community, creating a classroom dynamic, and talking to someone else other than the teacher about what is going on in the classroom. These interests are integral to educational success, and as such, strict enforcement of a rule such as "no side-talk" is counterproductive.

In sum, classroom discourse constitutes a distinct form of talk as manifested in its hierarchical and sequential organizations, its turn-taking system (i.e., how are conversational turns constructed and distributed?), and its specific set of activity types or unwritten rules along with the teacher and student control tactics deployed to enforce or contest such rules.

Learning and Classroom Discourse

While these scholars have taken an essentially descriptive stance (with perhaps the exception of Lemke, 1990) toward the distinctive nature of classroom discourse, some have sounded a more critical note by explicitly considering how classroom talk impacts student learning (Barnes, 1976/1992; Cadzen, 1988/2001; Edwards & Mercer, 1987). Douglas Barnes is a prominent British educationalist. His book *From Communication to Curriculum*

(Barnes, 1992), based on observations in a Leeds secondary school, was written almost 40 years ago when research on classroom talk was still in its infancy. In their introduction to *Exploring Talk in School*, Hodgkinson and Mercer (2008) present Barnes as offering this profound insight: "often the odds were stacked against pupils being able to use talk productively in the classroom, because of the rigid and formalised way teachers required children to engage in dialogue" (p. xi).

For Barnes, talk plays two roles in the classroom: as the communication system of the classroom and as a means for learning. The classroom communication system contains a set of tacit rules such as that teachers ask known-answer questions, which do not necessarily advance learning. Talk also serves as a means of learning, and as such, the kinds of talk that happen can determine the kinds of learning that ensue. Ultimately, there is no such thing as curriculum on the one hand and communication that delivers the curriculum on the other. Communication *is* curriculum, and communication can materialize as exploratory talk or presentational talk: the former is hesitant and incomplete (e.g., *if that is the case, how come such-and-such happens?*) and the latter definitive and final; the former serves to sort out own thoughts, and the latter to fit audience needs.

Barnes believes that both exploratory and presentational talk are important for student learning, but exploratory talk should be allowed and encouraged at earlier stages of the learning sequence because it is an important means of working on understanding rather than getting at the correct answer. Significantly, the teacher plays a crucial role in engineering what kind of talk ultimately happens. An assessing or judging teacher role, for example, calls for a *presenting* role of the students, whose talk is expected to be presentational or the *final draft*. In other words, the classroom communication system over which the teacher has a great deal of control determines to a large extent what kinds of talk transpire, what counts as an appropriate learning activity (rote memory or sorting out understanding problems), and what eventually gets learned.

Like Douglas Barnes who sought to uncover the "hidden curriculum" or "the communication system of the classroom," the psychologists Derek Edwards and Neil Mercer (1987) were interested in making explicit the implicit educational ground rules. Examples of such rules include: the teacher asks known-answer questions, repeated questions imply wrong answers, abstract principles are to be drawn from concrete experience via elicitations rather than telling, learning is to happen by doing, and contexts in math problems are irrelevant. "What concerns us here," as they write, "is not so much the patterning of the discourse itself, but rather the understanding that participants must possess in order to be able to take part" (Edwards & Mercer, 1987, p. 45). Such understanding, unfortunately, is largely kept implicit because, as Edwards and Mercer speculate, it is treated as self-evident, and restricted access is maintained for the purpose of control. Unfortunately, education (teaching, learning, and assessment) often fails "when incorrect assumptions are made about shared knowledge, meanings and interpretations" (Edwards & Mercer, 1987, p. 60). As they so perceptively write:

> Part of the problem for pupils is that much of the process remains mysterious to them. In however friendly and informal a manner, they are frequently asked to do things, learn things, understand things, for no apparent reason other than that it is what the teacher wants them to do. The goal and purposes of the lesson are not revealed. Indeed, neither often are the concepts that the lesson may have been designed to "cover." In the ethos of pupil-centred inductive learning, it is not acceptable to tell the pupils what they were supposed to discover for themselves, even after they have completed the various activities involved.
>
> (p. 158)

They argue:

> It is essentially through the pervasive phenomena of teacher control over the expression of knowledge that pupils' understandings of things are frequently created as procedural rather than principled—saying and doing what seems to be required, rather than working out a principled understanding of how and why certain actions, expressions and procedures are appropriate or correct. (Edwards & Mercer, 1987, p. 130)

The relationship between classroom talk and learning is also addressed in Cazden (1988/2001). As an American psychologist and educational anthropologist, Courtney Cazden proposes a reappraisal of the IRF sequence in the traditional classroom, arguing that its value should be "judged for [its] contribution to learning" (p. 47). The typical critique of IRF is that teachers ask display or known-answer questions and evaluate student responses in the third turn. In reality, observes Cazden, not all questions in the I slot of IRF are display questions, and teachers accomplish a range of tasks in the F slot beyond evaluation (cf. van Lier, 1996). Cazden also identifies some lessons as being nontraditional, where teacher turns are short and student answers are expanded, explanations are valued as much as answers, reference to others' talk is expected, correct answers are accepted but not positively evaluated, and alternative answers are sought (cf. Barnes's exploratory talk). In the end, Cazden argues that both traditional and nontraditional lessons play important roles in promoting student learning.

Clearly, the relationship between talk and learning in the classroom is a complicated one, where (1) teachers play a critical role in what goes into the IRF sequence, whether the talk would be exploratory or presentational, and whether the ensuing understanding would be procedural or principled and where, unfortunately, (2) the hidden curriculum or the mysterious nature of educational ground rules of the classroom often inhibit student learning, making it difficult to achieve principled understandings.

Home Practices and Classroom Discourse

Given the distinct nature of classroom discourse, children from diverse home environments are essentially faced with the daunting task of learning a new "language" as they begin formal schooling (Mehan, 1979) or, in Schieffelin and Ochs' (1986) words, of going through language socialization. Schieffelin and Ochs are anthropologists with a primary interest in how children are socialized into members of a society across different cultures. Without being classroom discourse analysts themselves, their work has a strong impact on subsequent work on classroom discourse that takes a language socialization approach. Briefly, socialization is process of becoming members of a social group (e.g., native speakers of American English, kindergarteners, physicians, and discourse analysts), and language socialization is a process of socialization in which language plays a central role as both the means (i.e., socialization through language) and the end (socialization to use the language of that particular social group). Becoming members of a social group also entails, for example, learning its structure of role and status (e.g., is society primarily structured around dyads or multiparty relationships?), its ways of expressing affect (e.g., is affect to be restrained or displayed?), and its literacy practices (e.g., what counts as a story?).

One of the most compelling arguments for how children's socialization at home impacts their school performance is detailed in Shirley Brice Heath's (1983) decade-long ethnographic work on two working-class communities in North Carolina in the 1970s—a time of desegregation when teachers were dealing with children from different communities and confronted with the question: how can their different ways of speaking, thinking, and behaving be bridged? Roadville is a white community with a textile industry, and Trackton a black community with farming and mills. Heath found that because of their different home backgrounds, the children from Roadville and Trackton would exhibit behaviors in various ways incompatible with what the teacher would expect to be "normal" school conduct. Roadville children, for example, were used to realistic play and Trackton children outside play. Neither style was suited to the school setup of play. Roadville children were aware of space-function and time-task ties, while Trackton children were not. Roadville children would respond to the same name for everyone, and Trackton children would not respond to names at all. Roadville children would misbehave in the absence of adults, and Trackton children would interrupt and chat freely during class discussions. Roadville children were prone to factual accounts, and Trackton children fanciful accounts.

As a result, Roadville children had no trouble making their non-fictive stories adhere to actual experience, but Tracktown children did. And neither group would summarize their stories with factual recapitulations.

All these practices were at odds with school rules. Instead of making school rules explicit, however, the teachers conveyed the rules through modeling and indirect requests, which failed to effectuate any change. Only after the teachers learned how the children functioned at home did they become much more explicit with their expectations. Some went so far as driving a van around neighborhoods to demonstrate how school was done. In the end, what Heath (1983) was arguing for was, I believe, building school practices on children's existing resources and strengths.

A very similar theme is found in Cazden (1988/2001). Having studied various K–12 classrooms in the United States, Cazden found that depending on their family backgrounds, children during sharing time told two kinds of narratives: topic-centered versus episodic. In a topic-centered narrative, a child would, for example, talk about how a man made a paper boat out of a dollar bill. In an episodic narrative, on the other hand, a child would jump from "Old Ironsides at the ocean" to "a fancy restaurant" and then the food she ate at that restaurant. While the topic-centered narrative received a positive response from the teacher, the episodic one received a negative one. After learning the sources of these variations, according to Cazden, the teachers (1) restructured the sharing time and took themselves out of it and (2) created an environment where different types of discourses were appreciated, and the children helped each other with their narratives.

Thus, our contemporary appreciation for the impact of home environment on school performance and the importance of building upon students' existing resources owe a great deal to the foundational work of Heath and Cazden as well as the framework of language socialization.

Sociocultural Foundations of Teaching and Learning

The final group of classic thinkers and scholars are those who have laid down the sociocultural foundations of teaching and learning for much of the work on classroom discourse today (Tharp & Gallimore, 1988; van Lier, 1996; Vygotsky, 1978; Wells, 1999). L. S. Vygotsky was a psychologist in postrevolutionary Russia (1917–1930s), who was interested in establishing a unified theory of how human psychological processes (e.g., voluntary attention, thinking, memory, planning, and problem solving) were developed. Synthesizing the contending views at the time (e.g., the inherent mind vs. society dualism of Western psychology), Vygotsky (1978) was the first modern psychologist to suggest "a mechanism by which culture becomes a part of each person's nature" (Introduction by Cole and Scribner [1978] to *Mind in Society*, p. 6), arguing that

> [e]very function in the child's cultural development appears twice: first, on the social level, and later, on the individual level; first, *between* people (*interpsychological*), and then *inside* the child (*intrapsychological*). . . .
> All the higher functions originate as actual relations between human

individuals. *The transformation of an interpersonal process into an intrapersonal one is the result of a long series of developmental events.*
(Vygotsky, 1978, p. 57)

Take, for example, how the child learns the gesture of pointing. It begins with a grasping movement directed toward an object. That grasping movement gradually takes on a social meaning as the adult reacts to it. The child begins to understand that the meaning of the gesture (its success or failure) is determined by other human beings. He starts to design that movement for another person, and with that, the grasping movement changes to the true gesture of pointing.

Contrary to the common belief that a child must be developmentally ready for learning to proceed, Vygotsky (1978) contends that "the developmental process lags behind the learning process; this sequence then results in *zones of proximal development*" (p. 80), which is "the distance between the actual developmental level as determined by independent problem solving and the level of potential development as determined through problem solving under adult guidance or in collaboration with more capable peers" (p. 86). With regard to good learning, Vygotsky (1978) writes:

> . . . learning which is oriented toward developmental levels that have already been reached is ineffective from the viewpoint of a child's overall development. It does not aim for a new stage of the developmental process but rather lags behind this process. Thus, the notion of a zone of proximal development enables us to propose a new formula, namely that the only 'good learning' is that which is in advance of development.
>
> (p. 89)

> . . . an essential feature of learning is that it creates the zone of proximal development; that is, learning awakens a variety of internal developmental processes that are able to operate only when the child is interacting with people in his environment and in cooperation with his peers. Once these processes are internalized, they become part of the child's independent developmental achievement.
>
> (p. 90)

Vygotsky's zone of proximal development (ZPD) is without a doubt one of the most influential concepts in educational research and practice. ZPD-based instructional approaches emphasize the importance of either pitching instruction to the appropriate levels of the students or making instructional activities meaningful and relevant to the students (Wells, 1999, p. 318). Wells (1999) proposes an expanded version of ZPD with the following features (pp. 330–331):

1. ZPD is created in interaction with an unknown and indeterminate upper bound.
2. ZPD applies to all participants, not simply to the less skillful or knowledgeable.
3. The sources of guidance include a range of semiotic resources beyond humans.
4. Learning involves not simply cognition but also acting, thinking, and feeling.

Of all the classics in educational discourse, Tharp and Gallimore (1988) are perhaps the most explicit in articulating a theory of teaching within the Vygotskyan sociocultural framework. As they so unambiguously proclaim, "[t]eaching must be redefined as assisted performance. Teaching consists in assisting performance. Teaching is occurring when performance is achieved with assistance" (p. 21). As educational psychologists, Roland Tharp and Ronald Gallimore lamented the lack of attention to the teaching practice itself despite the recurrent national conversations on impoverished teaching in the United States. In an almost poetic appeal, they urge us:

> Students cannot be left to learn on their own; teachers cannot be content to provide opportunities to learn and then assess outcomes; recitation must be deemphasized; responsive, assisting interactions must become commonplace in the class. Minds must be roused to life.
>
> (Tharp & Gallimore, 1988, p. 21)

Drawing examples from a small elementary school they designed and built, the authors demonstrate how teaching must be redefined as assisted performance, with means of assisting performance including *modeling, contingency management, feeding-back, instructing, questioning* (assessing vs. assisting), and *cognitive structuring*. Some of these terms warrant a brief explication. *Contingency management* refers to arranging rewards or punishments to follow on behavior depending on whether that behavior is desirable. *Feed-back* is information offered with reference to a standard. According to Tharp and Gallimore (1988), "[s]imply providing performance information (e.g., a test score; example mine) is insufficient; there will be no performance assistance unless the information provided is compared to some standard" (p. 55). *Instructing* appears to be equated with giving directives (e.g., *Read again.*) and is referred to as "that heard, regulating voice, a gradually internalized voice, that then become the pupil's self-regulating 'still, small' instructor" (p. 57). *Questioning* is considered an important means of assistance: "if he [Socrates] only lectures, he will never see the images of his pupils' minds, projected on the screen of their language" (p. 59). There are two kinds of questions. The assessment question "inquires to discover the level of the pupil's ability to perform without assistance" (e.g., *What was the last thing we talked about yesterday?*), and the assistance question "inquires to produce a mental operation that the pupil cannot or will not produce alone" (e.g., *What else could you use, Jimmie? How about those things you use in a parade . . . [to spread the news]*) (pp. 59–60).

According to Tharp and Gallimore (1988), "many teachers do not distinguish the two types (assessment vs. assisting questions). Unfortunately, this lack of discernment usually results in the teacher assuming that a request for information constitutes *teaching*. It does not. Though necessary to teaching, assessment is not itself a means for directly assisting performance" (p. 60). Finally, *cognitive structuring* refers to "the provision of a structure for thinking and acting. In science, it is theory; in religion, it is theology; in games, it is rules" (p. 63). It includes two types: (1) structures of explanation (e.g., *this is a story about a little girl's search for truth*) and (2) structures for cognitive activity (e.g., *when you encounter a new word, here are the things you can do . . .*). Ultimately, these means of assistance make *instructional conversation* possible:

> It is through the instructional conversation that babies learn to speak, children to read, teachers to teach, researchers to discover, and all to become literate. The concept itself contains a paradox: "instruction" and "conversation" appear contrary, the one implying authority and planning, the other equality and responsiveness. The task of teaching is to resolve this paradox. To most truly teach, one must converse; to truly converse is to teach.
>
> (p. 111)

This sentiment is very much shared by Leo van Lier, an educational linguist whose 1996 book *Interaction in the Language Curriculum* may be considered a manifesto of sociocultural theory in language education. A firm believer in the centrality of social interaction in driving language learning, van Lier, however, is critical of Tharp and Gallimore in what they consider to be instructional conversation:

> For all their professed abhorrence of the recitation script, Tharp and Gallimore quite happily embrace the structural format in which it typically occurs: the IRF exchange, where a student response is called forth by a teacher initiation, and vetted by a teacher feedback move. Interaction remains teacher-centered and teacher-controlled rather than becoming learner-centered and learner-controlled.
>
> (van Lier, 1996, p. 165)

For van Lier (1996), true conversation features symmetry and contingency, where "connectedness, co-construction of meaning, affirmation of communication, and emotional sharing" thrive (p. 159), and such conversation is "the most stimulating environment for learning" (p. 171). While symmetry refers to "equal participation rights and duties" (p. 14), contingency is characterized by *dependency* and *uncertainty* (p. 170). Contingent utterances, according to van Lier, relate new material to known material, set up expectations for what comes next, validate both preceding and next utterance, are neither entirely predictable nor entirely unpredictable, promote intersubjectivity, and ensure continued attention" (p. 184). Contingency is a crucial element in the interaction in ZPD, which is "easiest to achieve when interactants are oriented toward symmetry" (p. 193).

In sum, the sociocultural view of learning, which undergirds much of our classroom discourse research today, treats social interaction within the ZPD as crucial for learner development. Teaching, by extension, is a matter of offering optimal assistance or creating true conversation within the ZPD. Inspirational efforts have been made to depict what such assistance or conversation might look like, leaving us much food for thought and terrain for exploration.

APPROACHES TO CLASSROOM DISCOURSE

In this section, I offer a sample (rather than a comprehensive review) of various approaches to classroom discourse: (applied) linguistics, sociolinguistics, critical discourse analysis, education and educational psychology, ethnography, language socialization, and sociocultural theory, highlighting the kinds of questions that have driven the different strands of work (see Box, Creider, & Waring, 2013 for a review of classroom discourse studies in second and foreign language classrooms). These categories entail a mixture of methodological and theoretical stances. They are assembled for ease of presentation, not to signal any factual or definitive demarcations. In addition, since the focus of this book is on conversation analytic insights, I discuss relevant CA work in the next chapter, where I introduce the methodology.

(Applied) Linguistics

Scholars who take a linguistic or applied linguistic approach typically use a coding scheme to specify the nature of classroom interaction and to answer questions such as whether learning occurs, what constitutes success in school, or what types of teacher talk support learning. Fanselow (1977), for example, offers an instrument called Foci for Observing Communications used in Settings (FOCUS) to capture the characteristics of communication in the classroom (i.e., who communicates, what is the pedagogical purpose, what mediums are used to communicate content, how are the mediums used to communicate areas of content, and what areas of content are communicated). In her study on prekindergarten children's second-language discourse learning, Kleifgen (1990) asks: how do nonnative speaker (NNS) of English children learn the classroom discussion cycle (CDC) or

IRF compared to their NS peers? She video recorded six children (English, Chinese, and Korean) and their teachers during the first seven weeks of class and coded the data by solicitation, response, and reaction in the CDC. She found that while two-year-olds did not participate in any CDC, three- and four-year-olds learned CDC with no differentiation between the NS and NNS children. In other words, being an NNS of the language does not necessarily prevent children's learning of CDC.

Within the linguistic approach, the work of systemic functional linguists (SFL) features prominently. SFL is a linguistic theory developed by Michael Halliday (1978), according to which every language offers its speakers and writers a range of choices for construing meaning. There are, for example, three abstract functions *(metafunctions)* that are simultaneously realized in every clause we speak or write: ideational, interpersonal, and textual. The ideational function refers to aspects of grammar that represent the world and its experiences (e.g., lexis, transitivity, and logical connectors); the interpersonal function refers to aspects of grammar that realize the relationships of interlocutors (e.g., mood, modality, and person); the textual function refers to aspects of grammar that assist in organizing language as a message (e.g., theme, information, and cohesion). Taking a systemic functional linguistic approach, Christie (2002) asks: what constitutes success in morning news giving that includes show-and-tell and anecdotes? Based on observations of Susy, Ken, and Christopher (pseudonyms) in an Australian early childhood education classroom, Christie found that to be successful at the morning news giving, the child needed to choose an appropriate (i.e., happy) aspect of personal experience and (re)create it in sustained talk (with elaboration) that was either dialogic or monologic. While Susy could assume this ideal position, Ken and Christopher could not. As Christie observed, the morning news genre was not accessible to every child, and it did not allow for sufficient scaffolding, being a one-off activity with no lead-up or follow-up.

Using a combination of SFL and Vygotskyan theory, Sharpe (2008) asks: how can teacher talk support learning? Based on video recordings and field notes of two beginning-of-the-year high school history lessons in Australia, Sharpe found that the teacher used a range of strategies such as repeating, recasting recontextualization, and cued elicitation to promote use of technical language. The teacher also created in the feedback move "a discursive pressure that leads to an increased challenge for students by requiring them to elaborate or reformulate responses" (Sharp, 2008, p. 138). In addition, the teacher used what Wood (1992) calls "low control" moves such as telling, speculating, acknowledging, or suggesting rather than questioning. In so doing, he was able to "give students the opportunity to give their own viewpoint, reveal what they know and are uncertain about and find answers to questions of their own" (Sharpe, 2008, p. 140). Finally, the teacher used meta comments to create conceptual hooks and recycled ideas via busy clusters of words. Learning, according to Sharpe, was evidenced in student uptake documented in group discussions, tests, and interviews.

The theme of what kinds of teacher talk support student learning finds strong resonance among researchers of English language teaching (ELT) as well (e.g., Clifton, 2006; Cullen, 2002; Walsh, 2002). Cullen (2002) examined the pedagogical roles of the F move in IRF and the features of effective follow-up. Based on video recordings of secondary English as a foreign language (EFL) classrooms in Tanzania, he found that the F move took on evaluative and discoursal roles that included reformulation, elaboration, comment, repetition, and responsiveness. Walsh (2002) investigated how teacher talk in adult EFL classrooms facilitates or hinders student learning based on his observations of eight experienced teachers during eight hours of audio recordings of teacher-fronted activities. According to his analysis, direct error correction, content feedback, checking for confirmation, extended wait time, and scaffolding facilitated student learning, and turn completion, teacher echo, and teacher interruptions hindered student learning. Similarly, treating facilitation as an alternative to teacher-fronted classrooms, Clifton (2006) considered facilitator talk using audio recordings of facilitator-learner interaction in a language school in north France with three French-speaking adult students and identified its features as learner initiation, teacher back-channeling, asking referential questions, and coauthoring narratives. In the end, Clifton speculated that facilitating may be better suited to small groups of motivated, mature, and relatively advanced learners.

In sum, aside from further conceptualizing classroom discourse with instruments such as FOCUS, (applied) linguistics have further demonstrated learner access or lack of access to classroom discourse structures such as CDC or morning news genre, given their language and cultural backgrounds. In particular, (applied) linguists have made important strides in identifying the kinds of teacher talk that supports or inhibits learning in the (language) classroom (e.g., speculating rather than questioning and wait time vs. interruption).

Sociolinguistics

The interest of sociolinguists, on the other hand, revolves around specifying the variations in classroom language (Shuy, 1988), directing their attention to issues such as language play (Tarone, 2000) or the cross-culturally problematic discourse strategies used by the international teaching assistant (ITA) (Davies & Tyler, 2004). Based on video recordings of six language arts classrooms, for example, Shuy (1988) showed teacher talk varied by where and how it took place. As it turned out, to his great dismay, the majority of talk did not involve doing content but was devoted to form and control. In addition, some teacher questions were doing probing and others socializing; horizontal questions (i.e., asking the same questions repeatedly) did not engage probing, while vertical questions did. Some teacher talk was explicit with clarity and some implicit without clarity. Some used natural language and others ritualized. Teacher talk also varied by who controlled the topic, what counted as a safe topic, and whether the topic flowed naturally. Some teacher talk was conversational without stereotypical teacher intonation, and some encouraged "one-upping." Shuy concludes that effective teaching entails probing content rather than prioritizing form and control and that it utilizes, values, and builds on natural language.

Tarone (2000) drew attention to the aspect of classroom language that had not been accorded much legitimacy in second-language acquisition research—that of language play. For Tarone (2000), the purpose of play is "not primarily to transmit information, but rather to entertain," and play is "a socially-constructed phenomenon which is non-literal, inherently entertaining, and rule-oriented" (p. 32). Having established that play (with phonology, lexis, and pragmatics) does indeed exist in child and adult second-language talk, Tarone argues, drawing upon evidence from naturally occurring interaction between NS teachers and their NNS students, that play serves an important role in second-language learning by lowering the affective filter, stretching learners' sociolinguistic competence through double voicing, and destablizing the interlanguage system.

Working within an interactional sociolinguistic framework, Davies and Tyler (2004) examined transcripts from video recordings of a Korean ITA interacting with undergraduates in a physics lab, along with interviews and observational notes. They asked: (1) what discourse strategies does the ITA use in his interaction with the undergraduates, and (2) why is that strategy considered problematic by the students and the analysts? Their analysis showed that the ITA used an assertive and deductive discourse strategy in the discussion of cheating (i.e., *Please don't cheat.*), where the positive transfer of the inductive approach would have served him better as Americans would typically use an inductive and collaborative strategy in a similar situation.

In sum, by foregrounding variations, sociolinguists have (1) offered us yet another way to appreciate the nature of teacher talk (i.e., is it directed toward content or form and control? Is it doing probing or socializing? Is it explicit or implicit?), (2) forced us to pay attention to the less-than-legitimate aspect of classroom language (i.e., play) and its value for learning, and finally, (3) illuminated our understanding of the miscommunications incurred by clashing cross-cultural discourse conventions in classroom interaction.

Critical Discourse Analysis

Critical discourse analysis (CDA) is an extension of (or used interchangeably with) critical linguistics (CL-1970s) (Fairclough, 1989; Fowler, Hodge, Kress, & Trew 1979; Kress & Hodge, 1979; van Dijk, 1984; Wodak, 2011), specializing in the study of language and ideology. Ideology is defined in two related ways: (1) a system of ideas and practices that operate to the advantage of a social group; and (2) a system of ideas and practices that disguise or distort the social, economic, and political relations between dominant and dominated classes (Mesthrie, Swann, Deumert, & Leap, 2000, p. 320). The key concepts in CDA are: power, dominance, ideology, hegemony (i.e., ruling with the consent of the governed), naturalization, and hidden agenda. For CDA analysts, reality and thought are constructed to favor the powerful, and social change is manifested in changing constructions of reality and thought.

Kumaravadivelu (1999) summarizes the questions confronting classroom CDA analysts as follows (note: some are specific to L2 classrooms):

- If discourse participants bring to the classroom their racialized, stratified, and gendered experiences, how can we identify the way(s) in which these experiences motivate the style and substance of classroom discourse?
- If the objective of language education should be not merely to facilitate effective language use but also to promote critical engagement among discourse participants, then how can we analyze and assess the extent to which critical engagement is facilitated in the classroom?
- If the learners' voices have to be recognized and respected, how might their personal purposes, attitudes, and preferred ways of doing things be reconciled with classroom rules and regulations and with instructional aims and objectives?
- If learners bring to the classroom their own forms of cultural capital, which may be different from the capital hierarchy of the external world or even of the school they attend, how can we make sure that their cultural capital is recognized, rewarded, and enriched?
- If learners and teachers are using subtle forms of subversion in the practice of everyday classroom discourse, how can we investigate the source and substance of such tactics?
- If the learners' linguistic needs and wants cannot be separated from their sociocultural needs and wants, how can we analyze and interpret the impact of one on the other?

Thus, the prevailing concerns appear to be: (1) how does the larger context of who we are or what our motivations are affect what goes on in the classroom and what gets learned, and (2) what is the nature of power in the classroom, e.g., resistance, subversion, and so on? Perhaps not surprisingly, for example, IRF is considered to be a critical resource for exercising teacher domination and marginalizing student voices (Gutiérrez & Larson, 1994; Gutiérrez, Larson, & Kreuter, 1995).

A more nuanced view of power also exists. As Gutierrez, Rymes, and Larson (1995) memorably write with regard to their investigation of how power was locally constructed in the various social spaces during the "current events" activity in a ninth-grade Los Angeles classroom with mostly African American and Latino students:

We resist both glorifying the marginal student and simply blaming the teacher . . . all participants are complicit in maintaining a communicative barrier, although in very different ways, and in constructing the social and power relationships that unfold in particular communities of practices.

(p. 448)

Drawing on a combination of video recordings, field notes, and interviews, the authors found that while the teacher's monologic script conveyed the importance of reading the *Los Angeles Times* and constructed the students as incompetent, the students counter-script rekeyed the interaction via mocking, joking, and "mis-reading." According to the authors, it was the unscripted third space, where the script and the counter-script intersected, that offered some (fleeting) potential for dialogic learning:

> The students and teacher occasionally meet in the same "key" and share information that is not characteristic of either the teacher or student script. It is in this unscripted third space that student and teacher cultural interests, or internal dialogizations, become available to each other, where actual cross-cultural communication is possible, and where public artifacts such as the newspaper text, and even historical events are available for critique and contestation.

(p. 465)

The moment documented by the authors as exemplifying the third space occurred during a discussion of *Brown v. Board of Education*, where the Supreme Court found that the public education doctrine of "separate but equal" in the South in the 1950s (i.e., black and white children can go to different schools as long as the schools are equal) "is not equal" (p. 463). A half-black and half-white kid asked, "What if they're half black and half white?" This genuine but unexpected question took the teacher into a space where no stock answer was available, which made authentic communication possible. Unfortunately, as the authors write:

> This particular classroom community does not have enough interactional experience in the third space to mediate participation and, thus, learning in this new key. The students are quick to relegate the personal yet relevant to a joke about "Tania," who is half Black and half White. Almost simultaneously, the teacher re-invokes his own script and continues the quiz with the next question about the Supreme Court. Thus, the opportunity for contesting class standards such as the history of racism in this country or attitudes about miscegenation, goes unheeded.

(p. 466)

The notion of *third space* appears analogous to what Canagarajah (1997) refers to as the academic contact zone, where different communities interact. With an interest in discovering how minority students negotiate power in the academic contact zone, Canagarajah collected observations and recordings of oral and written communications at different levels of formality at a special summer writing course for predominantly African American undergraduates. He found that students represented themselves in academically favorable identities in initial online discussions but displayed conflicting stances in later messages. In addition, topic-centered discourse (that features carefully reasoned positions with clear explanations and relevant evidence) was found in the official space, whereas topic-associated discourse (that prioritizes collaborative exploration along with narratives, anecdotes, and pop culture motifs) and person-centered discourse (with a strong oral character and a distinct spoken idiom) were found in the *safe house*, where safe house refers to:

> social and intellectual spaces where groups can constitute themselves as horizontal, homogeneous, sovereign communities with high degrees of trust, shared understandings, and temporary protection from legacies of oppressions within the threatening atmosphere of the contact zone.
> (Pratt in Canagarajah, 1997, p. 174)

The safe house, argues Canagarajah, is a space for opposition and learning. The author concludes that it is important to consider how to tap into the pedagogical value of the safe house and bring those values into the public space of the contact zone. Canagarajah (2004) also shows how ESL students in a secondary school engaged in code- and style-switching and experimented with vocabulary and syntax in the safe house of off-task or between-task talk outside the official IRF format.

The concern for power negotiation is also manifested in Hanrahan's (2006) research question of how teacher discourse enhances or limits student access to science. Using a combination of CDA and SFL to analyze audio recordings of two 40-minute lessons from two secondary science classes along with interviews, Hanrahan shows that talk that limits access emphasizes material processes with an exclusive focus on scientific content without reference to people or appraisals and incurs minimal interaction, given its focus on correct answers. Such talk is also characterized by implicit transitions, ellipsis, formal language, more lexical density, and a style that reinforces difference. Talk that enhances access, on the other hand, foregrounds mental and verbal processes with people as participants and actors. It contains appraisals and personal narratives of actual events delivered with humor. It is characterized by student initiations, explicit transitions, informal language, little ellipsis, less lexical density, and a style that shows deference.

Finally, in a rare study that documents how a teacher is marginalized by student resistance an EFL classroom in Sri Lanka, Canagarajah (1993) showed that the students who were used to teacher-centered, grammar-based classes resisted the student-centered, discussion-based classroom promoted by the teacher. Many went so far as dropping the class and enrolling in private tutoring instead to ensure development of the necessary L2 skills for the next course in the sequence.

As can be seen, critical discourse analysts are concerned predominantly with how power is distributed and negotiated in the classroom, and their work has brought us such thought-provoking analytical concepts as the *third space* (Gutierrez, Rymes, & Larson, 1995), the *academic contact zone* (Canagarajah, 1997), and the access-enhancing versus access-limiting nature of teacher discourse (Hanrahan, 2006).

Education and Educational Psychology

For scholars with their intellectual homes in education or educational psychology, what drives their pursuits is the exclusive preoccupation with the question of what promotes learning, as opposed to, for example, explicating the nature and structure of classroom discourse or elucidating the power distributions in the classroom. Marton and Tsui (2004), for example, identify the conditions for successful learning as discernment, variation, as well as simultaneity and awareness:

> We can only experience simultaneously that which we can discern; we can only discern what we experience to vary; and we can only experience variations if we have experienced different instances previously and are holding them in our awareness simultaneously (in the diachronic sense).
>
> (p. 20)

For Marton and Tsui, the teacher's primary professional task is to create such conditions for the specific object of learning at hand, and *the space of learning* that accommodates these conditions is linguistically constituted, as demonstrated by the authors and their colleagues in a series of empirical studies.

In another attempt to specify the relationship between discourse and learning, Michaels, O'Connor, and Resnick (2007) outline the features of Accountable Talk that highlight the importance of listening to each other, logical reasoning, and factual accuracy. Such Accountable Talk, according to the authors, would "support and promote equity and access to rigorous academic learning" (p. 283). They also make specific recommendations of how such academically productive talk may be achieved in the classroom by outlining nine talk moves that promote such talk (Michaels & O'Connor, 2012). The specific link between discourse and learning is also dealt with in Mayer's (2012) book *Classroom Discourse and Democracy*, where she explores the affordances and constraints of the different forms of learning experiences related to classroom discussion (teacher-led, student-led, and co-led learning) in fostering one's academic growth and intellectual authority.

A sizable body of work done in education is ethnographic—a method that entails extended time in the classroom as participant or nonparticipant observers, collection of recordings in combination with field notes, and the use of interviews, journals, and stimulated recalls to obtain the emic perspective (Tsui, 2013). According to Watson-Gegeo (1997):

> Classroom ethnography refers to the application of ethnographic and sociolinguistic or discourse analytic research methods to the study of behavior, activities, interactions, and discourse in formal and semi-formal educational settings such as school classrooms, adult education programs, and day-care centers.
>
> (p. 135)

Under this extremely broad umbrella of classroom ethnography, Watson-Gegeo (1997) has placed four approaches that include (1) ethnography of communication that underscores contrasting patterns of language use in home communities and classroom settings as exemplified by the work of Gumperz, Cazden, and Heath, (2) micro-ethnography that analyzes the organization and management of one slice of social life in great detail as exemplified by the work of Erickson, (3) discourse analysis that highlights the structures and functions of classroom talk as represented by the work of Sinclaire and Coulthard, Lemke, and van Lier, and finally, (4) critical ethnography that focuses on how power relations in the larger society is reflected in the classroom as exemplified in the works of McDermott (1976) and Bernstein (1977).

For scholars engaging in ethnographic work in the classroom, the connection between discourse and learning is mediated by the notion of participation, with the assumption that participation is a necessary condition for learning. Revealing insights have been obtained regarding the various factors that shape student participation and, in particular, how building upon culturally different participation styles can promote student learning (e.g., Au, 1980; Erickson & Mohatt, 1982; McCollum, 1989). Au (1980), for example, shows that when the participation structures (e.g., chorus vs. a single child speaking to the teacher) in the reading lessons resembled those of talk story in the Hawaiian culture, a group of young Hawaiian children's reading achievements were promoted. Foster (1989) (also see Lee, 1995) examines how a black teacher in an urban community college incorporates familiar ways of speaking and appropriate performance norms into her classroom, how her teaching style affects student participation, and how participants themselves interpret this style. The analysis shows that the teacher used call and response, cross-speaker anaphor, coherence and meter, repetition, vowel lengthening, catchy phrasing, figurative language, symbolism, metaphors, and gestures to underscore her point, that the style engaged the students and promoted learning via, for example, mnemonic device, and that both the teacher and the students considered the style positive and productive. Foster concludes that a group-centered collective ethos has the potential of promoting the academic achievement of (black) students. The notion of building upon students' cultural repertoire needs to be approached with great caution, however. McCarty, Lynch, Wallace, and Benally (1991), for example, report on a project that successfully involves Navajo children in open-ended questioning, inductive and analytical reasoning, and student verbalization in both small- and large-group settings, thereby challenging the stereotype of Navajo children being "nonverbal" learners.

The theme of how teaching style affects student participation continues in Oyler's (1996) work on how teachers and students share authority in classroom interaction. In her year-long ethnographic study in an urban U.S. first grade classroom, Oyler found that during 14 read-alouds of information books with the teacher's support, students initiated in a variety of ways through directing process, questioning for understanding, understanding text, personal experience, intertextual link, claiming expertise, and affective responses. Thus, students regardless of backgrounds can engage with texts and contribute to classwork in a variety of ways, and by sharing authority, the teacher in fact extends her authority.

Rather than looking at the entire class, Rex's (2000) full semester study of a ninth grade academic foundations for success (AFS) class with mixed abilities focuses on the telling case of one lower-ability student named Judy and how the teacher creates opportunities of participation for her. As Rex shows, the teacher listens to, tries to understand, validates, positively evaluates, and diffuses any possible negative reading of Judy's questions, and he also takes the time to answer her questions. In the meantime, Judy also positions herself as an active inquirer. In other words, the teacher plays an important role in creating interactional inclusion.

In sum, while (applied) linguists have identified some features of teacher talk that support student learning, scholars in education and educational psychology have addressed the broader issue of what teachers can do to create particular conditions for learning that, for example, promote certain kinds talk that favor logical reasoning and factual accuracy, as epitomized in concepts such as *space for learning* or *Accountable Talk*. Treating participation as a key path to learning, classroom ethnographers in particular, have offered convincing evidence of how building upon learners' linguistic and cultural repertoire may promote or inhibit participation and how the teacher can play an important role in engaging student participation by sharing authority or validating student questions, among other practices.

Language Socialization

The theoretical framework of language socialization is a result of a joint proposal based on Schieffelin's study on how Kaluli children acquire language in Papua New Guinea (1975–1976) and Ochs' study on how Samoan children acquire language (1977–1978) (Ochs & Schieffelin, 1984). What Schieffelin and Ochs found from their respective studies was that "language acquisition is deeply embedded in the process of becoming socialized to be a competent member of a social group and that socialization practices and ideologies impact language acquisition in concert with neurodevelopmental influence" (Ochs & Schieffelin, 2008, p. 4). For Ochs and Schieffelin (2008),

> [a] primary goal of language socialization research is to analyze children's verbal interactions with others not only as a corpus of utterances to be examined for linguistic regularities but also, vitally, as socially and culturally grounded enactments of preferred and expected sentiments, aesthetics, moralities, ideas, orientations to attend to and engage people and objects, activities, roles, and paths to knowledge and maturity as broadly conceived and evaluated by families and other institutions within a community.
>
> (Heath, 1983, p. 4).

Language socialization concerns, in other words, "how children and novices become both communicatively and culturally competent within their homes, schools, and other discourse communities," with particular attention to: (1) "the social, cultural, and interactional contexts in which language and other kinds of knowledge are learned" and (2) "the role of teachers, peers, siblings, and other more experienced members of the culture who explicitly or implicitly help novices gain expertise in the ways of the community" (Duff, 2008, p. xiii).

Some have looked at how particular linguistic resources or discourse conventions have served as the means (and end) of socialization. IRF or the recitation script, for example, has been reported as a default socialization tool. Poole (1992) recorded verbal interactions as a participant observer in beginning-level adult ESL classes in the United States and found that the teachers, themselves middle-class European Americans, tended toward speaking to the students in ways akin to what Ochs and Schieffelin (1984) uncovered in their observations of white, middle-class American caregivers and their children. For instance, like mothers with their young, teachers often used IRF sequences to guide novice L2 speakers through language production. In Duff's (1995) work on an EFL history classroom in a Hungarian dual-language high school, the students were also well socialized into the recitation script embodied in the IRF structure. By contrast, they were novices in the student-centered, cooperative classrooms typical of Hungarian dual-language programs. When initially given the task of leading lectures, the students were dependent on formulaic expressions provided by the teacher to frame or conclude their talks. As the year progressed, the students exhibited their adeptness at using language more creatively through asking for clarifications from the teacher and providing their peers with feedback on improving student lectures. Duff concluded that the students were being socialized into becoming future EFL history teachers, performing as increasingly competent apprentices of this particular community. Beyond the recitation script, Agnes He (2000) in her study on Chinese heritage language schools suggested that the interactional and grammatical organizations of teacher's directives offered rich resources for socializing the children into Chinese cultural values.

Others have focused on how learners are socialized into academic conventions. Morita (2000), for example, investigates the nature of TESOL graduate students' discourse socialization into oral academic presentations (OAPs). Based on an eight-month ethnographic study of two graduate TESOL courses with a mix of native and nonnative speakers that involved classroom observations, video recordings of oral presentations, interviews, and questionnaires, Morita (2000) found that (1) the goal of discourse socialization entailed communicating epistemic stance, engaging the audience, and working collaboratively, that (2) the students learned by negotiating instructor expectations as well as preparing, observing, performing, and reviewing OAPs, and that (3) the NNSs experienced linguistic, sociocultural, and psychological difficulties and coped by, for example, rehearsing the OAPs, preparing organized handouts, and making extra written notes. Based on these findings, Morita posits that the NS–NNS dichotomy warrants reexamination, that the OAPs provide a useful forum for participation, and that OAP can be usefully analyzed for tacit rules of classroom interaction. Based on research conducted in a Canadian secondary school social studies classroom where some English language learners (ELLs) were being mainstreamed for the first time, Duff and Oliver (2009) also showed how students were socialized, through management interactions, content exchanges, communicative focused exchanges, and language focused exchanges, into making effective presentations when talking about current events and leading classroom discussions. The socialization of academic discourse also features prominently in a recent Mehan and Cazden (2015) review article on historical and contemporary trends of classroom discourse research. The authors observe that increasingly, teachers strive to socialize students into academic discourse by encouraging them to engage the "big ideas" of science, soliciting the grounds for student reasoning, and deploying discourse moves that promote such reasoning, thus evidencing a shift in the classroom language game from recitation to reasoning.

Still others have shed light on how the language socialization process can exhibit great variations and complexities. In her year-long research in an American elementary school classroom, Willet (1995) focused on a group of four L2 students as they completed phonics seatwork (working on their phonics workbook while sitting in their seats) and noticed a growing disparity in language development. Indeed, three of the four L2 learners had banded together, helping one another with tasks and experimenting with increasingly larger language chunks while conversing. Their active participation and linguistic independence increased during the year. By contrast, the fourth child's participation decreased, with his sparse linguistic contributions signaling an "outsider" status. Hall (1998) also found that students in a first-year Spanish class did not have equal access to opportunities for linguistic interactions. In fact, it appeared that two status groups had formed, the "primary" group receiving considerably more interactional opportunities from the teacher than the "secondary" group. The primary group was able to successfully initiate turns, overlap other students' talk, and engage the teacher in discussing content. On the other hand, the teacher often either ignored initiations by secondary group members or critiqued their contributions based on linguistic form, blocking them from elaborating on content. The variations and complexities of language socialization can also be experienced by the same group of learners at different times. Morita (2000) tracked six adult ELLs during their year-long sojourns in a Canadian university. She found that socialization is indeed a dynamic process, involving constant and evolving negotiating of identities as students socially construct their roles as members of varying classroom communities. At times, the students struggled to find or use their voice, silenced by peers or instructors, while at other moments, their presence and opinions were valued.

Finally, and unfortunately, socialization does not always move in the direction of growth or greater gains. Wortham (2005) focused on a ninth grade student Tyisha's trajectory of academic socialization from a promising student to a disruptive outcast. The two-year research involved field notes, informal conversations, interviews, and audio recordings of the classes in a U.S. public high school with 50 hours in one particular joint English and history class, where Tyisha was the focal student. Wortham showed that Tyisha's descent from a promising student to a disruptive outcast was accomplished through both denotationally explicit descriptions (e.g., "You're a bad student.") and implicit interactional positioning (e.g., position as outcast). The quality of teacher talk also can contribute negatively to socialization. In a first-year Spanish class, Hall (1995) found that the teacher's talk had no overarching topic to lend it any coherence. Instead, it was a string of loosely connected topics in the IRF format, with the same information repeated and recycled. The highly constrained nature of the interactions precluded students from becoming active participants through elaboration or inquiry.

In sum, work on language socialization has made important contributions to our understandings of the means and end of socialization as well as its pitfalls and complexities. Great insights have been gained, for example, into the features of academic discourse (e.g., communicating epistemic stance) and how such discourse may be learned through practices such as rehearsing and reasoning. While the IRF structure appears to be an important social-ization tool, its repetitive deployment without any overarching coherence can hamper rather than enhance learner socialization. And finally, the expe-rience of socialization can vary a great deal by individuals or by different time periods for the same group of individuals.

Sociocultural Theory

Although language socialization (LS) and sociocultural theory (SCT) stem from separate intellectual roots—LS championed by the linguistic anthro-pologists (Ochs & Schieffelin, 1984; also Schieffelin & Ochs, 1986) and SCT grounded in the Vygotskyan tradition of Soviet psychology—the two have much in common in their stance toward the learning process (Duff, 2007). Both emphasize the importance of social interaction, especially interaction over time between novices and those who are capable peers, caregivers, or experts. In sociocultural theory, the centrality of social interaction between more or less competent members is epitomized in classic concepts such as scaffolding (Wood, Bruner & Ross, 1976), mediation (Lantolf & Thorne, 2006), and the ZPD (Vygotsky, 1978). Among sociocultural scholars, dia-logic teaching has emerged to be an optimal mode of classroom interac-tion that promotes student learning (Mercer, 2002; O'Connor & Michaels, 2007; Wells & Arauz, 2006). Alexander (2008), for example, notes the following indicators of dialogic teaching: more focused questions, fewer stock responses to children's contribution, and children speculating, think-ing aloud, and helping each other rather than competing to spot the right answer. More specifically, sociocultural scholars have focused on the type of teacher (e.g., Jarvis & Robinson, 1997; Scott, 2008) or peer assistance(e.g., Ohta, 1995) as well as the type of interaction (e.g., Gutierrez, 2008; Skid-more, 2000) that best scaffolds learning within the learner's ZPD.

Jarvis and Robinson (1997) examined how teacher responsiveness con-tributed to student learning. Based on audio and video tapes from two lessons drawn from a large corpus of 17 primary-level EFL lessons in Malaysia, Malta, and Tanzania, as well as teacher interviews, they catego-rized teacher responses into *accept, model, clue, develop, clarify*, and *reject* and found that such responsiveness entails building upon pupil talk and addressing a potential problem. While showing that teacher discourse fea-tured the *focus, build, summarize* pattern, they found that too much *focus* with insufficient *build* and *summarize* hampered learning. Indeed, as Jarvis and Robinson (1997) claim, elaboration of *focus, build, summarize* may be a step toward identifying what type of teacher talk supports learning. Utiliz-ing the framework of scaffolding (Wood, Bruner, & Ross, 1976), McCor-mick and Donato (2000) demonstrated how one university ESL teacher's use of questions facilitated comprehension, comprehensibility, and partici-pation. Scott (2008) investigated how in a secondary school science class, the teacher helped students understand the scientific concept of "normal force" against a backdrop of everyday thinking. He found that the teacher's communicative approach featured four types of discourse defined along two dimensions: interactive and dialogic. Over the course of three lessons, the teacher moved from a style that was more dialogic (with a focus on everyday thinking) to more authoritative and then back to more dialogic (with a focus on scientific thinking). As Scott argues, intellectual relevance may be established by engaging an existing point of view, for meaningful learning to occur, the teacher needs to problematize the content under discussion, and dialogic teaching is accumulative rather than one shot.

Peer assistance is featured in Ohta's (1995) analysis of learner-learner collaborative interaction in the ZPD. Based on 100 minutes of audio and video recordings of a second-year university-level Japanese as a foreign language (JFL) class, Ohta showed that while limited language use opportunities were taken up "safely" during teacher-fronted activities, a greater variety of opportunities became available during pair activities as the higher-proficiency Becky and the lower-proficiency Mark progressed via shared strengths in the ZPD. Ohta concluded that pair work offered important opportunities for second-language acquisition in the ZPD, where both higher- and lower-proficiency learners can benefit from pair work.

Aside from the nature of teacher or peer assistance, others focused on the type of interaction that scaffolded learning. Skidmore (2000), for example, asked what type of teacher-pupil interaction during guided readings sessions might promote pupils' independent powers of comprehension in English primary schools. Showing two discussion sequences that involved a true-or-false task and the "Who is most to blame?" question, respectively, Skidmore pointed to the first sequence as an example of authoritative discourse and the second as internally persuasive discourse. He concluded that task type plays a role in the type of discourse it engenders and that teachers can choose to adopt more participatory modes of organization in the relative autonomy of the classroom. Using data from an intermediate-level Spanish language classroom where learners worked in dyads or triads across three different problem-solving tasks, Gutierrez (2008) investigated the nature of microgenesis affordance—characteristics of the assistance provided by the more knowledgeable peer or of the linguistic environment that drive the learner's L2 forward. She found that with assistance as microgenesis affordance, such assistance may be (1) requested and supplied in the form of *straightforward reply, paraphrase followed by a reply*, or *co-constructed*, or (2) unrequested and provided in the form of corrective feedback. Learners also cocreated learning affordances via interwoven consciousness (i.e., making language more manageable and benefiting from each other's mental activities) or mapping knowledge (i.e., questioning partner's utterance and mapping it against one's own knowledge).

In sum, sociocultural scholars who work in a variety of classroom contexts have contributed much specificity to the kinds of assistance and interaction that drive learning. They have shown, for example, the effectiveness of teacher questions, peer assistance, teacher responsiveness, and dialogic (vs. authoritative) discourse in promoting student learning.

CONCLUSION

From the classic works in classroom discourse, we have learned that (1) it is a distinct form of talk characterized by its own hierarchical and sequential organizations, its turn-taking system, and its specific set of activity types, (2) these rules of classroom discourse are often unwritten and mysterious (to students), and (3) their mysterious nature in part explains why children from particular backgrounds face difficulties in school. An important insight that this classic scholarship affords us is the relationship between talk and learning and the teacher's role in manipulating that relationship. Presentational talk, for example, would lead to ritualized understanding, and explorative talk to principled understanding. And most notably, talk that provides assistance in the ZPD facilitates learning.

Continuing explorations of these themes find manifold iterations in subsequent work carried out by scholars working with various approaches to classroom discourse. The distinct and mysterious nature of classroom discourse and its potential hindrance to specific groups has inspired scholars in (applied) linguistics and sociolinguistics to pursue inquiries into the features and functions of teacher talk as well as the varied, nonconforming, and cross-culturally problematic aspects of language use in the classroom. For critical discourse analysts and classroom ethnographers, the interest in classroom language has taken a more critical turn as they proceed to interrogate how power is distributed in the classroom and how teacher talk can play a crucial role in structuring access, participation, inclusion, and engagement. Others have foregrounded learning as their explicit focus of investigation. While language socialization researchers have produced careful portrayals of learners' varying trajectories of socialization into academic conventions and cultural values, (applied) linguists, educational psychologists, and sociocultural scholars have identified specific ways in which teacher talk might support student learning.

Clearly, the scholarship accumulated over the past five decades has formed a substantial knowledge base that anchors our current understandings of the nature of classroom discourse as well as the various ways in which such discourse promotes or hinders learning. In the next chapter, I introduce a specific approach to classroom discourse that has not been dealt with in these prior pages—that of conversation analysis (CA), where I also hope to articulate, with some clarity, the unique insights that CA work can bring to our existing body of knowledge. As will be made evident, for example, one distinct feature of CA is its microscopic focus on the "discourse" of classroom discourse, where its interactional details are maximally attended to—a practice not prioritized in most of the works reviewed so far.

REFERENCES

Alexander, R. (2008). Culture, dialogue and learning: Notes on an emerging pedagogy. In N. Mercer & S. Hodgkinson (Eds.), *Exploring talk in school: Inspired by the work of Douglas Barnes* (pp. 91–114). London: Sage.

Au, K. H.-P. (1980). Participation structures in a reading lesson with Hawaiian children: Analysis of a culturally appropriate instructional event. *Anthropology & Education Quarterly, 11*(2), 91–115.

Barnes, D. (1992). *From communication to curriculum* (2nd ed.). Harmondsworth, UK: Penguin.

Bellack, A., Kliebard, H., Hyman, R., & Smith, F. (1966). *The language of the classroom*. New York: Teachers College Press.

Bernstein, B. (1977). Class, codes and control. In *Towards a theory of educational transmission* (2nd ed., Vol. 3). London: Routledge & Kegan Paul.

Box, C. D., Creider, S. C., & Waring, H. Z. (2013). Talk in the second and foreign language classroom: A review of the literature. *Journal of Contemporary Foreign Language Studies, 396*(12), 86–97.

Canagarajah, A. S. (1993). American textbooks and Tamil students: Discerning ideological tensions in the ESL classroom. *Language, Culture and Curriculum, 6*(2), 143–156.

Canagarajah, A. S. (1997). Safe houses in the contact zone: Coping strategies of African-American students in the academy. *College Composition and Communication, 48*, 173–196.

Canagarajah, A. S. (2004). Subversive identities, pedagogical safe houses, and critical learning. In B. Norton & K. Toohey (Eds.), *Critical pedagogies and language learning* (pp. 116–137). New York: Cambridge University Press.

Cazden, C. (2001). *Classroom discourse: The language of teaching and learning* (2nd ed.). Portsmouth, NH: Heinemann.

Christie, F. (2002). *Classroom discourse analysis: A functional perspective*. London: Continuum.

Clifton, J. (2006). Facilitator talk. *ELT Journal, 60*(2), 142–150.

Cole, M., & Scribner, S. (1978). Introduction. In L. S. Vygotsky, *Mind in society: The development of higher psychological processes* (pp. 1–14). Cambridge, MA: Harvard University Press.

Cullen, R. (2002). Supportive teacher talk: The importance of the F-move. *ELT Journal, 56*(2), 117–127.

Davies, C. E., & Tyler, A. E. (2004). Discourse strategies in the context of crosscultural institutional talk: Uncovering interlanguage pragmatics in the university classroom. In K. Bardovi-Harlig & B. S. Hartford (Eds.), *Interlanguage pragmatics: Exploring institutional talk* (pp. 133–156). Mahwah, NJ: Lawrence Erlbaum.

Duff, P. (1995). An ethnography of communication in immersion classrooms in Hungary. *TESOL Quarterly, 29*(3), 505–537.

Duff, P. (2007). Second language socialization as sociocultural theory: Insights and issues. Language Teaching, 40, 309–319.

Duff, P. (2008). Introduction to Volume 8: Language socialization. In P. Duff & N. Hornberger (Eds.), *Language socialization: Encyclopedia of language and education* (Vol. 8, pp. xiii–xx). New York: Springer.

Duff, P., & Oliver, R. (2009). Language socialization in a Canadian secondary school: Talking about current events. In R. Barnard & M. Torres-Guzman (Eds.), Creating communities of learning in schools (pp. 165–185). Clevedon, UK: Multilingual Matters.

Edwards, D., & Mercer, N. (1987). *Common knowledge: The development of understanding in the classroom*. London: Methuen.

Erickson, F., & Mohatt, G. (1982). The cultural organization of participation structures. In G. Spindler (Ed.), *Doing the ethnography of schooling: Educational anthropology in action* (pp. 136–173). New York: Holt, Rinehart, and Winston.

Fairclough, N. (1989). *Language and power*. London and New York: Longman.

Fanselow, J.F. (1977). Beyond RASHOMON—Conceptualizing and describing the teaching act. *TESOL Quarterly, 11*(1), 17–39.

Foster, M. (1989). 'It's cookin' now': A performance analysis of the speech events of a black teacher in an urban community college. *Language in Society, 18*(1), 1–29.

Fowler, R., Hodge, B., Kress, G., & Trew, T. (Eds.). (1979). *Language and control*. London: Routledge and Kegan Paul.

Gutiérrez, A.G. (2008). Microgenesis, method and object: A study of collaborative activity in a Spanish as a foreign language classroom. *Applied Linguistics, 29*(1), 120–148.

Gutiérrez, K., & Larson, J. (1994). Language borders: Recitation as hegemonic discourse. *International Journal of Educational Reform, 3*(1), 22–36.

Gutiérrez, K., Larson, J., & Kreuter, B. (1995). Cultural tensions in the scripted classroom: The value of the subjugated perspective. *Urban Education, 29*(4), 410–442.

Gutiérrez, K.D., Rymes, B., & Larson, J. (1995). Script, counter-script, and underlife in the classroom: James Brown vs. Brown vs. Board of Education. *Harvard Educational Review, 65*(3), 445–471.

Hall, J.K. (1995). 'Aw, man, where we goin'?': Classroom interaction and the development of L2 interactional competence. *Issues in Applied Linguistics, 6*(2), 37–62.

Hall, J.K. (1998). Differential teacher attention to student utterances: The construction of different opportunities for learning in the IRF. *Linguistics and Education, 9*(3), 287–311.

Halliday, M.A.K. (1978). *Language as social semiotic: The social interpretation of language and meaning*. London: Edward Arnold.

Hanrahan, M.U. (2006). Highlighting hybridity: A critical discourse analysis of teacher talk in science classrooms. *Science Education, 90*(1), 8–43.

He, A.W. (2000). The grammatical and interactional organization of teacher's directives: Implications for socialization of Chinese American children. *Linguistics and Education, 11*(2), 119–140.

Heath, S.B. (1983). *Ways with words*. Cambridge, UK: Cambridge University Press.

Hodgkinson, S., & Mercer, N. (2008). Introduction. In N. Mercer & S. Hodgkinson (Eds.), *Exploring talk in school: Inspired by the work of Douglas Barnes* (pp. xi–1). London: Sage.

Jarvis, J., & Robinson, M. (1997). Analyzing educational discourse: An exploratory study of teacher response and support to pupil learning. *Applied Linguistics, 18*(2), 212–228.

Kleifgen, J. (1990). Pre-kindergarten children's second discourse learning. *Discourse Processes, 13*, 225–242.

Kress, G.R., & Hodge, R.I.V. (1979). *Language as ideology*. London: Routledge and Kegan Paul.

Kumaravadivelu, B. (1999). Critical classroom discourse analysis. *TESOL Quarterly, 33*(3), 453–484.

Lantolf, J.P., & Thorne, S.L. (2006). *Sociocultural theory and the genesis of second language development*. Oxford, UK: Oxford University Press.

Lee, C.D. (1995). A culturally based cognitive apprenticeship: Teaching African American high school students skills in literary interpretation. *Reading Research Quarterly, 30*(4), 608–630.

Lemke, J. L. (1990). *Talking science: Language, learning, and values.* Norwood, NJ: Ablex.

Marton, F., & Tsui, A. B. M. (2004). *Classroom discourse and the space of learning.* Mahwah, NJ: Lawrence Erlbaum Associates.

Mayer, S. J. (2012). *Classroom discourse and democracy: Making meanings together.* New York: Peter Lang.

McCarty, T. L., Wallace, S., Lynch, R. H., & Benally, A. (1991). Classroom inquiry and Navajo learning styles: A call for reassessment. *Anthropology & Education Quarterly, 22*(1), 42–59.

McCollum, P. (1989). Turn-allocation in lessons with North American and Puerto Rican Students: A comparative study. *Anthropology & Education Quarterly, 20*(2), 133–156.

McCormick, D. E., & Donato, R. (2000). Teacher questions as scaffolded assistance in an ESL classroom. In J. K. Hall & L. S. Verplaetse (Eds.), *Second and foreign language learning through classroom interaction* (pp. 183–202). Mahwah, NJ: Lawrence Erlbaum.

McDermott, R. P. (1976). Kids make sense: An ethnographic account of the interactional management of success and failure in the first grade classroom. Unpublished Ph.D. thesis, Stanford University, Stanford, California.

McHoul, A. W. (1985). Two aspects of classroom interaction: Turn-taking and correction. *Australian Journal of Human Communication Disorders, 13*(1), 53–64.

Mehan, H. (1979). *Learning lessons: Social organization in the classroom.* Cambridge, MA: Harvard University Press.

Mehan, H., & Cazden, C. B. (2015). Classroom discourse: From recitation to reasoning. In L. B. Resnick, C. Asterhan &. S. N. Clarke (Eds.), *Socializing intelligence through academic talk and dialogue* (pp. 13–34). Washington, DC: AERA.

Mercer, N. (2002). Developing dialogues. In G. Wells & G. Claxton (Eds.), Learning for life in the 21st century: Sociocultural perspectives on the future of education (pp. 141–153). Oxford: Blackwell.

Mesthrie, R., Swann, J., Deumert, A., & Leap, W. (2000). *Introducing sociolinguistics.* Edinburgh: Edinburgh University Press.

Michaels, S., & O'Connor, C. (2012). *Talk science primer.* Cambridge, MA: TERC.

Michaels, S., O'Connor, C., & Resnick, L. (2007). Deliberative discourse idealized and realized: Accountable talk in the classroom and in civic life. Studies in Philosophy and Education, 27(4), 283–297.

Morita, N. (2000). Discourse socialization through oral classroom activities in a TESL graduate program. *TESOL Quarterly, 34*(2), 279–310.

Ochs, E., & Schieffelin, B. (1984). Language acquisition and socialization: Three developmental stories. In R. Shweder & R. LeVine (Eds.), *Culture theory: Essays on mind, self, and emotion* (pp. 276–323). Cambridge, UK: Cambridge University Press.

Ochs, E., & Schieffelin, B. (2008). Language socialization: An historical overview. In P. A. Duff & N. H. Hornberger (Eds.), *Encyclopedia of language education, Volume 8: Language socialization* (2nd ed., pp. 3–15). New York: Springer.

O'Connor, C., & Michaels, S. (2007). When is dialog 'dialogic'? *Human Development, 50,* 275–285.

Ohta, A. S. (1995). Applying sociocultural theory to an analysis of learner discourse: Learner-learner collaborative interaction in the zone of proximal development. *Issues in Applied Linguistics, 6*(2), 93–121.

Oyler, C. (1996). Sharing authority: Student initiations during teacher-led read-alouds of information books. *Teaching and Teacher Education, 12*(2), 149–160.

Poole, D. (1992). Language socialization in the second language classroom. *Language Learning, 42*(4), 593–616.

Rex, L. (2000). Judy constructs a genuine question: A case for interactional inclusion. *Teaching and Teacher Education, 16*(2), 315–333.

Sacks, H., Schegloff, E. A., & Jefferson, G. (1974). A simplest systematics for the organization of turn-taking for conversation. *Language, 50*(4), 696–735.

Schieffelin, B., & Ochs, E. (1986). Language socialization. *Annual Review of Anthropology, 15*, 163–191.

Scott, P. (2008). Talking a way to understanding in science classrooms. In N. Mercer & S. Hodgkinson (Eds.), *Exploring talk in school: Inspired by the work of Douglas Barnes* (pp. 17–36). London: Sage.

Sharpe, T. (2008). How can teacher talk support learning? *Linguistics and Education, 19*(2), 132–148.

Shuy, R. (1988). Identifying dimensions of classroom language. In J. L. Green & J. O. Harker (Eds.), *Multiple perspective analyses of classroom discourse* (pp. 115–134). Norwood, NJ: Ablex.

Sinclair, J. M., & Coulthard, M. (1975). *Towards an analysis of discourse: The English used by teachers and pupils.* London: Oxford University Press.

Skidmore, D. (2000). From pedagogical dialogue to dialogical pedagogy. *Language and Education, 14*(4), 283–296.

Tarone, E. (2000). Getting serious about language play: Language play, interlanguage variation and second language acquisition. In B. Swierzbin, F. Morris, M. E. Anderson, C. Klee, & E. Tarone (Eds.), *Social and cognitive factors in second language acquisition: Selected proceedings of the 1999 second language research forum* (pp. 31–54). Somerville, MA: Cascadilla Press.

Tharp, R. G., & Gallimore, R. (1988). *Rousing minds to life: Teaching, learning, and schooling in social context.* New York: Cambridge University Press.

Tsui, A. B. M. (2013). Ethnography and classroom discourse. In J. P. Gee & M. Hanford (Eds.), *The Routledge handbook of discourse analysis* (pp. 383–395). New York: Routledge.

van Dijk, T. (1984). *Prejudice in discourse.* Amsterdam: John Benjamins.

van Lier, L. (1996). *Interaction in the language curriculum.* London: Longman Group Limited.

Vygotsky, L. S. (1978). *Mind in society: The development of higher psychological processes.* Cambridge, MA: Harvard University Press.

Walsh, S. (2002). Construction or obstruction: Teacher talk and learner involvement in the EFL classroom. *Language Teaching Research, 6*(1), 3–23.

Watson-Gegeo, K. A. (1997). Classroom ethnography. In N. H. Hornberger & D. Corson (Eds.), *Encyclopedia of language and education, Volume 8, Research methods in language and education* (pp. 135–144). Dordrecht: Kluwer.

Wells, G. (1999). *Dialogic inquiry: Towards a sociocultural practice and theory of education.* New York: Cambridge University Press.

Wells, G., & Arauz, R. M. (2006). Dialogue in the classroom. *Journal of the Learning Sciences 15*(3), 379–428.

Willet, J. (1995). Becoming first graders in an L2: An ethnographic study of L2 socialization. *TESOL Quarterly, 29*(3), 473–503.

Wodak, R. (2011). Critical linguistics and critical discourse analysis. In J. Zienkowski, J-O. Östman & J. Verschueren (Eds.), *Discursive pragmatics* (pp. 50–70). Amsterdam: John Benjamins.

Wood, D. (1992). Teaching talk: How modes of teacher talk affect pupil participation. In K. Norman (Ed.), *Thinking voices: The work of the National Oracy Project* (pp. 201–214). London: Hodder & Stoughton.

Wood, D. J., Bruner, J. S., & Ross, G. (1976). The role of tutoring in problem solving. *Journal of Child Psychiatry and Psychology, 17*(2), 89–100.

Wortham, S. (2005). Socialization beyond the speech event. *Journal of Linguistic Anthropology, 15*, 95–112.

3 Conversation Analysis

Championed by sociologists Harvey Sacks, Emmanuel Schegloff, and Gail Jefferson, conversation analysis (CA) emerged as a radical approach to sociological inquiry in the 1960s.

For the past four decades, CA has been effectively deployed to yield in-depth understandings of professional practices in a wide variety of contexts, forming an important knowledge base upon which practitioners can draw to identify problems, devise solutions, and enhance efficacy (e.g., Antaki, 2011; Drew & Heritage, 1992). In this chapter, I introduce CA as both a theory of, and an approach to studying, social interaction. I then offer a review of existing CA work on classroom discourse. The chapter ends with a discussion on how conversation analytic insights have contributed to our understandings of classroom discourse and, in particular, how such insights have the potential of enabling a theory of pedagogical interaction—an endeavor to be presented in the three chapters thereafter.

CONVERSATION ANALYSIS AS THEORY AND METHOD

CA as a Theoretical Framework

As noted in Chapter 1, CA is not simply a method but a theoretical framework as well. Informed by Garfinkel's (1967) ethnomethodology and Erving Goffman's (1967) theory of interactional order, CA rests on a set of assumptions that prioritize analytic induction (ten Have, 2007) and participant orientations (Sacks & Schegloff, 1973): (1) social interaction is orderly at all points—that is, no detail can be dismissed a priori; (2) participants orient to that order themselves—that is, order is not a result of the analyst's conceptions or any preformulated theoretical categories; (3) such order can be discovered and described by examining the details of interaction.

CA's bearing on theory may be further appreciated in light of its goal and tools of analysis. First, by discovering and describing members' interactional competence (Wong & Waring, 2010), accumulative CA findings ultimately amount to a theory of social interaction. Second, CA relies on a range of empirically grounded theoretical tools for analyzing social interaction. First-generation CA findings have generated a range of analytically useful concepts such as turn-constructional unit (TCU), transition-relevance place (TRP), adjacency pair (AP), and preference, which constitute in ongoing CA work a lens through which social interaction may be viewed and understood.

CA as a Methodological Approach

With a commitment to "naturalistic inquiry" (Schegloff, 1997, p. 501), CA insists on using data collected from naturally occurring interaction as opposed to interviews, field notes, native intuitions, and experimental methodologies (Heritage, 1984, p. 236). Analysts work with audio or video recordings along with the transcripts of these recordings, using transcription notations originally developed by Gail Jefferson (see appendix for a modified version that accommodates nonverbal behavior and the pedagogical contexts). A CA transcript captures a full range of interactional details such as volume, pitch, pace, intonation, overlap, inbreath, smiley voice, the length of silence, as well as nonverbal conduct. For readers unfamiliar with CA transcripts, such details can be overwhelming, but the devil is in the details. To truly appreciate the complexities of teaching is to appreciate its details. I have chosen to preserve the full range of intricacies of each transcript in this book precisely for this reason. My mission in part is to gradually socialize the readers into understanding CA transcripts.

The goal of CA is to uncover the tacit methods and procedures of social interaction. In Creider's (2014) words: "our job is to uncover the usually unconscious—but nonetheless extremely skillful—discourse analyses speakers perform as they interpret and respond to their fellow conversationalists, pause by-pause, word-by-word, gesture-by-gesture, and turn-by-turn" (p. 39). Analysis begins with the meticulous inspection of single instances and is guided by the question "Why that now?" (Schegloff & Sacks, 1973), that is, why a particular bit of talk is produced in that particular format at that particular time: what is it accomplishing? It is in these minute details that evidence is located for how social actions such as requesting or complaining are accomplished by the participants themselves. This emic, and deeply ethnomethodological, obsession with participant orientation or members' methods as made evident in their own conduct is what distinguishes CA from other methods of qualitative research.

While sharing the ethnographic tradition of naturalistic observation, for example, CA is distinct in its insistence on directing its observation toward "conduct as it has been preserved in audio and video recordings" (Clayman & Gill, 2004, p. 590) as opposed to conduct as *reported* by the participants. As McHoul (1985) reminds us:

The materials in their fine-grained detail often disclose versions of inter-actional events which are markedly counter-intuitive. That is, what people actually do in interaction often turns out to be quite unlike either professional sociological or members' own versions of what they do. To that extent, conversational analysis claims to produce findings which are both empirically grounded and (at least potentially) "news."

(p. 57)

CA is also distinct from grounded theory (GT) (Glaser & Strauss, 1967), where abstract concepts and theories are arrived at through empirical generation. Central to GT is the activity of coding, where bits and pieces of data extracted from their specific time and place are treated as indicators of theoretical concepts. This split between data and theory that characterizes GT, according to ten Have (2004), is nonexistent in ethnomethodology (i.e., the study of members' own methods of making sense of and participating in social order)—the foundation of CA (p. 146). He writes:

In a serious way, then, ethnomethodology does not strive to "add" any-thing to the social life it studies, no "theory," no "concepts," not a dif-ferent level of reality. It just brings to light what is already available for all to see; it is, then, just an eye-opener.

(p. 146)

In other words, rather than doing coding or using codes, the job of a CA worker is to crack the codes of social interaction. As a code-cracking enter-prise, CA is not equipped to answer questions such as whether X leads to Y (e.g., excessive television watching leads to violence), but it is well equipped to make substantive contributions to our understandings of what consti-tutes X in the first place.

Validity, Reliability, and Generalizability

Concepts such as validity (i.e., the extent to which an instrument measures what it is supposed to measure) and reliability (i.e., the extent to which an instrument yields consistent results across time and users) assume there is an objective reality to be unveiled (Tracy in Wood & Kroger, 2000, p. 163) and are typically applied to quantitative research. Given their sta-tus as long-standing measures for research soundness, however, it is not surprising that these same terms have sometimes been borrowed to judge the credibility of qualitative research as well (Peräkylä, 2004). Still, the transfer is not a simple and straightforward one, especially when it comes to CA—a rather distinct form of qualitative research in and of itself. To consider the validity in CA is to think about whether the analysis pro-duced by the researcher is in fact uncovering participants' practices of social interaction or "measuring" what it is supposed to "measure." Put otherwise, how do we ensure that the practices we are reporting (e.g., *What are you doing?* is a pre-invitation) are indeed the practices engaged by the participants in the interaction? Obviously, we need high-quality recordings that faithfully capture the interactions in the first place, and we need detailed transcripts that accurately represent the recordings. Most importantly, however, we need to be able to show in the publicly displayed transcripts, for instance, that *What are you doing?* is indeed produced and interpreted by the participants as a pre-invitation; that is, our description of the practices based on the data are convincing to the reader, who has equal access to the data. Ideally, readers of an analysis should have access to the recordings, not just the transcripts. The transparency of analytical claims grounded in specific participant conduct, therefore, is an important validation procedure in CA.

The reliability of CA findings is also tied to the highly detailed and public nature of its transcripts. Since these transcripts (and ideally recordings) are subject to repeated scrutiny by multiple readers, to ensure that the same data would yield consistent analyses across time and viewers, the onus is on the analyst to produce findings that can stand the test of such public scrutiny, e.g., to combat the multiple-interpretation problem. A practicing analyst often attends data sessions regularly, where participants hold each other accountable for the analyses they produce vis-à-vis a particular transcript along with its audio and video recordings—a process that typically yields increasingly finer observations of the interaction (i.e., greater validity) and, at the same time, discourages any open-ended "reading into" the transcripts or recordings. As in quantitative research, a valid CA finding is bound to be a reliable one (although not vice versa; e.g., consistent analysis can be performed on inaccurate transcripts). Mehan (1979) speaks of reproducibility or reliability as such:

> An independent investigator would be presented with this description of the lessons on the one hand, and the corpus of materials on the other. The description would serve as "instructions for looking." It would be that independent investigator's task to try and reproduce the same model of interaction described in this report. The extent to which he was successful would indicate the extent to which this is not a private model but a publicly verifiable one.
>
> (p. 177)

Key to understanding the generalizability in CA research is the concept of *possibility*: CA findings produce what is possible in other settings rather than what is generalizable—in the sense of "the traditional 'distributional' understanding of generalizability" (Peräkylä, 2004, pp. 296–297)—to other settings. Pomerantz (1990) draws upon the distinction between empirical generalization and analytical generalization (Yin, 2003) and writes, "[i]t should be clear that conversation analysis is not achieving 'empirical

generalization'" (p. 233). While empirical generalization involves generaliz-
ing from a sample to a population, in analytical generalization, each case is
related to a "theory." That is, by analyzing individual instances, the machinery that produced these individual instances is revealed (Benson & Hughes,
1991, pp. 130–131). Each instance is evidence that "the machinery for its
production is culturally available, involves members' competencies, and
is therefore possibly (and probably) reproducible" (Psathas, 1995, p. 50).
Additional instances provide "another example of the method in the action,
rather than securing the warrantability of the description of the machinery itself" (Benson & Hughes, 1991, p. 131). The value of CA analysis,
in Pomerantz' (1990) words, is that "we have identified a method (assuming sufficient evidence to support non-idiosyncratic use) and proposed how
it works sequentially and interactionally," and "subsequent research can
establish patterns of occurrences" (p. 233).

CA and Context

As opposed to treating context as external to the talk data, conversation
analysts insist on demonstrating in the details of talk that a particular
aspect of context (1) is treated as relevant by the participants themselves
(i.e. "demonstrable relevance") and that it (2) proves to be consequential
for how the interaction unfolds (i.e., "procedural consequentiality") (e.g.,
Schegloff, 1987, 1991, 1992). In other words, the evidence of context needs
to be located in the talk, although not necessarily explicitly so (Schegloff,
2009). In the following example, the identity of a *single mother* is shown
to be relevant to the complainer (i.e., demonstrable relevance) as she calls a
mediation center for neighborhood disputes (Stokoe, 2009):

1. single mother

10 C:		An,=
11 M:		=Yeah.
12		(0.3)
13 C:	→	By that ti- a- cos I'm a single mother,
14 M:	→	M:mm.=
15 C:	→	By that time, (0.3) I'm ti:red.
16		(0.2)
17 C:		.hhh
18 M:		Yeah.=
19 C:		An' I don't have many resources left for
20		co:ping with things.

For procedural consequentiality, the analyst would show how a particular
aspect of context affects how the interaction is conducted. In the following
example, the interview context has a clear effect on the interaction as Bush
withholds speaking until a question has been asked (Schegloff, 1992):

2. interview

```
01 Rather:  .hh Mister Vice President, tha:nk you for being with us tonight,
02          .hh Donald Gregg sti:ll serves as y'r tru:sted advisor.=he w'z
03          dee:ply involved in running arms t'the Contras an'he didn'
04          inform you. { . . . hhhh-(0.5)} Now when President Rea:gan's,
05          (0.2) trusted advisor: Adviral Rointdexter: (0.6) failed to inform
06          hi:m, (0.8), the president- (0.2) fired'im.hh
07    →     (0.5)
08          Why is Mister Gregg still: (.) inside the White House'n still a
09          trusted advisor.=
10 Bush:   =Because I have confidence in im, (0.3) en becuz ((continues))
```

Contrary to the popular misconception that CA does not address, or recognize the importance of, context, Schegloff (1991) writes:

> The point is not that persons are somehow *not* male or female, upper or lower class, with or without power, professors and/or students. They may be, on some occasion, demonstrably members of one or another of those categories. Nor is the issue that those aspects of the society do not matter, or did not matter on that occasion. We may share a lively sense that indeed they do matter, and that they mattered on that occasion, and mattered for just that aspect of some interaction on which we are focusing. There is still the problem of *showing from the details of the talk or other conduct in the materials* that we are analyzing that those aspects of the scene are what the parties are oriented to. *For that is to show how the parties are embodying for one another the relevancies of the interaction and are thereby producing the social structure.*
>
> (p. 51)

This view of context is often critiqued for being too narrow, which has remained an issue of great controversy among scholars (e.g. Billig, 1999; McHoul, Rapley, & Antaki, 2008; Nelson, 1994; Pomerantz, 1998; Schegloff, 1997, 1998, 1999; van Dijk, 2008, 2009; Wetherell, 1998). For the various positions on CA and context, interested readers should consult the special issues of *Research on Language and Social Interaction* (1990/1991 and 1998), *Discourse & Society* (1997–9), and *Journal of Pragmatics* (2008). Briefly, routine critiques of CA's approach to context typically concern its disinterest in external social and natural causes, its limited analysis of tiny bits of conversation, and its limited explanation of conversational activities ("unnecessarily" narrow sense of participant orientation). In defense of CA's "restricted" treatment of context, on the other hand, Schegloff (1991) cautions that "[i]nvoking social structure at the outset can systematically distract from, even blind us to, details of those domains of event in the world" (p. 62).

Some scholars have managed to exploit a broader context without compromising the fine details of interaction by combining CA and ethnography. Exemplary endeavors may be found in book-length studies such as Clemente (2015), Goodwin (2006), and Sidnell (2005). Based on his intense fieldwork in a Barcelona hospital on children' participation in conversations about their own cancer treatments throughout uncertain trajectories, for example, Clemente (2015) combines ethnographic descriptions of social and medical events with detailed analyses of questions that children asked their clinicians during videotaped medical interactions. In so doing, he vividly portrays child cancer patients' attempts to participate in their own treatment decisions.

CONVERSATION ANALYSIS AND CLASSROOM DISCOURSE

As shown in the previous chapter, existing research on classroom discourse has furnished a strong knowledge base of the nature of classroom interaction as well as the relationship between classroom talk and learning. Conversation analytic work makes similar contributions. What sets CA work apart, however, is not only its microscopic focus on the details of interaction but, more importantly, what such fine-grained attention enables—the unveiling of not classroom order per se but the order *oriented to by the participants themselves* (see Mehan, 1979 in the previous chapter), and not how talk contributes to learning per se but that talk-learning link *specifically oriented to by the participants themselves*. As McHoul (1985) put it, the goal is to uncover "the 'orientationals' observed during 'classroom life as usual'" (p. 55). Such "orientationals" would include, I believe, what Macbeth (2011) refers to as the type of understanding that precedes the formal or disciplinary sense of understanding. It is the understanding that makes instruction a possibility in the first place. In a telling exhibit, for example, Macbeth shows that in response to the teacher prompt *Do you want to change something?* addressed to a student after her writing on the board, everyone in the room knows that the answer is *yes* and that *yes* would not be sufficient without actually producing the change, and the student's decision to *leave it like that* (i.e., not changing anything) operates precisely upon this understanding. This is the type of understanding, as Macbeth observes, that "organize[s] the routine grounds of classroom instruction" (p. 448).

What also organizes the routine grounds of classroom instruction is, of course, such structural resources as turn-taking (i.e., practices for constructing and allocating conversational turns) and repair (i.e., practices of addressing problems of speaking, hearing, and understanding in talk). McHoul (1985) explores how the turn taking (Sacks, Schegloff, & Jefferson, 1974) and repair organizations (Schegloff, Jefferson, & Sacks, 1977) may be modified in the Australian secondary classroom. In an effort to uncover that "something" participants "simply seem to be able to reply on" "for their regular turn-allocation practices" (p. 55), McHoul found that teachers and students have access to separate turn-allocation machineries. Notably, the next-speaker-self-selects option is not available to students, the current-selects-next option is only minimally available to them, and the current-speaker-continues option is less prevalent for student use. With regard to correction, other-initiated self-correction is the most prominent in student-produced trouble sources, where teachers "appear to prefer to note the *existence* of correctables in student talk but to refrain from providing corrections proper" (p. 60). McHoul's (1990) study on geography lessons in Australian high school classrooms further explores how the classroom repair system may depart from the one reported in Schegloff, Jefferson, and Sacks (1977). He found, for example, that the predominant repair trajectory in the classroom is other-initiated self-correction, where other initiation is produced after the trouble source turn without any delay, but other correction is routinely withheld with much clueing. Sahlstrom (2002) investigates the interactional organization of hand raising in eighth grade classrooms in the Swedish comprehensive school and shows that, interestingly, late hand raisers are selected for the benefit of increasing participation, and as such, through hand raising, students systematically influence the length and content of the teacher's initiating turns. Others have documented various features of floor management in the second-language classroom (Mortensen, 2008, 2009; Waring, 2013b, 2013c).

In their meticulous pursuit to reveal the classroom order oriented to by the participants, conversation analysts also have produced revealing descriptions of how instruction is accomplished in the sequential organization of talk. Focusing on a sequence of grammar instruction in a fifth grade classroom of 10-year-olds, Macbeth (1994) unravels the intricate instructional technology deployed by the teacher to make visible the problem of pronoun usage in a pair of sentences written down by a student on the board (also see Macbeth, 2000). Based on video recordings of a problem-based learning (PBL) tutorial in an American medical school, Zemel and Koschmann (2011) ask: how does the tutor engage in an extended interaction with six students to elicit a proper description of X? They show that the teacher revises his earlier questions to pursue the correct description, with (1) an additional term as an explicit resource for yielding an alternative understanding, (2) an alternative question to suggest a different kind of response is in order and what that response may look like, or (3) a reversed polarity question (RPQ) to invite recognition of inconsistency (e.g., "And it *is* bactericidal." as a way of saying "it is *not* bactericidal."). As they observe, in the absence of explicit corrections, students can interpret a revised question as request for elaboration. They conclude that the teacher's question revisions serve as an important resource for guiding student reasoning. Hall and Smotrova's (2013) study on ESL and (under)graduate applied linguistics courses shows how teachers' self-talk serves to maintain student attention during moments of technical difficulty and to elicit empathetic student responses. They argue that such self-talk is an important resource for managing the complex contingencies of teaching and can contribute to establishing a more symmetrical classroom environment. Based on video-taped math lessons in Dutch secondary school, Koole (2010) distinguishes between two types of teacher explanations: discourse unit organization that involves the teacher's unilateral telling and a dialog organization where the teacher engages in IRF sequences. He found that the discourse unit explanation sequentially requires *a display* (or claim) *of understanding* (e.g., *yes* in response to *do you understand?*), and the dialog explanation *a display* (or demonstration) *of knowing* (e.g., *the author of* Iliad in response to *do you know who Homer is?*) (also see Koole & Elbers, 2014, on responsiveness in teacher explanations; Mortensen, 2011, and Waring, Creider, & Box, 2013, on vocabulary explanation).

Much of instruction entails the contingent management of learner contributions, such as how teachers answer student questions (Markee, 1995, 2004), deal with unexpected learner contributions (Fagan, 2012), or use epistemic status checks (ESCs) in response to student visual cues in the interest of moving the lesson forward (Sert, 2013). A rich locus for managing learner contribution, unsurprisingly, is the third turn after learner responses to teacher initiations. Lee (2007), for instance, takes issue with the "blank terms" attributed to the third turn such as "evaluation, "feedback" or "follow-up" and argues instead that the third turn accomplishes an "unforeseen range" of actions as it carries out the "contingent task of responding to and acting on the prior turns while moving interaction forward" (p. 1204). Yes-no questions in the third position, for example, can be used to "pull into view interpretative resources that are already in the room for students to recognize" (Lee, 2008, p. 237). A central aspect of managing learner contributions concerns error treatment or treatment of problematic learner contributions more generally (Park, 2014; Rolin-Ianziti, 2010).

As noted earlier, the conversation analytic treatment of how talk contributes to learning prioritizes learning as oriented to by the participants themselves. Based on data from both face-to-face and technology-mediated PBL tutorial meetings in a medical school, for example, Koschmann et al. (2005) detail how the participants collectively produce a problem in understanding. They found that, surprisingly, similar work is involved in both settings to produce a problem in understanding, that is, calling into question some sort of problem that projects some sort of action that is to be collectively undertaken (also see Waring, Box, & Creider, in press).

In mining for learning opportunities in the interactional data, CA scholars have repeatedly drawn our attention to learner practices of repair and various types of searches. Word searches, for instance, have been found to embody learners' cognitive states as they construct learning in a Japanese-as-a-foreign-language classroom (Mori & Hasegawa, 2009). Markee and Kunitz (2013) demonstrate how learners in an Italian-as-a-foreign-language classroom engage in word and grammar searches during task planning, again evidencing the socially distributed nature of cognition and, by extension, learning (also see Jakonen & Morton, 2015; Reichert & Liebscher, 2012). Participant orientation to learning is also embodied in learner initiatives (Garton, 2012; Jacknick, 2011; Li, 2013; Waring, 2011; Ziegler, Sert, & Durus, 2012), their management of tasks (Hellermann & Pekarek Doehler, 2010; Markee, 2005; Mori, 2004), multiple responses to teachers' questions (Ko, 2014), and humorous and playful sequences (Reddington & Waring, 2015; Waring, 2013c). Some scholars have focused on how learning a particular vocabulary item or grammatical structure is achieved within local interactional contexts in the short term (Markee, 2008). Others have documented how learning is accomplished over a longer period of time (Hauser, 2013; Hellermann, 2008; Waring, 2013d). For a review of recent development in CA research on learning and development, see Kasper and Wagner (2014).

CONCLUSION

CA is both a theoretical framework of and a methodological approach to social interaction. As a theoretical framework, it comes with a set of assumptions that prioritize participant orientations as made evident by the parties themselves in the very details of their interactional conduct. It takes as its point of departure the conviction that "the first analyst is already on the scene" (Macbeth, 2013), and the professional analyst's job is simply to "bring to light what is already available for all to see" (ten Have, 2004, p. 146). This is not unlike Mehan's (1979) observation of the goal of constitutive ethnography:

> I do not see the purpose of my analysis to be the presentation of unexpected findings. Instead, I see a major purpose of constitutive ethnography to be the presentation of information that the participants themselves already "know" but may have not been able to articulate.
>
> (p. 173)

As a methodological approach, CA insists on obtaining audio and video recordings of naturally occurring interaction, transcribing these recordings in ways that capture a full range of audio and visual details, asking the question of "Why that now?" throughout the analysis (Schegloff & Sacks, 1973), and finding the answer in the sequential details of interaction as demonstrated by the participants themselves. Rather than coding data, CA workers endeavor to crack the code of social interaction. The validity and reliability of CA findings are grounded in the quality of the recordings, the accuracy of the transcripts, and the routine engagement of group data sessions. Their generalizability, on the other hand, is of an analytical rather than an empirical kind (Pomerantz, 1990). CA findings uncover culturally available methods of social interaction in a specific set of data that can possibly but not necessarily be reproduced under other circumstances (Peräkylä, 2004).

As the rest of the research literature on classroom discourse, CA work has also furthered our knowledge of the nature of classroom talk and the relationship between that talk and learning. Rather than furnishing a professional analyst's interpretation of these matters, however, its interest is addressed specifically to how such nature and relationship are oriented to by the participants themselves. We are invited, for example, to a viewing of the structural resources such as repair and turn taking that enable classroom life as usual and the understandings that organize the routine grounds of social instruction. We are offered a microscopic look into how teachers explain problems, elicit descriptions, maintain attention, and respond to learner contributions. And the link between talk and learning is explored in the specific practices that embody participant orientations to learning such as learner initiatives, repair and search sequences, and learners' agentive management of classroom tasks.

In the ensuing three chapters, I aim to show how conversation analytic insights may be calibrated to illuminate the issues and challenges of pedagogical interaction more broadly—including but not limited to classroom discourse. Within this broader vision, I would also like to explore the very specific question of what teaching entails, or what it means to be doing teaching, and as will be demonstrated, my empirically driven answer will revolve around the three Cs:

1. Competence: achieving competence entails assuming competence.
2. Complexity: teacher talk is multivocal.
3. Contingency: teaching requires being responsive to the moment.

As noted in an earlier chapter, while *competence* underscores a primordial stance toward teaching that attends to learners' competence concerns, both *complexity* and *contingency* address the nature of teacher conduct, with *complexity* emphasizing its challenges, and *contingency* its optimal property.

REFERENCES

Antaki, C. (Ed.). (2011). *Applied conversation analysis: Intervention and change in institutional talk*. Basingstoke: Palgrave MacMillan.

Benson, D., & Hughes, J. (1991). Method: Evidence and inference for ethnomethodology. In G. Button (Ed.), *Ethnomethodology and the human sciences* (pp. 109–136). Cambridge, UK: Cambridge University Press.

Billig, M. (1999). Conversation analysis and the claims of naivety. *Discourse & Society, 10*, 572–576.

Clayman, S., & Gill, V. (2004). Conversation analysis. In M. Hardy & A. Bryman (Eds.), *Handbook of data analysis* (pp. 589–606). Thousand Oaks, CA: Sage.

Clemente, I. (2015). *Uncertain futures. Communication and culture in childhood cancer treatment.* Oxford and New York: Wiley-Blackwell.

Creider, S. (2014). *Encouraging student participation in a French immersion kindergarten class: A multi-modal, conversation analytic study.* Dissertation Proposal, Teachers College, Columbia University.

Drew, P., & Heritage, J. (Eds.). (1992). *Talk at work: Interaction in institutional settings.* Cambridge: Cambridge University Press.

Fagan, D. (2012). 'Dealing with' unexpected learner contributions in whole group activities: An examination of novice language teacher discursive practices. *Classroom Discourse, 3*(2), 107–128.

Garfinkel, H. (1967). *Studies in ethnomethodology.* Englewood Cliffs, NJ: Prentice-Hall.

Garton, S. (2012). Speaking out of turn? Taking the initiative in teacher-fronted classroom interaction. *Classroom Discourse, 3*(1), 29–45.

Glaser, B. G., & Strauss, A. (1967). *The discovery of grounded theory: Strategies for qualitative research.* Chicago, IL: Aldine.

Goffman, E. (1967). *Interactional ritual.* New York: Anchor Books.

Goodwin, M. H. (2006). *The hidden life of girls: Games of stance, status, and exclusion.* Oxford, UK: Blackwell.

Hall, J. K., & Smotrova, T. (2013). Teacher self-talk: Interactional resource for managing instruction and eliciting empathy. *Journal of Pragmatics, 47*, 75–92.

Hauser, E. (2013). Stability and change in one adult's second language English negation. *Language Learning, 63*(3), 463–498.

Hellermann, J. (2008). *Social actions for classroom language learning.* Clevedon, UK: Multilingual Matters.

Hellermann, J., & Pekarek Doehler, S. (2010). On the contingent nature of language-learning tasks. *Classroom Discourse, 1*(1), 25–45.

Heritage, John. (1984). *Garfinkel and Ethnomethodology.* Oxford: Basil Blackwell.

Jacknick, C. M. (2011). Breaking in is hard to do: How students negotiate classroom activity shifts. *Classroom Discourse, 2*(1), 20–38.

Jakonen, T., & Morton, T. (2015). Epistemic search sequences in peer interaction in a content-based language classroom. *Applied Linguistics, 36*(1), 73–94.

Kasper, G., & Wagner, J. (2014). Conversation analysis in applied Linguistics. *Annual Review of Applied Linguistics, 34*, 171–212.

Ko, S. (2014). The nature of multiple responses to teachers' questions. *Applied Linguistics, 35*(1), 48–62.

Koole, T. (2010). Displays of epistemic access: Student responses to teacher explanations. *Research on Language and Social Interaction, 43*(2), 183–109.

Koole, T., & Elbers, E. (2014). Responsiveness in teacher explanations: A conversation analytical perspective on scaffolding. *Linguistics and Education, 26*, 57–69.

Koschmann, T., Zemel, A., Conlee-Stevens, M., Young, N., Robbs, J., & Barnhart, A. (2005). How do people learn? Member methods and communicative mediation. In R. Bromme, F. Hesse, & H. Spada (Eds.), *Barriers and biases in computer-mediated knowledge communication and how they may be overcome* (pp. 265–287). Amsterdam: Kluwer Academic Press.

Lee, Y.-A. (2007). Third turn position in teacher talk: Contingency and the work of teaching. *Journal of Pragmatics, 39*, 1204–1230.

Lee, Y.-A. (2008). Yes-no questions in the third-turn position: Pedagogical discourse processes. *Discourse Processes, 45*(3), 237–262.

Li, H. (2013). Student initiatives and missed learning opportunities in an IRF sequence: A single case analysis. *L2 Journal, 5*(2), 68–92.

Macbeth, D. (1994). Classroom encounters with the unspeakable: 'Do you see, Danelle?' *Discourse Processes, 17*(2), 311–335.

Macbeth, D. (2000). Classrooms as installations: Direct instruction in the early grades. In S. Hester & D. Frances (Eds.), *Local educational order: Ethnomethodological studies of knowledge in action* (pp. 21–71). Amsterdam: John Benjamins.

Macbeth, D. (2011). Understanding understanding as an instructional matter. *Journal of Pragmatics, 43*, 438–451.

Macbeth, D. (2013). Some notes on the sociology of sequential analysis. Plenary address delivered at the 3rd meeting of the Language and Social Interaction Working Group (LANSI), Teachers College, Columbia University, New York.

Markee, N. (1995). Teachers' answers to students' questions: Problematizing the issue of making meaning. *Issues in Applied Linguistics, 6*(2), 63–92.

Markee, N. (2004). Zones of interactional transition in ESL classes. *The Modern Language Journal, 88*(4), 583–596.

Markee, N. (2005). The organization of off-task talk in second language classrooms. In K. Richards & P. Seedhouse (Eds.), *Applying conversation analysis* (pp. 197–213). New York: Palgrave Macmillan.

Markee, N. (2008). Toward a learning behavior tracking methodology for CA-for-SLA. *Applied Linguistics, 29*(3), 404–427.

Markee, N., & Kunitz, S. (2013). Doing planning and task performance in second language acquisition: An ethnomethodological respecification. *Language Learning, 63*(4), 629–664.

Mehan, H. (1979). *Learning lessons: Social organization in the classroom.* Cambridge, MA: Harvard University Press.

McHoul, A.W. (1985). Two aspects of classroom interaction: Turn-taking and correction. *Australian Journal of Human Communication Disorders, 13*(1), 53–64.

McHoul, A.W. (1990). The organization of repair in classroom talk. *Language in Society, 19*(3), 349–377.

McHoul, A., Rapley, M., & Antaki, C. (2008) You gotta light? On the luxury of context for understanding talk in interaction. *Journal of Pragmatics, 40*(5), 827–839.

Mori, J. (2004). Negotiating sequential boundaries and learning opportunities: A case from a Japanese language classroom. *The Modern Language Journal, 88*(4), 536–550.

Mori, J., & Hasegawa, A. (2009). Doing being a foreign language learner in a classroom: Embodiment of cognitive states as social events. *IRAL, 47*, 65–94.

Mortensen, K. (2008). Selecting next-speaker in the second language classroom: How to find a willing next-speaker in planned activities. *Journal of Applied Linguistics, 5*(1), 55–79.

Mortensen, K. (2009). Establishing recipiency in pre-beginning position in the second language classroom. *Discourse Processes, 46*(5), 491–515.

Mortensen, K. (2011). Doing word explanation in interaction. In G. Pallotti & J. Wagner (Eds.), *L2 learning as social practice: Conversation-analytic perspectives* (pp. 135–162). Honolulu: University of Hawaii, National Foreign Language Resource Center.

Nelson, C.K. (1994). Ethnomethodological positions on the use of ethnographic data in conversation analytic research. *Journal of Contemporary Ethnography, 23*, 307–329.

Park, J. (2014). The roles of third-turn repeats in two L2 classroom interactional contexts. *Applied Linguistics, 35*(2), 145–167.

Peräkylä, A. (2004). Reliability and validity in research based on naturally occurring social interaction. In D. Silverman (Ed.), *Qualitative research: Theory, method, and practice* (2nd ed., pp. 283–304). London: Sage.

Pomerantz, A. (1990). On the validity and generalizability of conversation analytic methods: Conversation analytic claims. *Communication Monographs, 57*(3), 231–235.

Pomerantz, A. (1998). Multiple interpretations of context: How are they useful? *Research on Language and Social Interaction, 31*(1), 123–132.

Psathas, G. (1995). *Conversation analysis: The study of talk-in-interaction.* Thousand Oaks, CA: Sage.

Reddington, E., & Waring, H. Z. (2015). Understanding the sequential resources for doing humor in the language classroom. *Humor: International Journal of Humor Research, 28*(1), 1–23.

Reichert, T., & Liebscher, G. (2012). Positioning the expert: Word searches, expertise, and learning opportunities in peer interaction. *The Modern Language Journal, 96*(4), 599–609.

Rolin-Ianziti, J. (2010). The organization of delayed second language correction. *Language Teaching Research, 14*(2), 183–206.

Sacks, H., Schegloff, E. A., & Jefferson, G. (1974). A simplest systematics for the organization of turn-taking for conversation. *Language, 50*(4), 696–735.

Sahlstrom, J. F. (2002). The interactional organization of hand raising in classroom interaction. *Journal of Classroom Interaction, 37*(2), 47–57.

Schegloff, E. A. (1987). Between macro and micro: Contexts and other connections. In J. Alexander, B. Giessen, R. Munch, & N. Smelser (Eds.), *The macro-micro link* (pp. 207–234). Berkeley and Los Angeles: University of California Press.

Schegloff, E. A. (1991). Reflections on talk and social structure. In D. Boden & D. H. Zimmerman (Eds.), *Talk and Social Structure* (pp. 44–70). Berkeley and Los Angeles: University of California Press.

Schegloff, E. A. (1992). In another context. In A. Duranti & C. Goodwin (Eds.), *Rethinking context: Language as an interactive phenomenon* (pp. 193–227). Cambridge, UK: Cambridge University Press.

Schegloff, E. A. (1997). Whose text? Whose context? *Discourse & Society, 8*(2), 165–187.

Schegloff, E. A. (1998). Reply to Wetherell. *Discourse & Society, 9*(3), 457–460.

Schegloff, E. A. (1999). 'Schegloff's texts' as 'Billig's data': A critical reply. *Discourse & Society, 10,* 558–572.

Schegloff, E. A. (2009). One perspective on conversation analysis: Comparative perspectives. In J. Sidnell (Ed.), *Comparative perspectives in conversation analysis* (pp. 357–406). Cambridge and New York: Cambridge University Press.

Schegloff, E. A., Jefferson, G., & Sacks, H. (1977). The preference for self-correction in the organization of repair in conversation. *Language, 53*(2), 361–382.

Schegloff, E. A., & Sacks, H. (1973). Opening up closings. *Semiotica, 7,* 289–327.

Sert, O. (2013). 'Epistemic status check' as an interactional phenomenon in instructed learning settings. *Journal of Pragmatics, 45,* 13–28.

Sidnell, J. (2005). *Talk and practical epistemology: The social life of knowledge in a Caribbean community.* Amsterdam: John Benjamins.

Stokoe, E. (2009). Doing actions with identity categories: Complaints and denials in neighbor dispute. *Text & Talk, 29*(1), 75–97.

ten Have, P. (2004). *Understanding qualitative research and ethnomethodology.* London: Sage.

ten Have, P. (2007). *Doing conversation analysis* (2nd ed.). Thousand Oaks, CA: Sage.

van Dijk, T. A. (2008). *Discourse and context: A sociocognitive approach.* Cambridge, UK: Cambridge University Press.

van Dijk, T. A. (2009). *Society and discourse: How context controls text and talk.* Cambridge, UK: Cambridge University Press.

Waring, H. Z. (2011). Learner initiatives and learning opportunities. *Classroom Discourse, 2*(2), 201–218.

Waring, H. Z. (2013a). Doing being playful in the language classroom. *Applied Linguistics, 34*, 191–210.

Waring, H. Z. (2013b). Managing competing voices in the language classroom. *Discourse Processes, 50*(5), 316–338.

Waring, H. Z. (2013c). Managing Stacy: A case study of turn-taking in the language classroom. *System, 41*(3), 841–851.

Waring, H. Z. (2013d). 'How was your weekend?': Developing the interactional competence in managing routine inquiries. *Language Awareness, 22*(1), 1–16.

Waring, H. Z., Box, C., & Creider, S. (in press). Problematizing vocabulary in the language classroom. *Journal of Applied Linguistics and Professional Practice.*

Waring, H. Z., Creider, S., & Box, C. (2013). Explaining vocabulary in the language classroom. *Learning, Culture and Social Interaction, 2*, 249–264.

Wetherell, M. (1998). Positioning and interpretative repertoires: Conversation analysis and post-structuralism in dialogue. *Discourse & Society, 9*(3), 387–412.

Wong, J., & Waring, H. Z. (2010). *Conversation analysis and second language pedagogy: A guide for ESL/EFL teachers.* New York: Routledge.

Wood, L. A., & Kroger, R. O. (2000). *Doing discourse analysis: Methods for studying action in talk and text.* London: Sage.

Yin, R. K. (2003). *Case study research: Design and methods* (3rd ed.). London: Sage.

Zemel, A., & Koschmann, T. (2011). Pursuing a question: Reinitiating IRE sequences as a method of instruction. *Journal of Pragmatics, 43*, 475–488.

Ziegler, G., Sert, O., & Durus, N. (2012). Student-initiated use of multilingual resources in English-language classroom interaction: Next-turn management. *Classroom Discourse, 3*(2), 187–204.

4 Principle of Competence
Achieving Competence Entails Assuming Competence

As early as the age of three, my daughter Zoe would resent being treated as knowing less than she actually did (or she thought she did): "I already knew that!" She would fling her arms with impatience and indignation. Her competence as a three-year-old was not to be questioned, and I didn't quite have the acuity to recognize how monumentally important that perceived competence was until I encountered this quote from the popular book *Parenting with Love and Logic*: "Kids say to themselves, I don't become what you think I can, and I don't become what I think I can, I become what I think you think I can" (Cline & Fay, 2014, p. 504). The sentiment carries a very familiar ring—one perhaps neatly fitted to our obsession with self-esteem in schooling. In a *New York Times* opinion article (Chua & Rubenfeld, 2014) on what drives success, for example, we learn that superiority complex—a deep-seated belief in one's exceptionality—is one of the three essential traits. On the other hand, as research has shown, imposing an identity of incompetence such as "poor reader" can impede a learner's engagement with reading and result in missed learning opportunities (Hall, 2009). In political philosophy, mutual recognition (e.g., recognition of the autonomous person) is considered key to human development (Honneth, 1992). In fact, as I heard that tiny voice of protest, I should have realized that adults say "I already knew that" all the time—although not quite in those four little words. Just think of the last time you were given some friendly advice you did not quite think you needed. Resisting uninvited advice that assumes or establishes knowledge asymmetry is not uncommon (Jefferson & Lee, 1992). We simply have learned to express our indignation with greater subtlety. Over my years of research on interactions in pedagogical settings, I have been repeatedly reminded of the omnipresent delicacy of competence in such interactions. Participants in a wide variety of ways defend, maintain, and assert their competence: a graduate student would foreground her efforts in understanding complex readings, a writing tutee would insist on having thought the same as his tutor, and a novice teacher would engage in "bright side telling" that downplays any problems that might cast her in a negative light during a post-observation conference. Looking competent, in other words, is a front-and-center issue for learners in various settings and, as such, integral to their journey to become competent. Hence the principle of competence to be explicated in this chapter: *achieving competence entails assuming competence*. As will be shown, expert teachers recognize and leverage that competence with great care and sophistication.

Importantly, having an abstract understanding of the magnitude of competence is not the same as witnessing its manifestation and cultivation in actual interaction. After all, its manifestation is almost never as obvious as Zoe's loud and clear proclamation and its cultivation never as simple as giving compliments or praise, especially if one were to keep the pedagogical goal of the moment in focus. Here is where conversation analysis (CA) becomes crucially relevant. As an approach devoted exclusively to uncovering the tacit methods of social interaction, it offers the much-needed tools for revealing how competence is subtly asserted and attended to in the microseconds of pedagogical interaction. Understanding *that* flossing is good for you is not the same as understanding *how* or *in what specific ways* it is good for you. CA specializes in making evident the *how*. I am reminded of my dentist's story of turning from a casual flosser into an obsessive one after being shown this grotesque exhibit in dental school of what not flossing can cause. My exhibits are of an interactional sort, and I hope they too have the potential of arousing a different, and more urgent, level of understanding. My proposal of *achieving competence entails assuming competence* is in part underpinned by the massive energy learners themselves devote to defending, maintaining, and asserting their competence in the course of their developmental journey. Leaving such competence concerns unattended to would, after all, constitute a great obstacle to helping learners achieve the competence they strive for.

In this chapter, I first show how looking competent is treated as being of paramount importance by the learners themselves in various types of pedagogical interactions. I then detail how learner competence may be carefully attended to. My focus, therefore, is on demonstrating how competence concerns matter for the participants and how assuming such competence is done in the interaction. As will be argued, understanding and practicing the principle of competence is foundational to one's pedagogical posture and instructional repertoire. I conclude with a discussion on the compatibility between the principle of competence and the concepts of play and prolepsis (i.e., a form of looking ahead) in Vygotsky's sociocultural theory. Before proceeding, I should note that for the purpose of this book, I use *competence* in its most vernacular sense of *know or can do X*.

COMPETENCE AS A PARTICIPANT ISSUE

As will be demonstrated in the ensuing pages, whether it is during graduate seminar discussion, post-observation conferences, ESL classroom interaction, or peer tutoring, the learner painstakingly ensures the preservation of his/her image of being competent. Although my data feature roles that are conventionally referred to variously as tutee, mentee, ESL student, or graduate student, for simplicity, I use "learner" as a generic label to capture and underscore what brings them to the interaction.

The Case of Graduate Seminar Discussion

In my data of graduate seminar discussion on second-language literacy, graduate students deploy various means to project the image of being competent, the incarnation of which may be either their reluctance in admitting not knowing (Waring, 2002) or propensity to forestall a competence-undermining course of action with a word string such as *yeah, yeah, yeah* (Waring, 2012a). In the event of not fully understanding the materials at hand, the student would ostensibly delay the explicit admission of non-understanding and offer an account to legitimize that non-understanding. In other words, s/he would clearly treat non-understanding as dispreferred (Pomerantz, 1984; Sacks, 1987)—something unexpected or out of the ordinary. In the following segment, Kelly is reporting on an article by the author Hudson that investigates how equipping L2 readers with background knowledge can affect comprehension. This purpose of the article is precisely what Kelly seems to have difficulty pinpointing. After two failed attempts earlier, Kelly continues to struggle with articulating the theme of the article:

1. had it before

```
01 Kelly:   ((reviews the literature on the three components of reading))
02          A:::nd (0.6) what Hudson (.) is (.) suggesting (.) is
03          that the ceiling isn't a::: (0.2) just a linguistic ceiling,
04          it's a::. hhh linguistic a:::nd psycho(.)linguistic? I think
05          he said? (0.2) ceiling? Um (.) a::nd that (2.0) by- by
06          running the study, he's trying to prove (.) that (2.0)
07  →       I'm having trouble putting this part in words, I had it
08          before maybe someone can help me. But (.) it- it's (.)
09          you know the second component (.) ceiling >some of the-<
10          they encounter (.) in >the second component<and to
11          prove that, he induces schemata (.) in (.) in (.) second
12          language (.) L2 readers, a:nd, fi:nds (.) that (.) uh:m (.)
13          you can effectively overcome (.) this (.) ceiling by
14          inducing (.) schemata (.) in readers. and (.) >there's
15          other things he found in his study< as well but it showed
16          it's not (.) strictly a first component (.) linguistic (.)
17          ceiling. That's just one (.) determinant that might (.)
18          play a role (.) in (.) um (.) not comprehending something
19          (.) in in a second language. uh:m (0.2)
20 Ellen:   I thought it had a lot to do with what Libby ((continues))
```

Beginning in line 05, Kelly starts for the third time to articulate the purpose of the study (*by running the study, he's trying to prove that . . .*). For the third time, she is unable to complete the clause, and it is at this juncture that she finally launches into an explicit admission, prefaced by the micropause and the (2.0) second pause in line 06, of not knowing (*I'm having trouble . . .*) starting line 07. We can thus safely say that this explicit admission is massively delayed.

Kelly's treatment of her competence as a keenly defendable commodity is also seen in her multiple attempts at articulating that ever-elusive understanding herself without soliciting others' help (which didn't come until line 08). Aside from the prior two failed attempts, in this very extract, we witness her final reach as she struggles to articulate what Hudson is *suggesting* (line 02). The effort is laced with much tentativeness as evidenced in the hedging verb *suggesting* (Hyland, 1996, p. 265), pauses (lines 06–08), rising intonations (lines 04–05), and a distancing device *I think* (line 04) (Goffman, 1981). By braving such great uncertainties, Kelly maximizes her display of effort, thereby competence, in managing the reading materials.

Such display is also evident in Kelly's immediate claim of *had it before* upon the admission and the ensuing full account of the significance of the article (lines 08–19). In other words, although Kelly's trouble with articulating the point of Hudson's study has been patently clear throughout the transcript, her admission of the trouble is withheld until she is able to formulate at least an independent understanding of the issue under discussion. There is, therefore, clearly a concern for maximally asserting her competence when that competence becomes questionable.

Learners also become defensive when their competence appears to be under siege. One linguistic resource deployed to fight this battle is the multiple-*yeahs*, which function to forestall an unnecessary course of action that may be heard as undermining the *yeah*-speaker's competence. Prior to the following segment, the professor has been recounting her experience with a dictionary project based on a corpus that has some authenticity problems, and in the process of that recounting, she used the phrase *collocational terms*. The segment begins with Libby initiating repair on *collocations*:

2. collocation

01	Libby:	<u>W</u>hat're collocations.
02	Prof:	What're collocations.
03	Ellen:	It's like- a tall building you will never say a high
04		building?
05	Libby:	>O̲h oh< O::H >okay thanks.<
06		°(Very go [o d.] °
07	Prof:	[It's-] it's <u>ways</u> that [w̲ o:::r d s]tend to=
08	Libby:	[>°Yeah.°<]

```
09 Prof:          =be used together.
10 Libby:         >°Ye[ah.]°<
11 Prof:               [C  ] O::::::llo:ca:tion.
12 Libby:         °Yeah.°=
13 Tamar:         =Rather than- s:et the table rather than
14                arra::nge [°the table or something like that.°]
15 Libby:    →             [Y  e  a  h.  y  e  a  h.   ] °yeah.
16                yea.° (°I know.°)
17 Prof:          and you know things like commit, where you
18                commit (0.1)
```

Instead of providing a direct answer, the professor redirects the question to the class (line 02), to which Ellen provides an illustration-based explanation: *tall building* versus *high building* (lines 03–04). Libby first receives the illustration as being informative (the three *oh*s), then indicates acceptance (*okay*) of, and finally expresses appreciation for (*thanks*) the explanation (line 5). The rushed quality of the closing-relevant *okay thanks* may be suggesting Libby's treatment of this just-completed question-answer sequence as a digression to be minimized. By now, Libby has clearly claimed her newly acquired understanding of what she previously had trouble with.

However, instead of returning to the main business of the discussion, the professor goes on to provide a pedagogical rendering of what *collocation* is—a formal definition delivered in elongated vowels, careful emphasis, and markedly clear enunciation (lines 07, 09, and 11). In so doing, she potentially treats Libby's claimed understanding as possibly not yet complete.

In lines 08, 10, and 12, Libby receives the professor's "teaching" with three quietly delivered single *yeah*s in marked contrast with the three *oh*s she produced earlier, thus withholding treating the professor's definition as informative (Heritage, 1984) and, in a sense, reclaiming her already arrived-at understanding. Again, rather than let the professor's definition be the final say on this "collocation" business, Tamar latches onto Libby's third *yeah* with yet another illustration-based explanation (*set the table* vs. *arrange the table*).

With another *yeah* (line 15) launched in overlap (Jefferson, 1983), Libby displays her understanding of where Tamar is heading. Rather than wait till a possible completion point of Tamar's turn to do the second *yeah* as she did before in line 10, this time Libby does her *yeah*s as a series of four, which outlasts Tamar's illustration. Again, each of the *yeah*s is produced in final prosody. The token *yeah* allows Libby to display alignment with Tamar's explanation in progress while treating the latter as nonnews. Note that the last two *yeah*s, which emerge out of the overlap after Tamar's turn, exhibit decreasing volume, and the final *yeah* comes in a reduced form. The differential volumes and articulation strengths of the tokens seem to suggest that they are produced incrementally in close synchrony with Tamar's unfolding turn with a specific design to outlast the latter. Once the task is accomplished, less articulatory force is applied. In other words, the multiple *yeah*s are in part designed to interrupt and to sequentially delete Tamar's explanation.

Thus, in a case where a co-participant has disregarded one's prior understanding display and has taken a course of action that exhibited such disregard (e.g., questioning, clarifying the assessed, or repeating an explication), the multiple *yeah* is mobilized to reject those competence-undermining actions.

The Case of Post-observation Conference

Let us now switch gears to a one-on-one setting, where teachers-in-training meet their supervising mentors in post-observation conferences at a graduate TESOL program. And typically, the teachers in training engage in competence preservation mainly by minimizing their responsibilities for any problems or engaging in bright-side tellings of the classroom events.

In the first case below, the mentor calls attention to some execution difficulty in a vocabulary game (lines 04–05) (M=mentor):

3. vocabulary game execution

```
01  M:          =((gaze to notes))-sometimes.°. hhh uh:::m
02              (1.5)
03              tch >I said< the vocabulary game was a cute
04              idea but there seemed to be some difficulty
05              in the execu((gaze to A))-tion.=
06  Amy:        =$yea[h.$] -((nods))
07  M:              [so ] why do you think that that happened.
08  Amy:        uhm some of it was:::::
09  M:          <cuz ↑I am not quite su:re.
10              [but- I'm just wondering ((gaze to notes))-why:.]
11  Amy:   →    [y↑ea:h I'm- I'm kinda try- I think some peo ]
12              ple:: >understood different things
13              [from the instructions?]<
    ((lines omitted))
14  Amy:   →    even though we covered it like two class periods,
15              in a row,. hh they didn't know all of it,=
16              =[that was one of the problems: with ()]=
17  M:           [            ((nods))                  ]
18  Amy:        <I think it was Hale.
    ((lines omitted))
19  Amy:   →               [((nods)) <s]o >I think some
20              of it was just-< (0.5) ((to A and nods))-confusion at
21              what they were supposed to do?
22  M:          ((no [ds)) ]
23  Amy:            [an' ] they {(((gestures))-finally (0.2) ca}me
24              together[r,]
25  M:              [ri]ght. cuz it started and then it
```

```
26              ((snaps fingers))-started kinda ramping up a little
27              bit [°(before its)-°] they kinda got into it?
28 Amy:         [yeah.-((nods)) ]
29 M:           [°u:m but it was ((gaze to notes))-a little bit°]
30 Amy:         [                    ((nods))                  ]
31 M:           (0.8) I was wondering like- it was like- the
32              execution of it someho:w (.) >°it wasn't quite
33              worki:ng, I wasn't sure if it was=°<
34              ((gaze to mid distance))-.hhh that it was:: (0.5) I w-
35              was wondering if this ((gaze to T))-was
36              vocabulary from like a couple of units ba:ck
37              and they were revisiting i:t >or it was
38              [something you did< last cl]ass [perio:d,   ] =
39 Amy:  →      [(syl) it was::::          ]    [Yeah. it w]
40              [as            continu]ation of >last class period<=
41 M:           = [°should've been°  ]
42 Amy:         = [they've been introduc]ed to the wo:rds=
43 M:           [        ((nods))       ]
44 Amy:         ((continues))
```

Note that Amy repeatedly attributes the execution difficulty to some failings on the part of the students. In line 11, she references the differential understandings among the students rather than any potential lack of clarity on her part. In lines 14 and 15, the students' failure to *know all of it* is juxtaposed with the suggestion that they should know it. In lines 20 and 21, her conclusion of *confusion at what they're supposed to do* makes no reference to her potential culpability in such confusion. In line 39, 40, and 42, she reiterates that it is the student's responsibility to know the materials. The transcript continues for another 31 lines (not shown) as Amy asserts the review nature of the vocabulary game and the students' familiarity with the activity, further distancing herself from any responsibility for the execution problem.

In the next segment, the mentor opens the meeting with a question that solicits the teacher's perspective on how the class went:

4. how it went

```
01 M:           °>.hh let me see< okay ° ((walks to chair))
02              -°(I was supposed to do it last week)
03              ((sits down))-but° (0.2) uhm so how did you think
04              ((gaze to A))-that (.) >it went.<
05 Amy:  →      .hh ↑fairly well um they had a class before us, so:::
06              >↓we got in there at the last minute at five to seven
((lines omitted))
22 M            ((looks down at notes and flips pages))-kinda°
23              (.) ° yeah.° .hh that's really hard to (°move
24              theirs and move themselves out of there.°).hhh
```

```
25              uhm (0.2) so:, I just- ((looks up at A))-but overall
26              do you think- >how do you think it went.<=
27 Amy:    →    =.hh >It was okay it was a little bit< unorganized,
28              u::m my: last activity: was::: >way over their
29              head so I changed it,<
30 M:           ((nods))
31 Amy:    →    u::m I had the:m >instead of ha- I had them<
32              do the- >go to the back of the room thing,<
((lines omitted))
39 M:           [°uh huh°-((nods))]
40 Amy:    →    [And that went- ] ((nods)) really [well.    ]
41 M:                                             >[that went]
42              really well? Okay< so flexibility then
43              [°(ended up working out)°-((looks down to notes))]
44 Amy:    →    [Yeah ((nods)) it worked out. >pretty well.<    ]=
45 M:           =((gaze on notes))->.hh That's good.< and the
46              more you ((gaze to A))-do it the more
47              you:: (0.2) understand like which parts you
48              can cut [out and which pa]rts °weren't°
49 Amy:                 [  yeah.-((nods))  ]
50 M:           ((gaze down to notes))-°>and stuff like that<.°
```

In line 05, Amy's self-assessment *fairly well* is prefaced by an inbreath that harbingers a multiunit turn. What ensues, however, is not further elaboration on the assessment but the procedural difficulty of getting into the classroom. As M brings her empathetic hearing to a close in line 22, she launches a reinitiation of her original query (line 26). In line 27, Amy's second attempt now involves a downgrade from the earlier *fairly well* to *okay* plus *a little bit unorganized*. It is worthy of note, however, that her elaboration on the negative assessment then becomes a display of her ability to competently manage an unforeseen situation, which ended up working *really well* (line 40), thus enhancing her positive face (Copland, 2012). In line 41, M repeats Amy's self-assessment and proceeds to articulate an analysis of what made it work really well, that is, flexibility. The sequence comes to a close soon thereafter.

In sum, Amy not only assumes an overall positive self-assessment on her performance even without any specifics, she also manages to achieve a bright-side telling of a *disorganized* event that ultimately presents her as a competent instructor with much pedagogical agility.

The Case of the ESL Classroom

In the ESL classroom, we may obtain a glimpse of learners' competence assertions in their responses to teachers' critique-implicative yes-no questions (Waring, 2012b). In particular, they either dis-align with the critical stance or produce their alignment in a dispreferred format (Pomerantz, 1984). They do so typically on behalf of their fellow classmates, thereby preserving the competence of the group. In the next segment, the class is doing a vocabulary exercise where they match each word in Column A with its definition in Column B (LL=learners):

5. immune

01 T:	=So wh- >what was your answer< for "immune."
02 Nina:	°uh fighting against disease or infection.°
03 T:	Okay?
04	(.)
05	u:h >d'y guys agree with that.<
06 LL: →	mhm [( )]-((*nodding*))
07 T:	[>"im]mune" is fighting against disease or
08	infection?<
09	(0.8)
10 T:	Now is that thee: would you say that's thee (0.5)
11	that's the (0.8) meaning of "immu:ne" i:n all
12	situations?=or is that the meaning of "immu:ne"
13	specifically for this: story? or-

In line 03, rather than positively assessing Nina's answer, the teacher produces an *Okay* in rising intonation. This is followed by a micropause and a lengthened *u:h*, both of which suggest incipient negative assessment. The teacher's question *d'y guys agree with that.* is therefore hearable as implicating a critical stance; that is, the answer is not agreeable. The learners, however, respond with an affirmative *mhm* accompanied by nodding without any delay (line 06), thus dis-aligning with the teacher's project.

The resistance to align with teacher critiques is also observed in cases where learner alignment is produced in a dispreferred format. In the next segment, the students have just finished putting on the board their proposed titles for a reading passage on dreams, and the class is reviewing the acceptability of each title. In lines 01 to 17, the teacher (T) in multiple ways hints at the problematic nature of the title *humans beyond world*, e.g., *I'm confused.* in line 02, *a matter or word order* in line 09, and *This- in my opinion-* in line 16. The teacher's yes-no question (line 18) then is raised in an environment of incipient critique and seeks such a critique from the students, which would be embodied in a *no* response to the question (LL=learners):

6. beyond the human world

01 T:	Can you explain to me the title?
02	I'm confused.
03 Kara:	[u::h ( )]
04 T:	[HUMANs beyond] world.
05	((*lines omitted*))

```
06 T:           ((turns to write on BB))-so, ↑here, you're trying
07              to say (.) beyo::nd (.) the huma::n (.) world.
08              (1.0)
09              So here it's a matter of (.) word order.-((group write))
10              °in this situation.° beyond the human world.
11              .hhh (0.5) h↑m. >what do we think.<
12              (0.8)
13 Cindy:       °very general.°
14 T:           .hhhh
15 Cindy:       heheh
16 T:           This (.) in my opinion- (0.2) what does this mean
17              when you hear beyo:nd the human world.
18              you think of dreams?
19 Cindy:   →  °No. de[ath.°]
20 Evelina:  → [spa  ]c[e.]
21 T:                  >[I ] think of< (.) d↓eath.-((points to C))
22 LL:           hmhh[hhmhh        ].hhh
23 T:               [and (.) s↓pace.]
```

The learners, however, appear to treat the *no* response as dispreferred in lines 19 and 20 through mitigation or avoidance. In line 19, Cindy's *No, death* is mitigated with a sotto voce delivery. In line 20, Evelina avoids a direct response to the yes-no questions by responding to the prior wh-question instead. In both cases, aligning with the question's critical stance would undermine the competence of Kara's group. By mitigating their responses that support the critique then, Cindy and Evelina display a concern for maintaining learner competence overall.

The Case of Graduate Peer Tutoring

Our final scene is from graduate peer tutoring. The data come from a writing center at a graduate school of education, where fellow students or graduates are paid to offer writing tutoring services. I will restrict my illustrations to two sorts of exhibits—those of advice resistance (Waring, 2005) and of advice acceptance (Waring, 2007). In particular, I show how resisting advice is a participant resource for asserting tutee expertise and how accepting advice may be done in such way that reconfigures the inherently asymmetrical relationships between tutor and tutee into more symmetrical ones.

Resisting Advice

Meet Priya, a doctoral student in art education from India, and her tutor (Tr), an MA graduate of the international education development program and a native speaker of English. A great deal of advice resistance is observed in the interaction between Priya and the tutor. Overall, Priya appears to be specifically resistant to mechanics of writing and content-related advice but relatively open to advice on nonsubject-specific academic writing matters. She minimizes the import of advice on the mechanics of writing and dismisses the tutor's agenda of doing micro-editing. She does so by initiating a new topic to prioritize, instead, general academic writing issues such as clarity or relevance. In the following segment, for example, the tutor suggests changing "was" to "is":

7. is it clear

```
01 Priya:        Make sense?=
02 Tr:           =Yea:h. It's very good.
03               (0.5)
04               I:s. The purpose of- °i::s°
05 Priya:   →    Yeah I'll change all my typos
06               [I want] someone check (   ).
07 Tr:           [ah::m ]
08               (1.0)
09 Priya:   →    >Is it clear?<
10               (1.8)
11 Tr:           Yeah this sentence I- ((continues))
```

In line 05, in her immediate response of *Yeah I'll change all my typos*, Priya acknowledges the necessity of fixing typos (*Yeah*; although the *was/is* issue is not exactly one of typos), asserts her competence in carrying out the task herself (*I'll change . . .*), and upgrades that assertion by indicating the thoroughness with which she can get the job done (*all my typos*). By using *typos* rather than, for example, *mistakes* or *errors* to characterize what the tutor is drawing attention to, Priya also effectively trivializes these problems, thus further buttressing the defense of her competence. In line 8, she quickly initiates a new sequence by prioritizing clarity over typos: *>Is it clear?<*, thereby indirectly resisting the advising agenda the tutor was putting forth. Note that in the subsequent turn, the tutor turns to a matter unrelated to typos (not shown).

When it comes to content-related issues, Priya would sometimes resist the tutor's advice by asserting her own agenda and invoking the voice of her professor as backup ammunition. Prior to the following segment, on four occasions, the tutor has explicitly advised Priya to make the link between her literature review and her research. As the segment begins, the tutor is advising Priya to acknowledge that she is looking at the artwork to learn something about the psychology of the groups of children (given the nature of her literature review). Note that the tutor initiates repair on the declarative format of *The link i:s* and reformulates the rest of the turn as a question instead. This cautious stance may be a result of Priya's earlier resistance to this particular line of advising the tutor has been pursuing:

8. the link is

```
01 Tr:           Okay.
02               (1.0)
03               The l↑ink i::s, (1.0) are you looking at the art work
```

```
04                 (.) to learn something about the two groups of (.) children?
05 Priya:    →     No? ((querulous))
06                 (.)
07                 I'm only looking at the art work to see how two groups
08                 of children depi- depict the incident. That's all.
09                 (.)
10                 depict a natural disaster.=what are the characteristics
11                 of drawing. That's all what we're looking at.=we're not
12                 looking at anything else.
13 Tr:             'cuz I found [>three different th]ings.< One,
14 Priya:    →                  [You know what? ]
15                 [I have Janine'sⁱ tapes.     ] You can listen to that.
16 Tr:             [stages of art development,]
17                 Two, creative and mental growth, co:nflict and growth.
18 Priya:    →     Creative and mental growth is totally (       ).
19                 Let me give what Ja- let me give you Janine's tape.
20                 What she said. She wants me to do.
21                 (0.2)
22                 I go:t it. You can listen to it.
23                 ((sounds of fiddling with a tape))
24                 It's ve:ry straightforward.
25                 (.)
26                 There's no complication at all.
27                 ((TR listens to the tape using the earphone))
28 Priya:          There's not even (.) a mention of doing °psychological.°
29                 (0.2)
30 Tr:             b- that's n↑ot- that's not the [pr↑oblem.]
31 Priya:                                         [No but I c]an't l↑ink it.
32                 becuz (.) if I link it it'll get so c↑omplicated.
33 Tr:             I don't w↑anchu to link it.
34                 (.)
35                 if you can't link it.
36 Priya:          >Then what do you want me< [to d↑o::::.]
37 Tr:                                        [I wanchu] to get r↑id
38                 of it.
```

Note that Priya's initial response to the tutor's carefully formulated suggestion is a dispreferred *No* (line 05) followed by a reassertion of her own agenda as *only* doing X (line 07) and *not* doing Y (lines 11–12). As the tutor proceeds to enumerate the three things that can be learned from looking at the artwork (line 13), Priya recruits additional ammunition by invoking the voice of her professor, and she does so interruptively (line 14), essentially offering an account for why the tutor's suggestion is incongruent with the specific needs of this paper. By accentuating *What she said. She wants me to do*, Priya puts forward someone at a higher rank, with greater credibility, and more important, someone with disciplinary expertise on the matter of her paper. She also characterizes her professor's words as being *very straightforward* (line 24) with *no complication at all* (line 26) and *not even a mention of doing °psychological°* (line 28) in contrast to the tutor's long-winded finding of *three different things* (line 13) and his attempt to delve into the complexities of psychology. As can be seen, the struggle between the two continues (line 30), and the segment ends with the tutor's directive to *get rid of* the irrelevant literature.

In both cases here, Priya asserts her competence not only as a graduate student but also as someone who is being formally trained in art education. This is evident in her rejection of the tutor's advising agenda on the mechanics of writing since advice on grammar and punctuation may undermine her basic competence as a graduate student. It is also evident in the unabated assertion of her own agenda when the tutor's advice steers into the content area of art education, where she clearly knows more.

Accepting Advice

Tutees' assertion of competence is also effectively embodied in methods of advice acceptance I have termed *complex advice acceptance*, which goes beyond the simple *okay* and its alternatives. They are complex not just because they are more elaborate in form but also because they are doing something other than mere acceptance. Briefly, while validating the acceptability of the advice, they qualify the nature of the acceptance and reconstitute the intrinsically asymmetrical event of consultation as a less asymmetrical one. In what follows, we consider two methods of complex advice acceptance (1) *accept with claims of comparable thinking* and (2) *accept with accounts*. Our protagonists in this case are Lena, a doctoral student in curriculum and teaching, and her tutor (Tr), a doctoral graduate of the applied linguistics program. In the transcript, to highlight the advice acceptance method, "acceptance" is marked with the '1→' and "claim of comparable thinking" with '2a→' ('2b'→ will be used later to indicate "account" in the second method of complex advice acceptance).

Lena asserts her competence using the method *accept with claims of comparable thinking*, which involves building a multiunit turn in which, minimally, Lena indicates acceptance of the tutor's advice while claiming that she herself knew, thought of, or has at one point done what is being suggested. In the following segment, the tutor formulates her advice initially as a modulated directive (*I was wondering if you could*) and then appends it with an assessment which accounts for that directive (*I don't think that's your focus.*). Lena accepts the directive with an *Okay?* in line 6 and subsequently aligns with the assessment with an explicit statement of agreement in line 7:

9. I agree

```
01 Tr:        ((reading the list of headings)). I was ↑wondering,=
02 Lena:      =Okay?
```

```
03 Tr:          if you ↑could (.) for the general organization I wanna
04              make the 'rejecting' part (.) part of your intro to
05              the chapter [°I don't th]ink that's your focus.°
06 Lena: 1→                 [>Okay?< ]
07       1/2a→>I agree.<
08 Tr:          Yeah [that's like a ba]ckground (  )
09 Lena: 1/2a→       [I totally agree.]
10       2a→  I didn't even know if I should just cut it.
11            [You kn]ow I mean,
12 Tr:        [Yeah. ]
```

Note that Lena's *Okay?* acceptance is done in overlap with the tutor's account, her rushed *I agree* is placed at the earliest possible completion of the tutor's account, and her reinforcing *I totally agree* is produced interruptively as the tutor continues her account. Thus, Lena designs her talk specifically to treat the tutor's account as unnecessary and her own acceptance as solid, thereby her thinking as in utter synchrony with the tutor's. Moreover, by alluding to her own earlier deliberations, which went further than the tutor's suggestion—cutting instead of repositioning certain materials (*I didn't even know if I should just cut it.*)—Lena effectively markets her agreement as not merely claimed but grounded in her own independent agenda.

Lena also asserts her competence using the method of *accept with account*, which involves detailing her rationale for doing the advised-against typically prior to officially accepting the advice. In so doing, she makes her acceptance contingent upon the understanding that whatever is problematic with the manuscript is not a matter of inadvertence and accident but a result of carefully wrought considerations. In the next exemplar, Lena's acceptance (line 12) of the tutor's advice to include *informants* in *methodology* (lines 01–02) is preceded by two accounts (lines 05–06 and 08–09):

10. remind the reader

```
01 Tr:          Informants should- °it- this should be included in
02              methodology.°
03 Lena:        °What is that?°
04 Tr:          The 'informants' part.
05 Lena: 2b→    °Okay.° .hh >YAH< I- I- I SAW it in somebody else's
06              u:m [(.) pilece.
07 Tr:              [Yeah.]
08 Lena: 2b→    then I thought w' maybe I need to remind the reader
09              who these people are.=That's why I put it in there.
10 Tr:          No: that's ((referring to methodology))
11              where [people go] to look for this.
12 Lena: 1→           [>Got it.< ]
```

In line 5, Lena produces a quiet *Okay*, which acknowledges the tutor's repair and, along with the ensuing inbreath and *YAH*, launches a two-part account for why she did what she did. She not only cites someone else's work as a precedent (lines 05–06) but also paints her decision as a reader-friendly one (lines 08–09). Further evidence of Lena's competence assertion is found in her interruptive launch >*Got it*< in line 12. By blocking the tutor's reiteration of her advice, Lena treats that reiteration as unnecessary and her acceptance as solid.

As can be seen, even in contexts where the advice recipient arrives at the interaction with the specific goal of seeking advice and the a priori asymmetry is the very basis for the encounter, such asymmetry is not automatically ratified or reinforced in interaction. For the advice recipient, the need for maintaining, defending, and asserting her competence remains interactionally relevant. With *accept with claims of comparable thinking* and *accept with accounts*, Lena forestalls the interpretation of acceptance as mindless compliance and asserts her identity as an independent, thoughtful, engaged co-participant in the advising process.

ATTENTING TO COMPETENCE CONCERNS

Having established the overwhelming concern for competence among learners in various settings, I now show how that delicate concern may be carefully nurtured as teachers (1) validate learner contributions (*I hear you.*), (2) favor learner potentials (*I see the best possible you.*), and (3) neutralize asymmetry (*I'm not better than you.*).

Validate Learner Contributions

The teacher can validate learner contributions by either (1) acknowledging or referencing learner talk or (2) ratifying diverging or playful initiatives.

Acknowledge or Reference Learner Talk

One way to validate learner contributions is simply to acknowledge learner talk. In the following segment from the graduate seminar discussion, the professor is explaining the concept *syntax-centered* as word order being a strong influence in a given language, using English as an example (lines 1–6; 8–9):

11. that's right

```
01 Prof:     I- I think (0.2) s- syntax centered means that the
02           ((lifts hands))-word {(((moves one hand away with
03           quick beats))-order} is is a stronger governing
04           factor in a language. and I think we would
05           probably say that that's true of Japanese.
```

```
06                     I mean >uh sorry.< where word order [is not]
07 Ellen:                                                 [(   )]
08 Prof:               so, so strong. In English word order makes a
09                     a huge difference.
10 Ellen:              (hm)
11 Prof:               u:m, (0.5) i- invariably we have a
12                     {(((lifts and moves hand to side at each word))-subject
13                     verb object[t} ((moves hand back and forth))- (   )]
14 Tamar:                          [(the) dog bit (men)               ]
15                     [against (men) bit dog.]
16 Prof:         →     [((nods))              ] ((nods))-that's right.
17 Tamar:              °(yeah.)°
18 Jack:               [mm-hm.]
19 Prof:         →     [that's   ] exactly right. man bit the dog versus
20                     the dog bit the man, makes a huge difference
21                     in meaning. ((lifts and moves hand to side in
22                     in quick beats))-simply by the syntax.=((moves
23                     hand back and repeats gesture))-the word order of it.
```

In line 10, Ellen utters a brief acknowledgement token without giving any substantive uptake, the absence of which the professor orients to by launching an elaboration on *word order* (line 11), specifying the invariable subject-verb-object (SVO) order in English. In line 14, Tamar gives a specific example of SVO in transitional overlap (Jefferson, 1983), which the professor immediately acknowledges (despite the overlapping talk in lines 13–14) both verbally and nonverbally (lines 16; 19–20). Notably, rather than continuing on her trajectory of elaboration (line 13), the professor drops out of the simultaneous talk to acknowledge and build on (*make a huge difference in meaning* in lines 20–21) Tamar's exemplification of SVO before returning to the main point of her explanation (*simply by syntax* in line 22). In other words, she validates Tamar's fleeting contribution without missing a beat in the midst of advancing her own explanation.

Validating learner contribution also is done by referencing learner talk. Consider another case from the graduate seminar. Immediately before the extract, Ellen was reporting on a finding of Gass's study reviewed in the article she was presenting, and Libby pointed out that the author of the review article never mentioned the proficiency level of the subjects in Gass's study. As the segment begins, Ellen responds to Libby's observation (lines 01–08) by citing the author's comment on a *major flaw with comparing data* (L=unidentified learner):

12. like you said

```
01 Ellen:              (um) somewhere in {(((glances down))-this
02                     article} she does say that a major fla:w with
03                     comparing data is (.) that (0.2) all the: subjects
```

```
04                  are so different.=the groups of subjects. so
05                  that you can see (what they) ↑(study)/(studied)
06                  and you can say it tells you something. but then
07                  you're comparing it to another study (   )
08                  totally different.
09  Libby:          (I guess my) (I-) I'm thinking that but I think
10                  my point is that it's a weakness in
11                  ((author's name))-(syl syl) because I can't believe
12                  that Ga:ss (.) who didn't mention the level the
13                  proficiency levels of her subject(s) and I think
14                  we're left with (1.0) ((author's name))-(syl syl)
15                  reporting Gass's conclusions and we can't
16                  interpret Gass's conclusions unless we kno:w
17                  (.) factors like (.) the proficiency level.
18  Ellen:          (but) we had that throughout the article
19                  (  [     )]
20  Libby:             [(    )] an interesting
21                  [experience.            ]
22  Prof:           [th- tha- that'd be some]thing to to check out
23                  [to see ] if it was (.) Gass's design weakness.
24  Libby:          [(right.)]
25  Prof:           in which case maybe ↑maybe she didn't report
26                  it. we don't know. at this point. and OR: u:m
27                  I mean because that was one of the criticisms
28      →           {(((slight nod to Ellen))-like you said} of a number
29                  of (.) people. I mean u:m (0.3) you know
30                  (Bernhardt) criticizes the {(((moving hands around,
31                  palms open, out in front))-sort of the (.)
32                  the slipshod the hodgepodge} nature of the
33                  research, so does Ba↑rnett. and so does
34                  ((author's name))-(syl syl). (and)/(in)
35                  >((author's name))-(syl syl)< in that sense
36                  [all of (them are) criticized.] look. nobody's
37  L:              [(((coughing))                ]
38  Prof:           looking at the same thing. here. u:m or
39      →           whether that's {(((gestures to Libby))-
40                  ((author's name))-(syl syl)'s misreporting of
41                  it} and so we really just can't get a clear
42                  picture of who's involved because she doesn't
43                  report it here. okay? {(((gaze to Libby))-I don't
44                  know. which one that is. I don't remember}
45                  enough about Gass's study to say whether
46                  to- to sa:y whether she mentioned (those).
```

In lines 09–17, Libby expresses a quick alignment with the critique but goes on to clarify that her issue is with the author not reporting the level of the subjects in Gass's study. In line 22, the professor interjects. As she responds to and summarizes the issues, she verbally and nonverbally attributes various points to both Ellen (line 28) and Libby (line 39), thus validating both contributions.

Ratify Diverging or Playful Initiatives

While it is relatively easy to validate learner contributions that align with the teacher agenda or discussion topic, a more valiant form of validation may be observed when the learner initiates a course of action that is divergent from the teacher agenda or nonconforming to the official tone of the classroom. In the following excerpt from math tutoring with children (Creider, 2013), The tutor (T) comments that Miguel, the child, has put out a row of dice, all of which have the three face on top. She then starts to count the dice (lines 01 and 03):

13. count cars

```
01  T:          °You're making it all three's in a row°
02              (.)
03              ((points at dice in line))-three dots, three dots.=
04  Miguel:     =all that this is a car.
05  T:          are those cars.
06  Miguel:     ((nods))
07  T:    →     >Yeah but let's see< (.) Let's count the colors of the cars.
08              (.)
09              Give me your finger.
10              ((M puts out finger)) (.)
11              ((T guides M's finger across line of dice)) pink car, green car,
12              red car, red car, blue car, black car, red car, with white dots,
13              red car with black do:ts.
14  Miguel:     ((places a red die in line))
15  T:          another red car.
```

As you can see, Miguel does not seem interested in the number three. Instead, he announces that *all that this is a car* (line 04). Rather than insisting on focusing on numbers, the tutor went with Miguel's car fantasy but at the same time was able to maintain her agenda on colors and counting. Creider has called this particular practice *weaving* as the tutor deftly weaves the child's initiative into her agenda without diminishing the latter's voice in any way.

An exhibit from the adult ESL classroom showcases the same teacher instinct in aligning with a learner's diverging initiative. The class is about to begin the activity of reenacting the discovery of silk. In lines 01 through 03, the teacher (T) is wrapping up the explanation of *reenact*. That the teacher's turn is coming to an end is shown in her (1) providing a summary of her explanation so far, (2) coming to a possible completion at the end of *historical events*, and (3) adding a *sotto voce* increment beyond the completion point (*free constituent* in Ford, Fox, & Thompson, 2002, p. 17). Now that the vocabulary item is out of the way, the teacher is positioned to give specific instructions for the reenacting activity. It is precisely at this point that, in latching, Carol launches a pre-sequence:

14. PBS

```
01 T:              ((lines omitted where T summarizing meaning of re-enact))
02                 and they act out things like- historical events. °
03                 what happened.°=
04 Carol:          =>yeah actually I don't know i- I j's-< ° I don't
05                 know if I can comment.°
06 T:         →    >y↑eah.<
07 Carol:          >yeah.< A:::::nd there're some channel see eh i- it's]
08                 u:h the public channel television?
09 T:         →    mm hm?
10 Carol:          >I don't remember< the:h the letters?
11 T:         →    P[BS?
12 LL:              [PBS.
13 Carol:          PBS?
14 George:         PBS (  )
15 Carol:          ((to G)) Yeah. they have som::e series, that they
16                 ((lines omitted))
17 T:         →    wow so th↑ey were re-enacti::ng [° (    )°
18 Carol:                                          [yeah yeah.
19                 they dre::ss exactly the way they di:d,
20 T:              Thank you for sharing ° that Carol.° Okay
21                 ((continues with task instruction))
```

Note also that Carol orients to her own initiative as an "intrusion" by littering her pre-request with speech perturbations and hedges (e.g., two self-repairs, *sotto voce*, and quick pace). The embedded question *I don't know if I can comment* (as opposed to *Can I comment?*) further distances Carol from the actual request. Note that rather than proceeding with her instruction, the teacher offers an enthusiastic go-ahead (line 06) to Carol's intricately designed pre-request. She goes on to support Carol's extended telling by producing a continuer (line 09), supplying the PBS as the searched-for item (line 11) and explicitly accepting the PBS story as an exemplar of reenacting—the theme of the lesson (line 17). In other words, although Carol's move temporarily stalls the teacher's agenda to move on, it is embraced by the latter nevertheless.

Finally, teachers' validating stances may become manifest in their willingness to align with playful initiatives that are not typical of the official classroom floor (Reddington & Waring, 2015). Join us in this scene from an intermediate-level class co-taught by two teachers. It begins with one teacher modeling for students how to give a presentation on a world record, a task they will be expected to perform shortly. He completes the modeling with an assessment: *Simple. Right?* (line 07):

15. for you

```
01 T1:                    [Ri::ght.  ] Each month it was
02                 nineteen dollars and ninety-five cents cha:rged (.)
03                 on the credit card. Goo:d. Umm, was a world record
04                 broken, yes, in two thousa:nd it was. Ma:ybe it was
05                 broken i:n two thousand o::ne, two thousand fou::r,
06                 two thousand five, we don't know, okay? That's all
07                 I want you to do. Simple. Right?
08 Carla:          For you.
09 LL:             [hahahahah      ]
10 T1:      →      [$For you ↑too.$]
11                 (1.2)-((students laughing; T1 hands a paper to a late student))
12 T1:             Okay, so. If you look at the little example on the top,
```

In line 07, the teacher's "Right?" prefers a *yes* response, and the adverbial phrase *for you* produced by Carla in line 08 appears at first glance to be such an aligning response: *Yes, simple for you.* However, by specifying a condition under which the teacher's assessment may be true, Carla in fact challenges the validity of that assessment. After all, the teacher's *simple* assessment is meant for the students, not the teachers. Compared to the more straightforward *No, not simple at all*, Carla's *for you* is done playfully and is treated as such by the class, as seen in the ensuing laughter. In fact, it constitutes a challenge to the teacher and his characterization of the pedagogical activity. Note that in line 10, the teacher extends the playful mood via the use of smiley voice as he restates his claim as *For you, too* (line 10), refuting Carla's challenge. By echoing Carla's turn composition and producing another extension then, he essentially "plays along" with her, and further laughter follows. Thus, the teacher, rather than shut down attempts at humor, laughs along and plays along (also see Lehtimaja, 2011; Pomerantz & Bell, 2011).

In sum, validating learner contributions is accomplished discursively as the teacher embodies his/her constant sensitivity by contingently acknowledging or referencing learner talk and as s/he deftly and confidently creates space for and sails along with learner initiatives that are divergent and/or playful. It is the teacher's way of saying *I hear you*.

Favor Learner Potentials

While *validate learner contributions* instantiates a vigilance about not dismissing or devaluing the "brave," *favor learner potentials* appears to be addressed to the "vulnerable" specifically—when one has produced a response that is less than ideal or when one's voice is not being heard. One might argue that in these cases, participants' competence concerns are at greater stake, and the teacher attends to those concerns by (1) highlighting success or (2) giving voice to the less vocal. In both cases, what becomes fore-grounded is learner potentials, whether that means adopting a glass-half-full outlook on less-than-ideal learner performances or refusing to take silence as an indication of incompetence.

Highlight Success

We begin with a simple example from an adult ESL classroom. The class is doing an exercise of supplying the correct preposition for certain phrases, and Bae in line 03 responds with *at charge of* instead of the correct *in charge of* (Fagan, 2013):

16. of is perfect

```
01  T:          Next one.
02              (1.8)-((Ann continues to look at paper: Bae picks his up.))
03  Bae:        Mr. Johnson is no:w? (0.6) at charge of office supplies.
04  T:      →   ((looks up and points paper at Bae))-"Of" is perfect.
05              (0.6)
06              ((to class))-but I think we're going to cha:ge (0.4)
07              [the first one.]
08  LL          [  In charge. ]
```

Note that rather than heading directly to the problematic *at*, the teacher first foregrounds the correct portion of Bae's response with the superlative assessment *perfect*. The glass-half-full outlook is sometimes indexed in ways that are less hyperbolic and more restrained. Consider a case from the grad-uate seminar, where Ling offers a less-than- thorough response (lines 04–05) to the professor's question (lines 01–02):

17. part of it

```
01  Prof:       what's all- what's that about. what
02              kinds of skills are they talking °about.°
03              (2.0)
04  Ling:       (it says) language classes in (syl)
05              like how do you uh (deal with some text.)
06  Prof:   →   okay, (0.2) that's part of it. [uh-huh,]
07  Tamar:                                    [isn't it  ]
08              part of first classes he:re [or the        ]
09  Prof:                                   [((nods))-mhm.]
10  Tamar:      universal is u:::m (   ) (it's I think) it's more
11              of a product. what you (.) [°ended with (   )°
12  Prof:                                  [(((nodding through
13              Tamar's turn))
```

```
14  Tamar:        what you got to, but ↑not how you got
15                there. how do you switch your: switches.
16                (0.5)
17  Prof:         [(I- I-)        ]
18  Tamar:        [how did you] [react to the:: to (the:,)]
19  Prof:                       [      ((nods))         ]
20            →   okay,=I think that would be part of it. The
21                other thing I (.) think of when I read this
22                is, (0.2) what is reading. ((continues))
```

In line 06, the professor acknowledges Ling's answer, and after a brief (0.2) gap where Ling does not continue, she proceeds to characterize that answer as partially on target. What we are not hearing is alternative formulations such as *What else?* or *That's not all of it.* The stress on *part* accentuates the desirable portion of Ling's response.

In line 07, Tamar orients to the professor's partial acceptance as requesting more, which she provides in the next few lines, and the professor supports her multiunit turn contribution with continuers and nodding. After a (0.5) gap in line 16, as she begins talking at the same time as Tamar continues, the professor immediately drops out and nods (line 19) through Tamar's continuation (see *validate learner contributions* earlier), which is eventually abandoned after some speech perturbation (line 18). In line 20, the professor again foregrounds the acceptable *part of* Tamar's response that constitutes an acceptable answer to her original question before supplying *the other thing* (line 21). The practice of highlighting success, then, involves foregrounding the positive portion of a less-than-adequate learner response.

It is also possible to highlight the positive without at all explicitly referencing what is left to be desired. In the following segment from graduate peer tutoring, the tutor (Tr) is taking issue with the multiple renditions of Lena the tutee's purpose of research and their lack of clarity for the most part:

18. this looks clearer

```
01  Tr:        A::::::nd, (0.5) and I thought the purpose- I've seen
02             that wor- worded different ways throughout (.) the
03         →   dissertation- throughout the chapter I thought this one
04             (.) looks (.) the clearest to me.
05             (0.5)
06             on page seven of your () proposal.
07  Lena:      °Okay.°
08             ((turns pages))
09  Tr:        (   ) So this one says examine the concepts of
10             democratic ((reading the rest of the sentence)) I- I-
11             it's hard for me to put a finger on it.
12  Lena:      Okay.
```

```
13 Tr:      →    what it is. an- an- this looks (.) clearer. ((reads))
14               This just looks much clearer [to me.]
15 Lena:                            [Okay.] All right.
16               This is what m:y (.) advisors and I worked out.
17 Tr:           O(hh)kay.
18 Lena:         But I a↑gree. An:d (0.5) purpose ((reads)) I- to me-
19               >↑ I wrote this one. ((laughs))<
```

Rather than noting the lack of consistency and clarity, which seems to be the problem, the tutor calls attention to what she considers to be the *clearest* version of the purpose statement without directly stating that the others are deficient. As it turns out, this *clearest* version is what Lena wrote herself, while the others were coauthored with her advisors. In this case then, the tutor's effort in foregrounding learner competence incidentally furnishes a unique opportunity for Lena to display her competence.

Give Voice to the Less Vocal

In any given classroom, some students are invariably more vocal than others, and teachers tend to be intuitively drawn to the vocal and equate their outspokenness with competence. Those who do not have the floor or are less adept at seizing and maintaining the floor are vulnerable to being viewed as less competent. The expert teacher, however, would see beyond the surface and behave in ways that treat the less vocal as just as competent. S/he would see the potentials of the less vocal and be very mindful about giving voice to them. This often involves actively selecting an alternative category of respondents vis-à-vis the ones who have spoken so far (Waring, 2014).

In the following segment, the class is discussing the culturally-specific nature of humor. In response to the teacher's elicitation in lines 11–12, Stacy, who typically manages to negotiate more than her fair share of the floor, self-selects to assert the differences between American and Danish humor (lines 16–17), which leads to a long sequence on the topic (not shown here):

19. what about Japanese

```
01 T:            Can you- Can you feel any big differences betwee:n
02               (.) say- (.) Am- American humor or English
03               humor?- ((to class))
04 Stacy:        Yeah.
05 Daisy:        Mhm.
06 Stacy:        Well not- (0.2) I- I can feel it from Danish humor
07               °to° (.) to American.
08 T:            Yeah?
((lines omitted))
09 Stacy:        I think that's (0.2) you have to be careful with.
10               °with that.°
```

```
11  T:            Okay. A'right, (0.2) ((to Naomi and Mo))-
12          →     Wha- What about- What about Japanese
13                humor.=Uh (.) Can y- Can you say anything about
14                (0.2) differences between a (0.4)}
15  Mo:           I don't know the difference.=But (0.2) ↑there is a
16                cartoon <South (.) Park,>
17  T:            [Uh huh.]
18  L:            [(Mhm.)]
19  Mo:           I think that's (0.2) >American Joke in there< (0.2)
20                that's not (.) um fo:r (.) someone li- (.) Japanese.
21  T:            Rea:lly.
22  Mo:           Yea:h. >Because it's< too black.
```

In line 11, the teacher receives Stacy's talk so far with a minimal acknowledgement and addresses his next question to Japanese humor (lines 12–13),
and in so doing, implicitly specifies the eligibility for potential next speakers
(Lerner, 2003), which effectively excludes Stacy, who has been occupying
the floor so far and gives voice to the typically quiet Japanese students.

The teacher also can target the "silent" by simply turning to the other
side of the room. In the next segment, in keeping with the "why English is so
difficult" theme, the class has been working on a task that involves figuring
out the pronunciation and vocabulary in a list of five sentences, an example
of which is "The bandage is wound around the wound." As the segment
begins, the class has just finished discussing the third sentence (lines 1–3):

20. this side over here

```
01  T:            So, the farm was used (.) to: produ:ce (0.2) produce.
02                (1.0)
03                {((to Sato))-°or fruits.°} Ok↑ay.
04                (0.5)
05          →     >Let's get someone< fro:m (0.5)
06                ((gestures to left))-°this side over here.=to do
07                number three.°
08                (0.8)-((T mild sweeping gesture))
09                Who's brave.=over here to do number three.
10                Robin, you wanna try?
11  LL:           heh heh [heh
12  Robin:               [well-
13  T:                   [Go ahea[d.   ]
14  Robin:                       [can] I- can I do the number four?
15  LL:           [heh hhe heh heh hahahahhahahhaha hahh]
16  T:            [You wanna do number four? hahhahahha ]
17                I'll let you do number four then.=
18                okay, [okay. ]
19  Robin:              [thank] you.
```

After a brief gap, the teacher in line 05 turns to treat those on his left side as potential next speakers. Without securing any volunteers in lines 08 and 09, where he does a nonverbal *this side* gesture as well as an invitation for the *brave* one, the teacher proceeds to select Robin as the next speaker. In line 12, Robin responds to the invitation with a disaffiliative *well* and requests a different item. Thus, Robin, who would not have otherwise spoken, gets a chance to make a contribution and does so on her own terms—in ways that best display her competence.

Finally, aside from actively selecting those who do not yet have the floor, the teacher can also give voice to the less vocal as they struggle to speak (Waring, 2013). In the next segment from an adult ESL classroom, the teacher asks Hiromi to complete the sentence *New York is so multicultural that . . .*:

21. just a second

```
      01  T:                 Tha:t, (.) what, Hiromi. (.) Ima:gine a sentence. New
      02                     York is so multicultural tha:t, ((gestures out toward her))
      03                     (1.6)
      04  Evelina:           (        )
      05  T:         →       ((holds up hand/nods/smiles to Evelina))
      06                     $ °>Just a second, just a second.<°$
      07                     (1.2)
      08  T:                 tha::t,
      09  Sato:              You never miss [your (homeland).=
      10  T:         →                      [(((holds hand up toward Sato/nods/smiles))
      11  Sato:              = (                    )]
      12  T:                 =$Just a second, let- let her try:$]
      13  Sato:              Sorry: hheh.
      14  T:                 I know, y- we have so many wonderful people who
      15                     wanna [ta:lk.]
      16  Hiromi:                  [So:  ] multicultural that (.) uh we have many
      17                     (     ) restaura:nts,
      18  T:         →       Perfect, perfect. Evelina. So multicultural tha:t,
      19  Evelina:           ° (            )°
      20  T:                 O::kay, Sato, go,
```

After a (1.6) second gap with no response from Hiromi, Evelina makes an unintelligible attempt, which is immediately put on hold by the teacher with nods and smiles in line 05 along with a hand gesture as well as the repeated and quickly paced *Just a second* in smiley voice. Another (1.2) second passes, and the teacher repeats the elicitation with a lengthened *tha:t* in continuing intonation in line 08, which receives Sato's volunteered completion *You never miss your homeland*. Again, the teacher extends to Sato the same on-hold gesture with nods and smiles and does so in terminal overlap (Jefferson, 1983), followed by the directive *just a second* delivered in smiley voice as well as the account *let her try.* (lines 10 & 12). After Sato's apology in the next line, the teacher proceeds to characterize the competing voices as *so many wonderful people who want to talk* (lines 14–15). Finally, in lines 16 and 17, after much persistence on the teacher's part to give Hiromi the space to try, the latter produces a sentence completion that receives two consecutive *perfects* in line 18. Immediately thereafter, the teacher returns the floor first to Evelina (line 18) and then to Sato (line 20). As shown, the teacher engages in a great deal of interactional work to carve out the space for Hiromi to exhibit what she *is* able to do and eventually succeeds in making public the latter's competence.

In sum, in favoring learning potentials, the teacher says *I see the best possible you.* This pedagogical posture becomes evident when s/he carefully calibrates his/her assessment of some less-than-desirable learner performance specifically to spotlight the latter's success, however miniscule or partial. It also becomes evident when s/h goes an extra mile to ensure that the competence of the silent and the struggling is not left underground but given a safe and proper platform.

Neutralize Asymmetry

In pedagogical interactions, an obvious threat to learner competence is the inherent asymmetry that such interaction assumes. Learning English, for example, presupposes one's yet-to-be-developed competence in English, and learning to teach presupposes one's yet-to-be-developed competence in teaching. One way of attending to such a priori competence deficiencies is to neutralize the undergirding asymmetry. In graduate peer tutoring, for example, the tutor frames her advice in ways that clearly show her not to be taking the asymmetry for granted. She displays, instead, great sensitivity toward the potential resistance that may come from the tutee. She does so by designing her advice as less than certain, less than serious, and by underscoring the caution she takes in reaching an assessment. Neutralizing asymmetry is also done by (1) claiming co-membership and (2) positioning the learner as professional.

Claim Co-membership

In my data of graduate tutoring, the tutor neutralizes asymmetry by claiming co-membership with the learner or positioning him/herself as experiencing similar issues as the latter. The following segment begins with the tutor (Tr) expressing her struggle with finding a proper heading in Lena the tutee's writing:

22. I go back and forth

    01 Tr: →   I- ↑I: go back and forth because >I first said
    02   I'll (go a' put this) I started to read your inclusion

```
03                    example I said they're all kind of different. So I- get
04                    rid of it, th(h)e ↑s(h)econd time I read it I pu- I put it
05                    back again< in the end I think it's better .hhh
06  Lena:             mhm
07  Tr:               so you- you use community as a larger category.=
08  Lena:             =>I think so [↑too.<
09  Tr:                            [Yea:h.
10  Lena:             I agree with you.=
11  Tr:               right?=
12  Lena:             =Totally. [↑Yeah ↑yeah. I- I [totally agree with you.
13  Tr:        →               [Yeah          [so, I- I-
14                    >even though< I went back and forth with it [(   )
15  Lena:                                                         [an'
16                    I ↑wanna do that I ↑wanna synthesize I ↑wanna it to
17                    be[come more-
18  Tr:                 [yeah.
19  Lena:             Yeah.
20  Tr:               °yeah°
21  Lena:             °'kay°
```

Notably, the tutor's advice of using *community as a larger category* (line 07) is presented as a result of much struggle on her own part (*I go back and forth . . .*) in lines 01 and 14.

In so doing, she manages to show that Lena's problem is not specific to her "deficient" competence but one that the tutor as an expert can experience as well. By positioning herself as a co-struggling participant then, the tutor is able to obviate the assumption that the tutee is necessarily less than competent—at least on this particular issue. Indeed, as can be observed, Lena subsequently positions herself as a co-participant on an equal footing by agreeing with, rather than accepting, the advice (lines 10 and 12).

In some cases, the tutor explicitly positions herself as a co-learner. In the next segment, the tutor notes the circular problem in Lena the tutee's writing (lines 01–04; 06), who then displays her understanding of the implicit advice by stating that what she should do is follow a particular line of thought without bringing in extraneous materials (lines 08–09; 11–12):

23. what do you do

```
01  Tr:                         = [(    ) exactly.
02                    yeah. INside each o:ne .hh sometimes the. hh the
03                    writing is a little bit circular .hh >You talk about A:
04                    and B: an' you go back to A a little agai:n< an' kind've-
05  Lena:             °'kay.°=
06  Tr:               =they're not as linear as (.) it- could be.
07                    (5.0)
08  Lena:             .hh >so< basically I'm watching out for like am I
```

```
09                  following that line of thought-
10 Tr:              ri:ght.
11 Lena:            right throu:gh without- (0.4)
12                  brin[ging in something else? °okay°
13 Tr:                  [ri:ght.
14            →      A friend of mine has this great (0.2) tactic
15 Lena:            °What does she do.°
16 Tr:        →     she uses this to- to write cuz I ↑love her ↑writing.
17 Lena:            aha?
18 Tr:        →     an' >I always say what do you ↑do what do you do =
19 Lena:                [>right right.<
20 Tr:        →     =[and I started to use it recently I think it ↑really
21                  ↑works.< =.hh Each time she begins a paragraph,
22 Lena:            [yeah.
23 Tr:             [she- she asks a question.
24                  (0.8)
25                  u:m >↓she says this is the question I'm going to
26                  answer in this paragraph.. hh and she (0.2) writes
27                  that paragraph.
28 Lena:            >an' then she gets [rid of the question.<
29 Tr:                                 [she ge-
30                  gets rid of the qu(h)estion! Cuz I always thought
31                  her writing is just rea:lly (0.2) clear. and really g↑ood.
32                  .hhhm and its- s(h)o I s(h)aid wh(h)at d'y do >°an' (.)
33                  she said this is what she does°<. hh >(an' I was like) oh
34                  tha- that's what she does< it- it sounds so simple and I-
35                  I >never really started to ↑use it until very recently.<
36                  .hh and (.) it ↓really ↑helps!
37 Lena:            (  !) [that's good.    [Exactly.
38 Tr:                    [y(h)eah hh yea:[h it-
39                  it really keeps you on track s' you don't go (.) like- (0.5)
40                  (sometimes) you wand(h)er o:ff [when you wri:te and=
41 Lena:                                           [°wander off°
42 Tr:              = your thou:ghts are taking [you places. .hhh
43 Lena:                                        [right.
```

In line 14, after briefly confirming Lena's understanding display, the tutor proceeds to offer a solution of her own—by sharing a *tactic* (line 14) she *learned* from a friend whose writing she greatly admired (line 16). Her learner identity is voiced in such reported speech as *what do you ↑do what do you do* (line 18). She also reports on her learning process (*and I started to use it recently* in line 20) and offers testimony to the success of the tactic (*I think it ↑really worked*) (lines 20–21) in much the same spirit of sharing a secret recipe with one's close friends. In so doing, the tutor again positions herself as sharing the same writing issues as the tutee does and benefiting from the same learning process that the latter is subject to. Asymmetry is neutralized and the issue of deficient competence rendered invisible.

Position Learner as Professional

While *claim co-membership* entails adopting a novice status to reach an equal footing with the learner, *position learner as professional* involves attributing an expert status to the latter. This is done in part by treating the learner as the decision maker. Prior to the segment from a post-observation conference, the issue of a particular reading activity having taken up too much time came up, and as the segment begins, the mentor appears to be tying the activity back to its purpose, with scanning or skimming as its possibilities:

24. if you wanna speed this up

```
01  M:       ((looks down))- a::nd um, Oh Yeah. so the:
02           um, (0.4) basically the ((looks at F))- purpose
03           of the reading.
04  Fay:     ((looks at report, nods))- mm hm, (.)
05           ((puts report down, looks at M)) yes.
06  M:       when- so basically when you have a
07           handout with (.) specific questions,
08  Fay:     ((nods))- mhm.
09  M:       they read the questions first, so it's
10           (.) scanning.
11  Fay:     ((nods))- mm hm?
12  M:       an' that usually takes longer.=although
13           ↑they- they did pretty well.
14  Fay:     ((nods)) [>they did-< yeah.    ]
15  M:                [cuz when they have to] write
16           answers to the questions? that usually
17           takes them [a while.]
18  Fay:                [exactly. ] they- they- {that was
19           taking them longer.- ((points down))} ((looks
20           down))- U:m, >becuz I was< going around?
21           they- they ((looks up))- read? (.) the whole
22           thing? bu:t writing it down was: ((nods))-
23                [taking a lot of time.]
24  M:       ((nods))-[right. right. right.    ]
25  Fay:     ((nods))- yeah.
26  M:    →  so::, um, if you wanna speed this up,
27  Fay:     ((nods))- [mm hm,]
28  M:                 [u:m,     ] (0.8) you can (.) have
29           them (.) not write it down.
30  Fay:     mm hm,
```
((lines omitted addressed to outside noise))

```
31 M:          °okay.° ((turns to Farah)) U:m, Or? you
32             can do ski↑mming? where you ask them
33             the wh-questions?=
34 Fay:        =okay.=
```

It is not clear whether the length of time taken by the reading activity is
treated as problematic by either the mentor or Fay. By noting that scanning
usually takes longer (lines 10 and 12), the mentor is at least providing an
account for the time taken. By adding *although ↑they- they did pretty well*
(lines 12–13), however, she seems at least to be insinuating the problematic
nature of devoting too much time to a single activity.

Keeping this in mind, we may then have a basis for hearing *speed this
up* (line 26) possibly as implicit advice to solve the time problem, and Fay
appears to be orienting to it as such: observe the *mm hm*, nods (lines 27
and 30) and the *okay* in line 34. What is noticeable for our purpose is this:
the advice, prefaced by *so::, um,* is formulated as conditionally acceptable
via the if-clause. In so doing, M treats its acceptance as entirely lying in the
hands of Fay without imposing on the latter skimming rather than scanning
as a purpose for *her* activity. In other words, Fay is positioned as someone
who has the ultimate say in her professional decisions.

This same theme of positioning learner as ultimate decision maker
becomes visible in the following segment from graduate peer tutoring,
where the tutor (Tr) is making a suggestion of reorganizing the materials:

25. don't know if you're going to buy this

```
01 Tr:         An:::d (0.2) I think the:se are the fou::r u::::m (1.0)
02             things right? °your ide- not- ( [)°
03 Lena:                              [commu[nity?
04 Tr:                                      [° ( ) ( )
05             learning ( ) learning.°
06 Lena:       ° ( ) learning basically yeah.°
07 Tr:         .hhhh
08 Lena        [°and inquiry.°
09 Tr:    →    [I'M TRYING TO (0.2) I- I don't know if you're
10             going to buy this but um (.) w- we'll look at some
11             specific examples too. I'm trying to get you to put
12             inclusion into com[munity, and power into voice.=
13 Lena:                         [okay?
14             =Yeah. I think I can do that?=
15 Tr:         =so you have three.
16 Lena:       =Three. Yeah.
```

In line 09, the tutor begins with *I'M TRYING TO* but stops to insert *I-
I don't know if you're going to buy this but um (.) w- we'll look at some
specific examples too* (line 09–11) before returning to *I'm trying to* with a

completion of her proposal this time. By inserting *I don't know if you're going to buy this*, the tutor treats Lena as someone to be persuaded rather than directed. Both the verb *buy* and the hedge *I don't know if* allude to the image of Lena being a professional with her own set of independent experiences, resources, and preferences—someone that would require serious efforts to persuade. By promising to *look at some specific examples too*, the tutor further positions Lena as a judicious party who is not to be persuaded without substantive evidence. Thus, the tutor is in the position of presenting a case, and Lena the tutee of assessing the feasibility of that case. The encounter is one of professional colleagues.

Continuing with the theme of *position learner as professional*, we return to the post-observation conference for our final case of the section. Here, the participants are discussing the issue of having only one student in the class just observed (M=mentor):

26. put you off your game

```
01 M:          a:nd, (0.2) you were telling me a little bit earlier
02             about having that {(( turns page ))-one student.}
03       →     (0.2) do you f↑ee:l tha:t (.) that sort of (.)
04             put you off of your (( gaze to A ))-game,=
05             >starting off the class with that,
06             [or d'y feel-]<,=
07 Ava:        [a little bit ].
08 M:          =(( nods ))-y[eah, ]
09 Ava:                     [yeah].
10 M:          >well tell me about it.<
11 Ava:        well I think (.) that (.) y'know I had tried to
12             think of contingencies for various things,
13 M:          m[hm.      ]
```

In line 01, the mentor begins his next question with a *pre* that refers back to Ava's own mentioning of the issue. A brief gap emerges before the actual inquiry commences, which is a yes-no question that foregrounds Ava's feelings (and thoughts). The phrase *put you off your game* (line 04) is carefully crafted to position Ava as a professional who has a game plan but may be momentarily "off the game." Line 05 may be an extension produced in the monitor space (Davidson, 1984) given the lack of immediate response from Ava, and that extension itself is followed up with an alternative (line 06) that overlaps with Ava's response *A little bit*. This *position as professional* move appears to be instrumental in creating a space for Ava to articulate her thoughts later as a professional (lines 11–12).

In sum, learner competence may be attended to by neutralizing the asymmetry inherent in pedagogical encounters. Subtle maneuvers such as *claiming co-membership* or *positioning as professional* do not overtly glorify leaners' competence but render invisible the assumption that learners are automatically deficient in their specific areas of pursuits, putting forward, instead, the understanding that their issues are not unique to their "deficient" status and that they are the ultimate decision makers steering their own intellectual advancement and professional growth.

COMPETENCE, PLAY, AND PROLEPSIS

Having begun with the proposal that achieving competence entails assuming competence, I devoted the bulk of the chapter to demonstrating the omnipresence of participants' competence concerns in pedagogical interactions as well as how such concerns may be attended to subtly and skillfully. As shown, in lieu of a three-year-old's *I already knew that!*, ESL students exhibit reluctance in aligning with teachers' critique-implicative yes-no questions, teachers in training engage in bright-side telling in assessing their own performance, and graduate students express noncomprehension, receive explanations, and resist and accept advice in ways that foreground their identity as hardworking, independent, and knowledgeable co-participants. Recognizing the range of conduct as indices of competence concerns rather than dismissing them as irrelevant, subversive, presumptuous, or even delusional can perhaps inspire an appreciation for the foundational power of competence as learners navigate their developmental paths. And in the best possible world, such appreciation would beget serious attention and modified behavior, where competence is recruited as a resource rather than neglected as a nuisance.

Throughout this chapter, we have become acquainted with the tutor, the teacher, the mentor, and the professor who recognize the centrality of competence in learner development and embody such recognition as they validate learner contributions, favor learner potentials, and neutralize asymmetries. Instead of being solely focused on their own agendas and interactional trajectories, they acknowledge or reference learner talk and ratify diverging or playful learner initiatives. Instead of following the instinctive urge to fix problems and yield to the sounds of ready and confident participation, they make a point of highlighting the success of learner performance and work hard to give voice to the less vocal. Instead of operating within the comfort zone of asymmetry, they claim co-membership with the learner and position the latter as professional. Importantly, in all these cases, competence is not attended to via any dramatic or perfunctory accolades. Rather, what the learners are given is a chance to be heard, a chance to be seen, and a chance to be leveled with as valuable contributors, discerning consumers, and equal partners. They are, in other words, given the opportunity to behave as though they were "a head taller" than themselves, which may remind us of the exciting possibilities envisioned by the Russian psychologist Vygotsky (1978) of what play brings:

> Play creates a zone of proximal development of the child. In play a child always behaves beyond his average age, above his daily behavior; in play it is as though he were a head taller than himself.
>
> (p. 102)

Arguably, the principle of competence—that is, *achieving competence entails assuming competence*—is simply yet another rendition of Vygotsky's theory of play. Insofar as the ZPD contains the distance between one's actual and potential development (Vygotsky, 1978, p. 86), play, according to Vygotsky, creates that zone that allows the child to go beyond his/her current abilities to reach his/her potentials, and such potentials are more specifically understood as what the child is capable of accomplishing with the assistance of an adult or a capable peer. Let us be clear that the tutor, the teacher, the mentor, and the professor in this chapter did not provide such assistance (see Chapter 6 instead). What they did do, however, was create the zone, set the stage, and establish the foundation so that the learner can have the courage and security to play. By treating the learners as valuable contributors, discerning consumers, and equal partners, they open up the space for the latter's development. Admittedly, my analysis does not produce evidence for such development. It does, however, offer glimpses into how attending to learner competence may, for example, engender open reflection in post-observation conferences—a key ingredient in teacher learning. More crucially, it specifies a range of discursive practices for building the playground or creating the ZPD for learning. While CA provides the methodological tool for discovering how assuming competence is accomplished in situ, Vygotsky's ZPD offers the much-needed theoretical lens to enable the leap from assuming competence to achieving competence.

An equally useful lens is the concept of prolepsis. In addressing the question of how language learning actually happens in his ecological theory of language education, van Lier (2004) calls prolepsis "a cornerstone of equal importance to scaffolding" (p. 153). Drawing upon Bakhtin (1981) and Rommetveit (1974), among others, van Lier (2004) defines prolepsis as "a form of looking ahead, of assuming something to be the case before it has been encountered, a foreshadowing in some sense" (p. 152). For him, prolepsis is an indicator of greater contingency—a feature of classroom interaction beneficial for language learning (van Lier, 1996, p. 182). As he writes,

> Prolepsis can be seen as a game of make-believe in which the educator pretends that the learner knows more than she actually does and can do more than she has shown to be capable of hitherto.
>
> (van Lier, 2004, pp. 152–153)

One might argue that to honor the principle of competence is to practice prolepsis, and in this chapter, we have become witness to how the game of prolepsis is being played out in the minute details of moment-to-moment interaction as the more competent participant subtly but effectively validates learner contributions, favors learner potentials, and neutralizes asymmetry.

REFERENCES

Bakhtin, M. M. (1981). *The dialogical imagination.* Austin: The University of Texas Press.

Chua, A., & Rubenfeld, J. (2014, January 25). What drives success? *New York Times.* Retrieved from http://www.nytimes.com/2014/01/26/opinion/sunday/what-drives-success.html

Cline, F., & Fay, J. (2014). *Parenting with love and logic: Teaching children responsibility.* Colorado Springs, CO: Navpress.

Copland, F. (2012). Legitimate talk in feedback conferences. *Applied Linguistics, 33*(1), 1–20.

Creider, S. (2013). The integration sequence: Responding to child initiations in a tutoring session. Unpublished manuscript. Teachers College, Columbia University.

Davidson, J. (1984). Subsequent versions of invitations, offers, requests, and proposals dealing with potential or actual rejection. In J. M. Atkinson & J. Heritage (Eds.), *Structures of social action: Studies in conversation analysis* (pp. 102–128). Cambridge, UK: Cambridge University Press.

Fagan, D. S. (2013). *Managing learner contributions in the adult ESL classroom: A conversation analytic and ethnographic examination of teacher practices and cognition* (Doctoral dissertation). Retrieved from ProQuest Dissertations & Theses Full Text.

Ford, C. E., Fox, B. A., & Thompson, S. A. (2002). Constituency and the grammar of turn increments. In C. E. Ford, B. A. Fox, & S. A. Thompson (Eds.), *The language of turn and sequence* (pp. 14–38). Oxford: Oxford University Press.

Goffman, E. (1981). *Forms of talk.* Philadelphia: University of Pennsylvania Press.

Hall, J. K. (2009). Interaction as method and result of language learning. *Language Teaching, 43*(2), 1–14.

Heritage, J. (1984). A change-of-state token and aspects of its sequential placement. In J. M. Atkinson & J. Heritage (Eds.), *Structures of social action: Studies in conversation analysis* (pp. 299–345). Cambridge, UK: Cambridge University Press.

Honneth, A. (1992). The struggle for recognition: The moral grammar of social conflicts. Cambridge, MA: MIT Press.

Hyland, K. (1996). Talking to the academy: Forms of hedging in science research articles. *Written Communication, 13*(2), 251–281.

Jefferson, G. (1983). Notes on some orderliness of overlap onset. *Tilburg Papers in Language and Literature, 28*, 1–28.

Jefferson, G., & Lee, J. R. E. (1992). The rejection of advice: Managing the problematic convergence of a "troubles-telling" and a "service encounter." In P. Drew & J. Heritage (Eds.), *Talk at work: Interaction in institutional settings* (pp. 521–548). Cambridge, UK: Cambridge University Press.

Lehtimaja, I. (2011). Teacher-oriented address terms in students' reproach turns. *Linguistics and Education, 22*, 348–363.

Lerner, G. H. (2003). Selecting next speaker: The context-sensitive operation of a context-free organization. *Language in Society, 32*(2), 177–201.

Pomerantz, A. (1984). Agreeing and disagreeing with assessments: Some features of preferred/dispreferred turn shapes. In J. M. Atkinson & J. Heritage (Eds.), *Structures of social action: Studies in conversation analysis* (pp. 57–101). New York: Cambridge University Press.

Pomerantz, A., & Bell, N. (2011). Humor as safe house in the foreign language classroom. *The Modern Language Journal, 95*(Suppl. 1), 148–161.

Reddington, E., & Waring, H. Z. (2015). Understanding the sequential resources for doing humor in the language classroom. *Humor: International Journal of Humor Research, 28*(1), 1–23.

Rommetveit, R. (1974). *On message structure.* New York: Wiley.
Sacks, H. (1987). On the preferences for agreement and contiguity in sequences in conversation. In G. Button & J.R.E. Lee (Eds.), *Talk and social organization* (pp. 54–69). Clevedon: Multilingual Matters.
van Lier, L. (1996). *Interaction in the language curriculum.* London: Longman Group Limited.
van Lier, L. (2004). *The ecology and semiotics of language learning: A sociocultural perspective.* Norwell, MA: Kluwer Academic Publishers.
Vygotsky, L.S. (1978). *Mind in society: The development of higher psychological processes.* Cambridge, MA: Harvard University Press.
Waring, H.Z. (2002). Expressing noncomprehension in seminar discussion. *Journal of Pragmatics, 34*(12), 1711–1731.
Waring, H.Z. (2005). The unofficial business of repair initiation: Vehicles for affiliation and disaffiliation. In A.E. Tyler, M. Takada, Y. Kim, & D. Marinova (Eds.), *Language in use: Cognitive and discourse perspectives on language and language learning* (pp. 163–175). Washington, DC: Georgetown University Press.
Waring, H.Z. (2007). Complex advice acceptance as a resource for managing asymmetries. *Text and Talk, 27*(1), 107–137.
Waring, H.Z. (2012a). Negotiating competence with multiple-*yeah* in academic contexts. *Language and Information Society, 16,* 141–172.
Waring, H.Z. (2012b). Yes-no questions that convey a critical stance in the language classroom. *Language and Education, 26*(5), 451–469.
Waring, H.Z. (2013). Managing competing voices in the second language classroom. *DiscourseProcesses, 50*(5), 316–338.
Waring, H.Z. (2014). Turn allocation and context: Broadening participation in the second language classroom. In J. Flowerdew (Ed.), *Discourse in context: Contemporary applied linguistics*(Vol. 3, pp. 301–320). London: Bloomsbury.

5   Principle of Complexity
Teacher Talk Is Multivocalic

Zoe began kindergarten last September. She loves school and would play school after school. Any passer-by would know she was playing school upon hearing installments such as *Does everybody get it?*, *Very good*, *What do YOU think the answer is?*, *Let's say . . .*, *I'll give you a clue*, and the like. We associate certain language specifically to being a teacher. We invoke that language in our caricatures of teacher talk. Yet, we rarely question what such talk actually does in interaction. Does it pursue understanding, provide encouragement, or promote independence? Does it do what we assume it does? It may come as a surprise that sometimes it doesn't. This is because teacher talk is multivocalic; a particular utterance or practice can be saturated with more than one voice or can do more than one thing, bringing into relief a range of concerns inhabiting the classroom: order, equity, learning, participation, progressivity, and inclusiveness, namely, the multiple and potentially competing demands that teachers manage on a moment-by-moment basis. Within the same utterance, for example, the voice of pursuing understanding may clash with the voice to achieve progressivity as progressivity can be pursued at the expense of ensuring an adequately patient space for learning. At the same time, however, the multivocality of teacher talk may be usefully recruited, with the deployment of a single practice, to strike a delicate balance between exercising necessary control and fostering an open space for participation. As will become evident throughout the chapter, multivocality is evocative of Bakhtin's (1981, 1986) notions of "heteroglossia," "hybridation," and "double-voiced discourse." This Bakhtinian connection will be elaborated in the conclusion of the chapter.

While *competence* evokes an overall ethos of teaching, both *complexity* and *contingency* (this and next chapters) address the nature of teacher talk, with *complexity* underscoring its challenges and *contingency* its desired quality, with inevitable overlapping between the two. In this chapter, we take a critical look at the multivocality of teacher talk, uncovering how such multivocality may constitute either an impediment or a resource as one navigates the pedagogical universe. As will be shown, as an impediment, the inherently conflicting nature of these voices can frustrate rather than facilitate the learning process. As a resource, the many voices can be deployed expertly to balance the competing agendas intrinsic to pedagogical encounters. In what follows, we first take a closer look at some of the routine teacher language by way of making evident its pitfalls, problems, and unintended outcomes as a by-product of multivocality. We then illustrate some specific ways in which certain competing agendas in pedagogical encounters may be delicately managed with multivocalic teacher talk.

MULTIVOCALITY AS AN IMPEDIMENT

Strikingly, evidence for multivocality as an impediment can be located readily in some of the most taken-for-granted renditions of teacher talk such as *very good*, *any questions?*, and the types of elicitations we engage in as we ostensibly do teaching. In such cases, two different voices reside in each utterance, and as will be demonstrated, they tend to work against each other.

Explicit Positive Assessment (EPA)

One routine bit of teacher talk is *very good* as teachers give explicit positive assessments (EPAs) on learner performance. Such positive reinforcement seems integral to building a healthy and nurturing learning environment. Yet, what my data from the adult ESL classroom show is that at least in some form-focused contexts, EPAs such as *very good* can stifle rather than promote learning as it conveys not just sequence closed, but "case closed" (Waring, 2008). Like other sequence-closing thirds such as *oh* or *okay* (Schegloff, 2007), and unlike negative assessments after learner talk (which would incur further expansions), positive assessments do not project any further within-sequence talk. It is the "preferred" (Pomerantz, 1984; Sacks, 1987) response that closes the sequence. As with any typical preferred response, it is delivered without any delay, mitigation, or accounts:

1. married

```
01 T:          ((looks up at class)) Nu::mber three:::::
02             ((points))-Kevin.
03             (1.0)
04 Kevin:      "Wow. I didn't know (.) you were married."
05             (0.8)
06             "Ho:::w lo:ng
07             have you:::[:::::: (.) b : e e n   m a r r i e d."        ]=
08 T:                     [((slight nod turns into large encouraging nods))]
09      →       =$Very good=how long have you been married.$
10             =Very good. Nu:mber four. Mai,
```

2. play saxophone

```
01 T:              °Good.° Number six, Yuka?
02                 (0.8)
03 Yuka:           ((reads)) >oh< come o:::::n. You really play the
04                 saxophone.
05                 (0.5)
06                 How lo:ng (.) have you been playing the sa- the
07                 saxophone.=
08 T:        →     =The ↓saxophone.↓Very good. °very good.°
09                 Number seven? Miyuki?
```

3. trying for Olympics

```
01 T:              ((reads instructions for the next exercise))
02                 Nu:mber one.=>Veronica.<
03 Veronica:       ((reads)) Oh really? I didn't know you were
04                 'tryning' for the Olympics. How long (.) have you
05                 been 'tryning' (.) for the Olympics?
06                 [((looks up at T))   ]
07 T:        →     [>°G o o d.° Ho ]w long have you been training
08                 for the Olympics.<=Excellent.
09                 (0.2)
10                 Nu:mber two. ((continues))
```

As Schegloff (2007) points out, sequences with preferred second-pair parts are "closure-relevant," while those with dispreferred second-pair parts are "expansion-relevant" (p. 117). Not surprisingly, the EPA turns typically are followed by silence or the initiation of a new sequence.

It is important to note that sequence closing does not necessarily block further topical talk. For example, once an invitation is accepted, a new sequence addressed to making arrangements with regard to the invitation may proceed, and this new sequence is still situated within the general activity of invitation (cf. "sequences of sequences" in Schegloff, 2007, pp. 195–216). What EPA does, however, is not just close a sequence, but insinuates "case closed," that is, treating further talk on the subject as unnecessary and unwarranted. The prosodic packaging, for example, of decreased volume, lowered pitch, and slower speed (see previous extracts) that accompany the delivery of EPA contribute to suggesting the closing of an activity (Goldberg, 2004), their dissolving effect not unlike the "trail-off silences" discussed in Local and Kelly (1986, p. 195). In addition, the EPAs often occur with other items such as *thank you* and repetitions that typically occupy the closing slots of transitions.

What also contributes to the "case closed" hearing of EPA is its undertaking of putting the learner response on a pedestal, so to speak. Observe the nodding, the smiley voice, the emphatic delivery and marked pitch (see (1)–(3)) as well as the repetition of the correct response that is deeply intertwined with accolades. What is repeated is specifically marketed as desirable, and that desirability is sometimes further bolstered by the marked delivery of that repetition. In short, a host of discursive resources are deployed to legitimize or set in stone the learner's response as *the* "perfect answer" and, as such, definitive and beyond negotiation. What this does is implicitly construct any other answer as deviant and less than competent.

Further cementing the "case closed" hearing of EPA is its appearance as an encouraging, congratulating, and rewarding gesture at the finish line of a "journey." The next segment concerns the following fill-in-the-blanks item:

The Harlem Globetrotters are a world-famous comic basketball team. They (1. play) _____ basketball since 1926, and they (2. travel) _____ to different countries of the world for more than 40 years.

4. Harlem Globetrotters

```
01 T:          [O k a:] y? u::::::h ((looks around the room)) Miyuki.
02             (1.5)-((Miyuki looks up and then down at textbook))
03 Miyuki:     ((reading)) The Harlem Glo-
04             (1.0)-((looks closer at the textbook)) °tera-°
05             [((looks up)) trotter.]
06 T:          [t r o t        ] te:rs,
07 Miyuki:     ((looks down)) Globe [trotters,]
08 T:                                [trotters,]
09             °mhm?°
10 Miyuki:     ((continues reading)) Globetrotters are a world-
11             famous comic basketball team. They have been
12             playing basketball since 1926. and they ((looks up))
13 T:          mh:m?
14 Miyuki:     ((looks down and continues reading)) and they have
15             been traveling to different countries of the world for
16             more than forty years.=
17 T:     →    =°↓Very good. Tha:nk you.°
18             (.)
19             K↑evin. We skipped ↑you. >Go ahead.<
```

In line 4, soon after beginning to answer the teacher's nomination, Miyuki initiates repair as shown in the cutoff at the very first syllable of *Globetrotters*. A full second passes before she produces the nontarget-like *tera*, which is followed by yet another cutoff. Looking up immediately thereafter, Miyuki completes her repair by uttering the remaining syllables—*trotters*. Her self-repair comes in overlap with the teacher's other-repair at line 9, which outlasts Miyuki's by one syllable as a result of the teacher's slower and emphatic delivery.

In line 07, Miyuki repeats *Globetrotters* in its entirety, the final two syllables of which are again collaboratively completed by the teacher. Meanwhile,

Miyuki also begins to disengage her gaze from the teacher toward her text-book. The teacher's continuer *mhm?* in line 10 aligns with Miyuki's closing agenda. In line 11, Miyuki completes the first clause with the correct verb form *have been playing*. Soon after beginning the second clause, she looks up at the teacher as if to confirm that she still has the floor, to which the teacher offers a confirming *mhm?*. Miyuki then proceeds to provide the second correctly conjugated verb.

Throughout the sequence, we have observed Miyuki's struggle with a pronunciation problem as well as her nonverbal quest for the teacher's assurance not only on the linguistic form but also on her floor rights. We also have observed the teacher's close monitoring of and sensitivity toward the interactional contingencies in Miyuki's emerging response. Given the eventful nature of this joint production, one may hear the teacher's *very good* in line 17 as a congratulatory applause for the entire journey Miyuki has traveled, with the assistance of the teacher, to bring the task, not without difficulty, to its completion. Thus, by treating the learner response as beyond reproach and by applauding the series of efforts devoted to achieving that response, EPA sounds a finale-like note. It delivers the meta-message of "case closed" and discourages (further) negotiation. Indeed, the teacher remains silent after the *very good* and proceeds to initiate a new sequence.

That such a "case closed" message can inhibit further negotiation may be observed in the following extract, which occurs 66 lines after Extract (1):

5. have a question

01	Miyuki:	I have one [ques]tion,
02	T:	[Yes.]
03	Miyuki:	Number three is if without "be:" °is not good?°
04	T:	How lo:ng (1.0) you've been marrie[d?
05	Miyuki:	[Have
06		you married. °have you married.°-((*looks at T*))
07	T:	°Oka::y?° ((*walks to BB*)) >Let's write this
08		d↑own.< ((*starts writing*))

Recall that in Extract (1), Kevin successfully provides the correct verb form, and the teacher immediately produced an EPA and moved on to the next person. The case was clearly closed, and no possibility was provided for otherwise. Yet, much later in the interaction, as the teacher is about to move on to the next item on the agenda, Miyuki raises an issue that was clearly unresolved at the time. Her question leads to a sequence that lasts two and a half minutes. It turns out to be the most complicated error-correction sequence in the entire two-hour class. Briefly, Miyuki has treated *marry* as a verb, in which case its correct present perfect form would be *have married*, except that the punctual aspect of *marry* is ill fitted to the duration query of *how long*. Since the mere form of *married* may be either a verb or an adjective, Miyuki's confusion is not surprising, but the earlier EPA closing may have made it difficult for her or anyone else to voice potential understanding problems such as this. Also note that Miyuki is simply exploring the possibility of *another* correct answer (*if without "be:" °is not good?°*) instead of questioning the earlier accepted corrected answer. What the EPA turns potentially block, then, is not only unvoiced understanding problems but also proposals for alternative correct answers.

Understanding-check Questions

Just as we routinely offer positive assessments on learner contributions, we routinely check learner understanding via *any questions?* and the like. It may be worth pondering how often we actually do receive questions when we openly invite them. In my data at least, the learners insist on treating such teacher solicitations as preferring *no-problem* answers (i.e., no questions) (Waring, 2012). This does not mean that questions are not asked after such invitations. It simply means that when they *are* asked, they are put forth with delay, mitigation, or accounts. They are delivered as "dispreferred" items—with the understanding that they are somehow unwanted. As will be shown, the learners persist in their orientation to the understanding-check (UC) questions as preferring *no-problem* both at activity boundaries and after teacher explanations or instructions.

In the following segment, the class has just finished practicing pronouncing a list of words on the board. In lines 01 through 05, the teacher surveys the class for the "success rate" of the practice, and Tomo emerges to be the "winner" who got everything right. This overall evaluative nature of the survey then serves to mark the completion of the pronunciation activity:

6. no questions

01	T:		Did somebody get everything right?
02	L:		°Yes.°
03	T:		°Yeah? Tomo?°
04			(0.2)
05	T:		°(You get) everything right?°
06	Tomo:		{0.2)-((*nods*))}[°Yeah.°]
07	T:	→	[°'kay.°] Okay. <u>Do</u> you have any
08			questions.
09	LL:	→	No. No questions. ((*several speaking not in perfect unison*))
10	T:		<u>No</u> questions. <u>Good</u>. A'right.
11			((*T sorts through papers on desk*))
12			Okay now, take out you:r stor- <u>home</u>work. ((*continues*))

Note that in response to the teacher's UC question in lines 07 and 08, the learners' *No. No questions* (line 09) is done without any delay, mitigation, or account. As such, they treat *no problem* as the preferred response to the teacher's UC question. The teacher then accepts the *no-problem* response and proceeds to move on to the homework segment of the lesson (lines 10–12).

The same pattern may be observed in responses to UC questions after teacher instructions as seen in the following segment, where the teacher has just finished giving instructions for an upcoming dictation activity:

7. very clear

```
01 T:              So no:::[: :  ]-((shakes head))
02 Jose:                   [Yea]h.-((waves T away)) I understand.
03 T:              (mhm,)-((steps away from Jose))
04                 (0.5)-((T approaches Amy and Mo))
05 T:              ((to Amy)) Do you have any questions?
06 Amy:    →       No.
07 T:              ((to Mi)) Very clear?
08 Mi:     →       Yes.
```

In line 06, Amy's *no problem* is produced without any delay, mitigation, or accounts, which is then solidified in her unequivocal *yes* in line 08 to the teacher's *Very clear?*

The preference for *no problem* is sometimes manifested in the dispreferred format in which *yes-problem* responses are delivered, as seen in the next segment that involves the teacher's explanation of the subjunctive mood (lines 01–10). Following the explanation, a (0.5) second gap emerges, along with the teacher's *sotto voce Mkay*, which precedes another (3.0) second silence before the UC question is produced:

8. regrets

```
01 T:              And like we practiced toda::y,=you know, well- if
02                 somebody: talks about >something that happened,<
03                 and the:n u:h (0.4) you also have a similar story
04                 (0.4) you could jump in and be (li-) {(((affected
05                 voice)) O:::h (0.2) I- (.) I want to share my story
06                 too::::, This happened to me:::} An:d i- if it's a: >if
07                 it w- if it's< a sa:d story, {((puts hand to heart)) °and
08                 you feel regret,} then you can say, O:h I wish that it
09                 hadn't happened. Like that.°
10                 (0.5)
11 T:              °Mkay.°
12                 (3.0)-((T looks at BB then turns to class))
13         →       Any questions?
14                 (1.8)
15                 Yes.-((points to Neela))
16 Neela:  →       Can you sa::y (0.5) could °instead of would°?
```

```
17  T:                  mm:::::: {((reads BB to self)) if they had studied
18                      English harder, ((continues))
```

Note that Neela provides her *yes-problem* response in the form of a question after a (1.8) second delay, thereby displaying her orientation to the UC question as preferring *no problem*.

In short, the teachers' UC questions appear to be treated by learners as preferring *no problem*. This is evidenced in their brief and quick delivery of *no-problem* responses as well as their delayed and mitigated delivery of *yes-problem* ones. Part of the problem is that the UC sequences appear to be performing a dual function, at least at activity boundaries. At the most literal level, by employing the syntactic resource of an interrogative and lexical resources such as *any questions*, UC questions provide learners opportunities to voice any unresolved understanding problems and engage in understanding-check. At the same time, however, they also serve to launch a possible activity-closing sequence before transitioning to the next activity. The environment is such that closing would be naturally expected. The specific wording of the questions also tends to be generic and formulaic, which contributes to the hearing of these questions as harbingers of closing. All UC questions found at the activity boundaries in my data, for example, take either the syntactic or phrasal form of *(Do you have) any (other) questions (about X)?* and to a less extent, *Anything else?* In particular, vocabulary items such as *else* or *other* as in *Anything else?* or *Any other questions?* typically are heard in conversational closings (Button, 1990). Heritage, Robinson, Elliott, Beckett, and Wilkes (2007), for example, report that the formulation "Is there something else you would like to address in the visit today?" is much more likely to receive patient concerns than if "something" is replaced by "anything".

In line with this closing agenda then, the teacher also treats *no-problem* responses as favorable, as seen in Extract (6) earlier. An additional exemplar may be found in Segment (9) below. The teacher has just finished answering some questions about a passage on lottery tickets by line 08, and the UC question is launched in line 09:

9. was it easy

```
01  Jen:          [It's true::, it's true::, not false. Yea:h.]
02  Rodrigo:      [(                                    )] hh hh I had
03                the question. I had the answer but (she) not
04                believe me.
05                ((laughter))
06  T:            (No:,) she wanted me to clarify.
07                ((laughter))
08  T:            Because she knew that you (.) had the right answer.
09                Okay? U:m, any questions about the vocabulary?
10                (0.2)
11  T:     →      Was it easy?
```

| 12 | [| ((*several Ss murmuring 'yeah'*)) |] |
| 13 Di: | [(What's) number <u>six</u>, in the vo<u>ca</u>bulary.] |

Note that after the brief (0.2) second gap, the teacher raises a second yes-or-no question that now prefers *easy*, which makes evident his pursuit to secure a *no-problem* response that would facilitate transitioning to the next lesson segment.

One final instance may be considered. The teacher has just finished answering a series of learner questions about a grammar exercise on the present perfect, and the UC question is produced after a (2.0) second gap and, again, follows a transitional *Okay?*:

```
10. are we done

    01  T:        ((looks down and reads TB))-So the team has won
    02            >98% of the games they have °played so far.<°
    03            (2.0)
    04            Okay? any other questions?
    05            (0.5)
    06      →     No:?=are we do:ne?
    07  LL:       Yea:[h.
    08  T:            [We're done with homework?
    09            (1.0)
    10            Okay. No:w, (1.0) ↑I want you:: to::
```

In line 06, after the brief (0.5) second gap, the teacher explicitly seeks *no problem* via the No:? followed by an explicit request for confirmation that the current activity has now been completed (*are we done?*), and she moves on to the next lesson segment in line 10.

Thus, at activity boundaries, the UC question carries the double voice of checking understanding and doing possible activity closing. In both cases here, the silence after the UC question delays this closing and can indicate that the students are not yet ready to move on. Herein lies the problem: what facilitates the closing aspect of the questions is not always congruent with the goal to fully assess learner understandings at the time. This explains, at least partially, the learner preference for *no problem* in their responses to such questions at activity boundaries. That is, even if they do have problems to voice, the pressure to move on is not in favor of such voicing.

Before leaving this section, I should point out that the teachers behave very differently in the environment of explanations and instructions (as opposed to activity boundaries), where they maintain, with UC questions, a singular focus on ensuring that the just-given explanation or instruction has indeed been adequately understood. The learners' persistent preference for *no problem* within that environment may lie in certain competing concerns intrinsic to the classroom ecology. To wit, admitting to not understanding the instruction or explanation may be detrimental to either self or the instructor: *yes problem* can imply a negative assessment of the teacher instruction or explanation; it also can be taken as a signal of problematic learner competence in grasping such instructions or explanations.

In sum, the UC question is a complicated item that embodies the complexity of teacher talk, where the voice of ensuring understanding competes with those of promoting progressivity (i.e., moving the interaction forward) and inferring competence, which makes solicitations such as *any questions?* not always the optimal tool for gauging understanding—a key ingredient of teachers' professional work.

Elicitations

Of all the talk teachers do, elicitation is perhaps the most rampant. This is consistent with the preference for eliciting rather than informing in middle-class North American culture (Koshik, 2005, p. 154). In dealing with learner errors, for example, teachers withhold telling (McHoul, 1985, 1990) and engage, instead, in "hints and cues" (Allwright, 1980, p. 167) or "intimations" (Macbeth, 1994, p. 316). Such elicitations can be multivocalic in the sense that the cues to push for understanding are often at the same time sources of great confusion (see "Cues and Confusion" below). The multivocality of elicitation also is found in cases where what appears to be an open invitation for learner perspectives is also hearable as an (impending) assessment (see "Invitation and Assessment" below).

Cues and Confusion

Elicitation rather than telling is often done to promote learner autonomy. It seems perfectly reasonable to assume that guiding learners to discover a solution on their own is superior to handing them the solution from the outset. A common conundrum for elicitation, however, is that this round-about approach often incurs confusion, which obfuscates rather than illuminates understanding. In the following segment from an after-school literacy program, the tutor is an undergraduate education major, and Nora a first grade native Spanish speaker. They have just finished reviewing the words with *ee* endings and have begun to spell *manatee* letter by letter on their own personal whiteboards. They have so far completed *m-a-n-a-t* with two more letters to go. As will be seen, the tutor (Tr) engages in a great deal of elicitations by way of getting Nora to discover the final two letters on her own (B=board):

11. manatee

```
01 Tr:          ((picks up B and tilts to N direction)) mana:,
02              [{tee::?-((glances at N's B and withdraws own))
03 Nora:        $[mh↑hmm[nnnnn]-((back to seat))$
04 Tr:      →              [Okay,] wha[t did-  ]
05 Nora:                              [°(yeh.)°]
```

```
06  Tr:          what did all {these- ((reaches for tree))-these}
07               [((picks up and repositions tree))
08  Nora:        [tre[e:::::::]
09  Tr:              [letter-] what did they {end in.-((brings closer
10               green book with "tree" and "bee" and "me"))}
11  Nora:        tree:-((looks to green book))
12  Tr:          [How did they e:nd. ((points to book)) ]
13  Nora:        [((N begins to look down and start writing))]
14               ((writes while M looks))-(5.0)
15  Tr:          How d- ho- okay so, write down
16               [the tree: the bee,] -((refers to book))
```

In line 04, the tutor begins with a *wh* question. She quickly comes to a cutoff and inserts *all*, switching the focus from *manatee* to *ee* words in general. The pronoun *these* in line 06 then refers to a general class of words such as *tree* or *bee*, but this reference clashes with her nonverbal gesture of reaching for *tree*, the specific object (line 06). She then quickly repairs that reference with *letter* (line 09), although like *tree* the object, a letter would not end in anything either (i.e., would not work for Tr's question *What did they end in?*). Another cutoff ensues as the tutor redoes the question in its entirety: *what did they end in*, substituting *letter* with *they* as she brings closer the green book with the *ee* words. By the time this five-word elicitation is completed, it has undergone three self-repairs. In her attempt to fill the X slot of *what did X end in*, the tutor has gone from what was mostly likely to be *manatee* to *all these*, to *letter*, and finally, *they*.

Nora's trouble following this elicitation can be observed in the next few lines. She responds with *tree* in line 11, which is clearly not a fitted answer to *what did they end in*. Her difficulty is evidenced further in her continuing nonresponse even after the tutor's attempt to rephrase her original elicitation (line 12). Note also that *what did they end in.* and *How did they e:nd.* are designed in such a way that makes a wide range of unrelated answers potentially acceptable: "in happiness," "quietly," "with a comma," and so on. Thus, the tutor's elicitations are rendered obscure or unfavorably multivocalic by (1) the multiple self-repairs in a short question, (2) the conflicting verbal and nonverbal referents for *these*, (3) the question design that fails to limit adequately the range of acceptable answers. The voice of cuing understanding or promoting self-discovery (Waring, 2015) also becomes, to a certain degree, the voice of confusion.

Observe another instance from the adult ESL classroom, where a vocabulary exercise is underway, and each word in one column is to be matched with an explanation in another. Daisy provides the answer for *endorphins* in line 3. As it turns out, although *chemicals that make us feel better* is the correct item to be matched with *endorphins*, it is not the response the teacher is looking for at the moment. What he appears to be seeking instead is the meaning of *endorphins* as literally given in the text (i.e., *a natural painkiller*), which should not be difficult for this advanced-level class. But

locating the answer, which involves the teacher's multiple elicitations, spans
a total of 10 turns and the 24 lines:

12. according to the sentence

```
01 T:              Oka:y, so from the s↑entence we can tell "endorphins"
02                 mea:ns (0.8)
03 Daisy:          °chemicals that make us feel better.°
04 T:              Oka↑y.
05                 (0.8)
06        →        a:nd uh Angie according to the sentence "endorphins"
07                 mea:ns (1.0)
08 Angie:          °It's the same word (    ) I can't explain (   )°
09 T:     →        w- bu- according to the sentence, if we use the (.)
10                 kind of context j's to help us.= The- the sentence
11                 really tells us what- another way to talk about °the
12                 meaning° right?
13 L:              °mhm °
14        →        (3.5)
15 T:     →        [What is that-    ]
16 Angie:          [(y' they crea:te-)] (     ) ↑I don't k↑now.
17                 °I ca(h)n't expla(h)in in the s(h)entence. When you know
18                 the word, it's difficult to explain.°
19 T:     →        I:: don't think it's difficult. If you ta- take a look at
20                 li:ne wh- wh- which line is it.
21 Angie:          °Twenty one.°
22 T:              Twenty one a:::nd twenty two.right?
23 Angie:          mhm
24 T:     →        so according to twenty one and twenty two the- th-
25                 so >I don't want you to give any-< you don't have to
26                 think of any (.) new idea.=I'm asking wha- what does-
27                 what does the story say.
28 Angie:          Oh. It's natural (.) °painkiller.°
29 T:              >Exactly. Yeah. so they v- they very very uh (.)
30                 explicitly tell us the ↑meaning here.< b' then they
31                 change to "chemicals >that make us feel better"?<
32                 (0.8)
33                 So ok↑ay.
```

The teacher first redirects the question to Angie (lines 06–07), which seems
to take the latter by surprise. After all, Angie is being asked to give an answer
that has already been accepted in line 04. In line 08, with *I can't explain . . .*,
she displays her interpretation of the teacher's question as a request *for her
to explain* what *endorphin* means based on the text. Rather than addressing
this problematic interpretation in the next lines (09–12), the teacher returns
to his original focus of *according to the sentence*, now highlighting *another*

way of referring to endorphins. Although one learner offers a quiet confirming *mhm* in line 13, no actual identification of this other way emerges in the subsequent long (3.5) second gap. This is the second opportunity for the teacher to notice that some sort of misalignment has occurred and to perhaps redesign his elicitations. Instead, he appears to be continuing on the same trajectory with a *wh* question in line 15, which overlaps with Angie's aborted attempt to articulate an explanation in her own words, followed by another account for her inability to answer. The misalignment deepens as the teacher rejects Angie's assertion of difficulty in line 19 and directs her to the line number that contains the answer.

Once the exact lines in the text are located, the teacher continues to pursue the answer to his original question, now emphasizing that no *new idea* is needed to complete this task (lines 25–28), which appears to be utterly and instantly liberating. Notice her use of the change-of-state token *oh* (Heritage, 1984) in line 28, which treats the teacher's *you don't have to come up with any new idea* as new information: what he has been looking for all along is merely a literal quote from the text, which she could have given much earlier. The multiple elicitations have, in fact, derailed rather than streamlined the process of reaching a particular understanding. Again, the voice of promoting self-discovery coexists with that of breeding confusion.

In both these cases, the drive to elicit rather than tell has decisively incurred multiple interfering messages along the way, and the clarity of teacher talk is severely compromised as a result. Such complexity of teacher talk is clearly to the detriment of student learning. I am reminded of Edwards and Mercer's (1987) critique of cued elicitations: "It is difficult to avoid the impression that the pupils were essentially trying to read all the signals available in a guessing game in which they had to work out, more by communicative skill than by the application of any known principle of measurement, what it was that the teacher was trying to get them to say" (p. 145).

Invitation and Assessment

Elicitation also becomes unfavorably multivocalic when an open invitation for learner perspectives is hearable as an (impending) assessment, which would constrain the possibility for carefree contribution. In post-observation conferences between mentors and teachers in training, for example, it seems almost impossible not to hear the mentor's questions as potential assessments. This testing frame (Copland, 2010; Goffman, 1974; Tannen, 1993) is evidenced in the presuppositions built into the questions (*strong* or *not so strong* aspects of the teaching) as well as the assessments following the responses (e.g., *bingo* or *great answer*). As such, learners can approach answering with great caution, treating any noticing preceding the question and the question itself as upcoming critiques. In the case below, the mentor (M) opens the meeting with a question that solicits the teacher's perspective on how the class went:

13. how it went

```
01  M:        °>.hh let me see< okay ° ((walks to chair))
02            -°(I was supposed to do it last week)
03      →     ((sits down))-but° (0.2) uhm so how did you think
04            ((gaze to A))-that (.) >it went.<
05  Amy:      .hh ↑fairly well um they had a class before us, so:::
06            >↓we got in there at the last minute at five to seven
((lines omitted))
22  M:        ((looks down at notes and flips pages))-kinda°
23            (.) °yeah.°. hh that's really hard to (°move
24            theirs and move themselves out of there.°).hhh
25      →     uhm (0.2) so:, I just- ((looks up at A))-but overall
26            do you think- >how do you think it went.<=
27  Amy:      =.hh >It was okay it was a little bit< unorganized,
28            u::m my: last activity: was::: >way over their
29            head so I changed it,<
30  M:        ((nods))
31  Amy:      u::m I had the:m >instead of ha- I had them<
32            do the- >go to the back of the room thing,<
((lines omitted))
39  M:        [°uh huh°-((nods))]
40  Amy:      [And that went- ] ((nods)) really [well.      ]
41  M:                                          >[that went ]
42            really well? Okay< so flexibility then
43            [ °(ended up working out)°-((looks down to notes))]
44  Amy:      [ Yeah ((nods)) it worked out. >pretty well.< ] =
45  M:        =((gaze on notes))->.hh That's good.< and the
46            more you ((gaze to A))-do it the more
47            you:: (0.2) understand like which parts you
48            can cut [out and which pa]rts °weren't°
49  Amy:              [ yeah.-((nods))    ]
50  M:        ((gaze down to notes))-°>and stuff like that<.°
```

Unlike *how did it go?*, which presupposes not having access to the events in question, *how did you think it went?* entails at least the possibility of equal access to the events, which indeed is the case given that M has observed part of the class. In other words, she is in the position to assess how it went, but she holds that assessment at bay as she focuses the query specifically on Amy's perspective with *did you think*. To a certain extent then, the question can be heard as an assessment of some sort (see "recipient side test question" in Antaki, 2013). That is, the mentor is not only testing Amy's ability to accurately assess her own performance but also heralding her own independent rating—one with greater authority given the epistemic asymmetry of the encounter.

In fact, we observe Amy's maneuver in escaping from this test in her initial response. In line 05, she utters an almost pro forma *fairly well*

without any further specification. She then proceeds to tell her class's difficulty in entering the room. By turning to an event that M was not privy
to, Amy sidesteps the risk of producing an assessment incompatible with
that of M's.

In response to M's persistent probing, Amy's second attempt in line 27
involves a downgrade from the earlier *fairly well* to *okay* plus *a little bit
unorganized*, orienting to the possibility of the mentor's assessment being
negatively valanced, although her elaboration on this negative assessment
then becomes a display of her ability to competently manage an unforeseen
situation, which ended up working *really well* (line 40). In other words,
M's elicitation for teacher reflection is responded to by Amy as a potential
assessment on her ability to accurately gauge her own performance as well
as an incipient (and possibly negative) assessment on her performance as the
teacher in the just-observed class.

In the adult ESL classroom, a particular type of elicitation may also be
deployed to convey an assessment. In particular, where evaluation is relevant, yes-or-no questions can be used by the teacher to convey a critical
stance regardless of what the object of the evaluation is, whether the question is positively or negatively formulated, and whether the critical stance
aligns or dis-aligns with the polarity of the question. In the following segment, the class is working on a textbook unit on humor that begins with
two *funny* cartoons. While the class agrees on the funny nature of the second cartoon, opinions vary with regard to the first one:

14. is there a joke

```
01 T:          Okay, so bu- bu- the issue i:s the
02             first one, (0.2) Sara sa:ys she doesn't g↑et it.
03 Sara:       N[o. ]
04 T:           [rig] ht? >What d'y guys< think.=
05        →    is- is there a joke in the first one?
06             (1.0)
07 Rose:       °It- it- it's not funny [( )°]
08 Sara:                        [No:.] Ye(hh)a:h.-((looks up at T))
09 T/LL:       huh huh
10 Rose:       I- I don't know.
```

Note that the teacher has characterized the first cartoon as being *the issue*
(line 01), followed by a report of Sara's report of not getting it (line 02).
With the *right?* in line 04, he rallies support for Sara's difficulty *getting* the
joke—an implicit critique of what the textbook presents as funny. He then
launches a general solicitation of opinion (>*What d'y guys< think.*) followed
by the latching yes-or-no question *is there a joke in the first one?* (line 05).
The yes-or-no question then is produced in an environment that suggests
the absence of humor in the first cartoon. It also is prefaced with a quick
cutoff, appearing to signal some delicacy of the critique that the question is
recruited to convey. As can be seen, Rose's response in line 07 aligns with

the critical stance (*not funny*). In fact, later on in the lesson, the teacher explicitly states his critique as: *if you don't have funny jokes in your chapter, then it's not so good.*

There is nothing inherently problematic with elicitations being used as a resource for conveying assessments. What *is* potentially problematic, however, is that when the voice of invitation meshes with that of assessment, teacher talk may not achieve its intended goal. If by choosing elicitation over telling, the teacher aims at stimulating reflection and engaging critical thinking, some serious reconsideration is in order since, as shown, the interfering element of assessment makes it impossible for such elicitations to be heard as open invitations for bold and unguarded ruminations. This does not mean that elicitation cannot be used productively. The challenge is to carefully craft its execution in ways that minimize any negative multivocality.

As demonstrated in this section, while *very good* and *any questions?* offer positive assessment and solicit understanding, they also announce "case closed" or time to move on. The former facilitates learning; the latter curtails it. While elicitations can stimulate thinking and promote autonomy, they also can convey a critical stance, invoke an assessment frame, and incur unnecessary confusion. The former facilitates learning; the latter curtails it. Undoubtedly, such complexity of teacher talk constitutes a confounding impediment of some sort. Too often, we are trapped in these tangles of conflicting voices and yet remain blissfully oblivious to their potential pitfalls, and as a result, well-intentioned efforts fall flat in the reality of actual encounters. Becoming cognizant of the unintended consequences of some of our routine discourse practices may indeed be the first step towards reclaiming the power of teacher talk.

MULTIVOCALITY AS A RESOURCE

Despite all the pitfalls of multivocality as already detailed, I also understand multivocality as a resource when it is carefully deployed to address the competing demands of pedagogical interaction. It is no news that the structure of classroom talk embodies a great deal of teacher control (e.g., Cazden, 2001; Edwards & Mercer, 1987; Lemke, 1990), and as Mehan (1979) reminds us, such control is a necessity—"a means to an end" or "a utilitarian stance adopted for the practical purposes of achieving educational objectives" (p. 81). Control breeds order and, by extension, the possibility of executing one's pedagogical agenda, but there are other concerns at play: the need to build rapport, promote participation, and respect learner voices, creating what van Lier (1996) so vividly portrays as the "dynamic struggle between centrifugal and centripetal forces" (e.g., diversity vs. homogeneity, conversation vs. monolog, and autonomy vs. control) (p. 183) or that between connection and control (Waring, 2014). Teacher talk is often charged with the delicate task of balancing the competing demands of control and connection. In what follows, I show how such delicate maneuvering is interactionally accomplished through complex teacher talk that involves (1) embedding conversation in IRF, (2) assimilating learner voice, and (3) alluding to institutional frame.

Embedding Conversation in IRF

The competing demands of control and connection may be attended to when the sequential structure of classroom talk is tweaked to accommodate conversational matters, where personal inquiries take the place of display questions, and appreciations take the place of assessments. In the following exemplar, the teacher launches an inquiry about *everyone's weekend* and explicitly nominates Ana as the next speaker in line 05:

15. how a:::re you

01	T:	((*talks about March being a strange month*)) So, next week it
02		might be 60 degrees. ((*shrugs*)) who knows.
03	Sato:	°yeah.°
04	T:	who knows. Anyway, >how was everyone's
05		w↑eekend.< ↑A:na::,
06	Ana:	hm [mm]
07	T:	[How] ↑A::RE you:.
08	Ana:	I'm fine. ((*coughs*))
09	T:	>are you feeling better?<
10	Ana:	Ye:s I feel [better.]
11	T:	[Oh g↑o]:od good.=did you relax
12		this week?
13		(0.2)
14	Ana:	Ye:s basically stayed at home.
15	T:	mm hm,-((*nods*))
16	Ana:	°Yes.° I didn't go (outside a lot).
17	T:	mhm, (that was) very smart.=
18	Ana:	°yeah.°
19	T:	Ve:ry >smart.=but you feel better.<
20	Ana:	Yes.=
21	T:	=Good. >I'm happy to h↑ear that.<

Note that the teacher is the one who initiates the sequence, asks questions, offers assessments, and closes the sequence (lines 04, 07, 09, and 11). These clearly are acts of control implemented within the IRF structure (Sinclair & Coulthard, 1975). Ana's talk, on the other hand, is restricted to brief answers, and she does not reciprocate the how-are-you initiated by the teacher.

Within this overarching frame of control, however, one cannot help but register the somewhat conversational tone of the interaction. Note that the teacher's delivery of *Ana* (line 05) is marked with raised pitch, elongated vowels, and a continuing intonation, which combine to signal a spontaneous and pleasant encounter between peers. In addition, the "big" how-are-you in line 07 is hearable as marking some "specialness;" for example, the participants have not seen each other for a while (Schegloff, 2007, p. 197). Further evidence for the teacher's effort to forge connection may be located in line 09, where his inquiry *Are you feeling better?* is a personal one that presupposes the sort of familiarity more likely to be found between peers than between teacher and student.

This grappling for connection becomes more pronounced in the following segment, where the teacher displays an intense interest in the students' personal lives and activities with a series of "machine-gun questions" (Tannen, 1981). Consider the segment below:

16. what show

16	T:		.hhh and Ma:yo is over here,
17			((*check in book*)) Miy↑ako. We missed you
18			last [week.]
19	Miyako:		[s(hh)o]r(hh)y.=
20	T:	→	=That's o↑kay.>that's okay.< did you have a
21			good weekend?
22	Miyako:		yes, last night I was he:re, (syl syl)
23	T:		At Col↑umbia.
24	Miyako:		at the University to see: my peer's show.
25			Miller (.) Theater.
26	T:	→	°what <u>sh</u>ow was it.°
27	Miyako:		It's a African dance show.
28	T:		O↑:h {w↓oo::.-((*leans back*))}
29	Miyako:		°(syl syl)° a peer of mine was in the show
30			( ) on the stage °so°
31	T:	→	w↑o:::w. ↑wonderful. Wonderful. So- (.)
32			did they perform well?
33			(0.2)
34	Miyako:		°i- ↑<u>y</u>eh. It was [goo::d,°]
35	T:	→	[((*nods*))] °nice.° do you also
36			do African dance?=
37	Miyako:		=<u>y</u>es.
38	T:	→	>°↑very interesting.°< how long have you been
39			doing it.
40	Miyako:		°(syl) about (0.2) four years.°
41	T:		w↑o:::w. >you must be an expert now.<
42			(0.5)
43	Miyako:		<u>not</u> ye[t.]
44	T:		>[n]ot yet [okay, okay<] .hhehe

Note that although the teacher performs the control acts of launching a series of questions, these are not known-answer questions but personal inquiries, and notably, his uptake of Miyako's contribution entails appreciations of the events (lines 20, 26, 31, 35, and 38) rather than autocratic assessments of correctness or acceptability. By embedding conversation into the sequential structure of IRF then, the multivocalic teacher talk attends to the competing concerns of both control and connection and, in particular, enables the building of rapport within the constraints of classroom discourse (Amory, 2013; Nguyen, 2007)—an important element of effective teaching (Cornelius-White, 2007; Ramsden, 2003; Torff & Sessions, 2005).

Assimilating Learner Voice

Aside from building rapport, another competing concern for many teachers is promoting student participation. As Paoletti and Fele (2004) have convincingly argued, teachers constantly endeavor to strike a difficult balance between the competing tasks of maintaining control on the one hand and soliciting student participation on the other (p. 78), where participation may entail not complying with a directive, taking initiatives outside the bounds of classroom order, or challenging the teacher's epistemic authority (Waring, Reddington, & Tadic, 2015). Again, in such cases, the multivocality of teacher talk may be exploited to maintain control in subtle ways that nevertheless validate learner contributions. This is in part done by assimilating learner voice, where the teacher makes use of potentially derailing or subversive learner talk in such a way that preserves his or her agenda.

In line 01 of the following segment, the teacher begins by announcing *question number one to everyone*. One might argue that with such a preface, the question to come is attributed a special degree of import. Indeed, *Why is English difficult?* (line 02) does not project a simple answer as would a *what/who/when/where* query. The teacher's quizzical look and smile in line 03 further suggests the potential complexity of the expected answer:

17. any foreign language

01	T:	Okay question number one to everyone.
02		Question number one. ↑Why is English difficult?
03		((*quizzical look and walks to SS in smile*))-(1.8)
04	Kara:	°be<u>ca</u>use (.) it's foreign language.°
05	LL:	[hmh hmh hmh]
06	T: →	[So,] <u>any</u> foreign language is very very difficult.
07		(1.0)-((*T1 smiles*))
08	Jasmin:	At the beginning uh you don't have a feel for
09		the language uh, and the grammar is different?
10		a::nd uh it's- and a lot of part of language for example

11   there's uh: more u:h Anglos, angl- I don't know
12   Anglo-°Saxton?° the language? than- mine? so its- uh:
13   quite different.-((*T1 nodding throughout the talk*))

In line 04, Kara subverts that "complexity" expectation by giving a radi-
cally simple answer, which is subsequently received as a joke of some sort
in line 05.

In line 06, rather than joining the laughter or taking issue with the challenging aspect of Kara's response, the teacher makes explicit the premise of
the syllogism that underlines her comment (i.e., All foreign languages are difficult. English is a foreign language. Therefore, English is difficult.), and he uses
such extreme case formulations (Pomerantz, 1986) as *any* and the repeated
very to further undermine the indefensibility of Kara's stance. By producing
such a sober and reasoned counter then, Kara is positioned as a competent
and conscientious student despite her mischievous attempt, and at the same
time, the teacher's original question continues to warrant a serious response
and now an even more poignant one. Indeed, that response appears in line 08
as another student, Jasmin, attributes the difficulty to the differences between
English and one's native language. In this case, the teacher is able to effectively
assimilate Kara's somewhat derailing challenge into a direction that furthers
his own pedagogical agenda, thereby ensuring both control and participation.

A similar maneuver may be observed in Creider's (2013) work on tutor–
child interaction, where the tutor assimilates the child's somewhat diverging
initiative into her own agenda via what Creider has so aptly called "weaving." In the following extract, the tutor is playing math games with Olivia
(age five), using poker chips and dice. Throughout the sequence, she proposes to categorize the chips by color, and Olivia attempts to do so by size.
In lines 01 and 02, the tutor directs Olivia to make a pile of red chips and
proceeds to notice specifically the *red ones* (line 04), further highlighting *red*
as the focus of the task:

18. color vs. size

01 Tr: ((*moves chips around*))-there's fat ones, (0.2)
02   and sma:ll o::nes,
03 Olivia: ((*picks up red chip*))-this is °(a huge) one,°=
04 Tr: =(n:h) make a {((*points to chips on floor*))-p-
05   start a pile of red ones °here >let's start a pile
06   of red ones.<°}. hh He:re's
07   ↓red [o:nes,   ]
08 Olivia: [a:nd the s]ame size.=
09 Tr: =Yeah those are all the same si:ze.
10   (0.2)
11   here's a lo:t of red ones.
12 Olivia: ((*picks up one red chip*))
13   °(why can't- we c' collect all of those)° we c'

```
14                  collect them into
15                  ((picks up a red chip and then a yellow one))-
16                  different si- into the same si:zes,=
17 Tr:      →       =we could collect them in same sizes
18                  [but let's collect them- we could collect them]=
19 Olivia:          [        ((picks up blue chip))                ]
20 Tr:      →       = by ↑colors ↑too.=we could make pi:les
21                  of each colo[r. ]
22 Olivia:                      [I-]
23                  I like to make my °own little pile.°-((with stack
24                  of red, yellow, and blue chips in hand and reaches for another))
25 Tr:              ((reaches for C's "pile")) make your p↓i::le, (0.2)
26                  take your pile 'n make l- make- see how
27                  high a pile of red ones, okay?
       ((lines omitted; interruption by O's baby brother—TR and O give him some chips))
28 Tr:              So you're making a pile of red ones. I think I'll make
29                  a pile of yellow ones.
```

Despite the tutor's focus on the *red ones*, however, Olivia adds in overlap *and the same size*, introducing *size* as a competing feature to work with and creating a possible obstacle to the tutor's proposal. In line 09, the tutor produces a simple confirmation without entertaining the potentially competing proposal. She goes on to notice *a lo:t of red ones* (line 11)—an upgrade from her earlier *Here's ↓red o:nes* (lines 06–07). At the same time, Olivia intensifies her pursuit of size with an explicit proposal (lines 12–16). Size as a criterion is now officially on the table, and Olivia begins implementing that proposal by starting to pick up chips of different colors but the same size (lines 12 and 15).

In line 16, the tutor continues her pursuit of color but does so in a manner that validates Olivia's initiative without compromising her own goal. She repeats Olivia's proposal almost word for word before articulating her own, where the initial *let's* is abandoned for Olivia's phrasing *we could* (line 18). The emphasis on both *color* and *too* (line 20) is also a powerful illustration of the delicate balance the tutor appears to be striking between pursuing her own agenda and validating that of Olivia's. In lines 20 and 21, the tutor continues to use Olivia's wording (*we could*) as she suggests making piles of each color. As can be seen, the struggle between color versus size continues as Olivia announces her preference for her *own little pile* (line 20), and the tutor struggles to morph that *own little pile* into *a pile of red ones* (lines 25–27). In line 28, after an interruption caused by Olivia's baby brother, the tutor observes that Olivia is *making a pile of red ones*, and the two go on to sort the chips based on color. Like the ESL teacher in the above extract then, the tutor assimilates the potentially derailing child proposal into her own agenda rather than either chastise or dismiss it. With such assimilation, learner voice is validated without compromising teacher agenda. The multivocality of teacher talk is usefully exploited to ease concerns for both control and connection.

Allude to Institutional Frame

The balance between control and connection is also achieved when the exercising of control is carried out implicitly and lightheartedly. This typically happens when the conversational tone of interaction so far is abandoned in the service of some institutional concerns, and the teacher invokes the institutional frame but does so with subtlety and levity. The following exchange takes place at the very beginning of the class:

19. male students

```
01 T:              ((looks around))-wo::w. La:dies, where are
02                 the ((scowls))-men.
03 LL:             hhhehehhe[heh
04 Janet:                   [((points to T))
05 T:        →     Yes. Besides me.=hehhehhahaha The male
06                 students >are not here today.< °interesting.°
07                 Okay let's see who is here °let's see° Ana.
```

In lines 01 and 02, as he scans the room, the teacher comments on the presence of the *ladies* and the absence of *men*. The employment of gender categories rather than, for example, on-time versus late students, keys the interaction as conversation that prioritizes connection. In the next line, however, Janet points to the teacher as the "man" he is looking for, thus exposing the absurdity of his question. In line 04, the teacher proceeds to exclude himself from the other males in the class with the increment *besides me* (line 4) followed by laughter, thereby implicitly prioritizing his teacher identity and invokes the institutional frame. In lines 05 and 06, the emphasis on *male students* further foregrounds the institutional frame, with *not here today* alluding to the institutional category of "late students." Crucially, this allusion to the institutional identities allows the teacher to proceed with the attendance-taking business (line 07), to which the earlier conversational frame has become an obstacle. At the same time, the implicitness as well as the laughter appears to have preserved at least a portion of the conversational tone initiated by *Wo::w, La:dies, where are the men?* Thus, control is exercised with an eye toward connection.

The allusion to the institutional frame may also be done with humor. In the next segment, the teacher's control over "speaking rights" is challenged when the selected student does not respond, and others step into her turn space (Waring, 2011). Prior to the extract, May has read a sentence containing the verb "refuse." The teacher subsequently confirms and reinforces the proper pronunciation of this word (line 01) and asks May for its definition (line 02). After a (0.5) second gap and no answer from May, other students respond:

20. many voices

```
01  T:              /z/. >it sounds like a /z:/.< Okay.
02                  >an' what does this word mean.< May. Refuse.
03                  (0.5)
04  LL:             refuse. reject (  )
05  T:      →       Okay.=May, you have many voices. [huh huh ]
06  LL:                                               [hah hah] hah
                                                      hah hh
07  T:              May, what do you think it is.
08  May:            (     )
09  T:              O:kay?-((nods)) and
10                  "reject" means ↑what.-((turns to class))
11                  (1.0)
12  T:              ((arm out in recognition))-deny:. ((nods)) reject.
13                  O:r-((arms points to S))
14  L:              °turn down.°
15  T:              °Okay.° >great.< Good synonym.=all of those. ((turns to BB))
```

In line 05, the teacher acknowledges the unsolicited responses with *okay* but immediately directs a comment to the nominated student: *May, you have many voices* humorously attributing the other responses to May. The class laughs in overlap with the teacher's own laughter following his observation. By delivering this playful remark, the teacher indirectly admonishes May for not responding as the selected party and others for responding when not selected. It is therefore both a renewed directive to May to respond (e.g., see the stress on *you* in line 07, which implicitly invites the contrast "not others") and a general reminder to the class of the "rule" that the floor belongs to the nominated student. By further delaying evaluation of other appropriate answers and pursuing an answer from the nominated student (line 07), the teacher subtly reinforces the "rules" of classroom turn taking without punishing the violators or stifling their participation.

Thus, the multivocality of teacher talk can be a resource for managing the competing demands of control and connection. In each of these cases, whether it involves embedding conversation in IRF, assimilating learner voices, or alluding to institutional frames, the complex teacher talk embodies both the centripetal forces of exerting control, maintaining order, and implementing agendas and the centrifugal forces of building rapport, encouraging participation, and validating learner challenges and initiatives.

MULTIVOCALITY, BAKHTIN, AND COMPLEXITY THEORY

This chapter has been devoted to elucidating the complexity of teacher talk, and I have used the term "multivocality" to portray the nature of such complexity. More specifically, there are two ways in which we understand the multivocality of teacher talk: (1) its conflicting voices that constitute a hindrance to learning (e.g., *any questions?* solicits understanding problems without encouraging the voicing of such problems), and (2) its tension-sensitive voices addressed to competing concerns such as control and connection that permeate pedagogical encounters (e.g., *May, you have many voices* serves as a reminder of the turn-taking rule while preserving a friendly stance through humor). In other words, multivocality can be an impediment or a resource. Understanding multivocality as an impediment can hopefully force us to reassess some of the routine teacher talk, be mindful of its unintended consequences, and as a next step, seek possible alternatives. How can we offer positive reinforcement without shutting down the conversation? How can we ensure understanding without betraying an urge to move on? How can we cultivate autonomy and promote independent thinking without the elicitations that so often derail more than enlighten and terrify more than inspire? At the same time, understanding multivocality as a resource can perhaps awaken us to the ingenuity of teacher talk and help us appreciate its carefully crafted texture that strikes a delicate balance between centripetal forces such as exercising control, maintaining order, and accomplishing agendas on the one hand and centrifugal forces such as building rapport, encouraging participation, and validating learner voices on the other. Remaining constantly alert to such ingenuity is, as I imagine, a precursor to becoming part of that ingenuity or part of the broader endeavor to enrich and fine-tune the magic of teacher talk.

I should acknowledge that the multivocality of teacher talk is not unlike the multivocality that saturates ordinary conversation. It is not, as noted at the beginning of this chapter, a novelty by any means. As the Russian literary critic Mikhail Bakhtin (1895–1975) writes: "[a]ny speaker is himself a respondent to a greater or lesser degree. He is not, after all, the first speaker, the one who disturbs the eternal silence of universe" (Bakhtin, 1986, p. 69), and "[e]ach utterance is filled with echoes and reverberations of other utterances to which it is related" (Bakhtin, 1986, p. 106). Indeed, the multivocality I speak of is filled with echoes and reverberations of powerful Bakhtinian concepts such as "heteroglossia," "hybridation," and "double-voiced discourse," all of which capture the idea of different voices co-inhabiting and dialoging with each other as well as with those that precede and ensue. In his analysis of a literary passage, Bakhtin (1981) observes:

> The ceremonial emphasis on glorification is complicated by a second emphasis that is indignant, ironic, and this is the one that ultimately predominates in the final unmasking words of the sentence. We have before us a typical **double-accented double styled hybrid construction** [emphasis mine]. What we are calling a hybrid construction is an utterance that belongs, by its grammatical and compositional markers, to a single speaker, but that actually contains mixed within it two utterances, two speech matters, two styles, two "languages," two sematic and axiological belief systems. (pp. 304–305)

I find myself fantasizing that over half a century later, Bakhtin becomes infatuated by classroom discourse and remarks on the use of *very good*: "[t]he ceremonial emphasis on positive assessment is complicated by a second emphasis that hastens to suggest case-closed, and this is the one that ultimately predominates in the final hearing of the utterance."

As I look through the lens of Bakhtin and marvel at the myriad echoes and reverberations, I also become alarmingly self-conscious of my failure at noticing the dialogic aspects of multivocality. In explaining heteroglossia, Bakhtin (1981) emphasizes that the "two voices are dialogically interrelated . . . Double-voiced discourse is always internally dialogized" (p. 324). Is it possible, then, that soliciting questions and pre-closing in *any questions?* are dialogically related in the inhibiting sense of multivocality, and so are control and connection in the facilitating sense of multivocality? Now that the notion of dialogic is brought to the fore of my consciousness, it seems obvious that the dialectical relationships between control and connection would be a classic example of dialogism as the two opposing forces interrelate. In fact, in their glossary of Bakhtin's vocabulary, Emerson and Holquist (1981) write: "[h]eteroglossia is as close a conceptualization as is possible of that locus where centripetal and centrifugal forces collide" (p. 428). Indeed, the teacher's *May, you have many voices.* is the locus where the centripetal voice of enforcing order and the centrifugal voice of inviting participation come into dialog. The same opposing relationship may be observed in the use of *any questions?*, where the voice of ensuring understanding and that of moving the lesson along are mutually defeating: ensuring understanding requires lingering, and pre-closing precludes such lingering. The dialectical tension between the centrifugal and the centripetal is neutralized in the case of *May, you have many voices* but tipped to the direction of the centripetal in the case of *Any questions?*.

The notion of interrelatedness is also highlighted in complexity theory, which "deals with the study of complex, dynamic, non-linear, self-organizing, open, emergent, sometimes chaotic, and adaptive systems" (Larsen-Freeman & Cameron, 2008, p. 4), a defining characteristic of which is that "its behavior emerges from the interaction of its components" (Larsen-Freeman & Cameron, 2008, p. 2). Clearly, teacher talk is a complex system of its own, and its feature of multivocality embodies "all the messiness it engenders" (Larsen-Freeman & Cameron, 2008, p. 9). As Larsen-Freeman and Cameron (2008) so confidently proclaim, "We expect data to be noisy and messy because the dynamics of complex systems produce variability" (p. 16). We observe such variability in the multivocality of teacher talk, most poignantly in the absence of a clear and linear one-to-one correspondence between talk and its function as the same linguistic assemblage can signal conflicting meanings and attend to opposing forces. Viewing teacher talk as a complex system is both comforting and exhilarating. Given the open and dynamic nature of a complex system, adjustment of any single element can have the ripple effect of system-wide change as elements constantly interact and self-organize. Herein lies the hope for growth and development: the pitfalls of multivocality can be sidestepped and its creativity harnessed and multiplied.

REFERENCES

Allwright, D. (1980). Turns, topics, and tasks: Patterns of participation in language learning and teaching. In D. Larsen-Freeman (Ed.), *Discourse analysis in second language research* (pp. 165–187). Rowley, MA: Newbury Houses.

Amory, M. (2013). *Developing teacher-student rapport.* Unpublished manuscript, Teachers College, Columbia University, New York.

Antaki, C. (2013). Recipient-side test questions. *Discourse Studies, 15*(1), 3–18.

Bakhtin, M.M. (1981). *The dialogic imagination.* Austin: The University of Texas Press.

Bakhtin, M.M. (1986). *Speech genres and other late essays.* Austin: The University of Texas Press.

Button, G. (1990). On varieties of closings. In G. Psathas (Ed.), *Interactional competence* (pp. 93–148). Washington, DC: International Institute of Ethnomethodology and Conversation Analysis and University Press of America.

Cazden, C. (2001). *Classroom discourse: The language of teaching and learning* (2nd ed.). Portsmouth, NH: Heinemann.

Copland, F. (2010). Causes of tension in post-observation feedback in pre-service teacher training: An alternative view. *Teaching and Teacher Education: An International Journal of Research and Studies, 26*(3), 466–472.

Cornelius-White, J. (2007). Learner-centered teacher-student relationships are effective: A meta-analysis. *Review of Educational Research, 77*(1), 113–143.

Creider, S. (2013). *The integration sequence: Responding to child initiations in a tutoring session.* Unpublished manuscript, Teachers College, Columbia University, New York.

Edwards, D., & Mercer, N. (1987). *Common knowledge: The development of understanding in the classroom.* London: Methuen.

Emerson, C., & Holquist, M. (1981). Glossary. In M.M. Bakhtin (Ed.), *The dialogic imagination* (pp. 423–434). Austin: University of Texas Press.

Goffman, E. (1974). *Frame analysis.* New York: Harper and Row.

Goldberg, J.A. (2004). The amplitude shift mechanism in conversational closing sequences. In G. Lerner (Ed.), *Conversation analysis: Studies from the first generation* (pp. 257–298). Amsterdam: John Benjamins.

Heritage, J. (1984). A change-of-state token and aspects of its sequential placement. In J.M. Atkinson & J. Heritage (Eds.), *Structures of social action: Studies in conversation analysis* (pp. 299–345). Cambridge, UK: Cambridge University Press.

Heritage, J., Robinson, J., Elliott, M., Beckett, M., & Wilkes, M. (2007). Reducing patients' unmet concerns in primary care: The difference one word can make. *Journal of General Internal Medicine, 22,* 1429–1433.

Koshik, I. (2005). *Beyond rhetorical questions: Assertive questions in everyday interaction.* Philadelphia: John Benjamins.

Larsen-Freeman, D., & Cameron, L. (2008). *Complex systems and applied linguistics.* Oxford, UK: Oxford University Press.

Lemke, J.L. (1990). *Talking science: Language, learning, and values.* Norwood, NJ: Ablex.

Local, J., & Kelly, J. (1986). Projection and "silences": Notes on phonetic and conversational structure. *Human Studies, 9,* 185–204.

Macbeth, D. (1994). Classroom encounters with the unspeakable: "Do you see, Danelle?" *Discourse Processes, 17*(2), 311–335.

McHoul, A. W. (1985). Two aspects of classroom interaction: Turn-taking and correction. *Australian Journal of Human Communication Disorders, 13*(1), 53–64.

McHoul, A. W. (1990). The organization of repair in classroom talk. *Language in Society, 19*(3), 349–377.

Mehan, H. (1979). *Learning lessons: Social organization in the classroom.* Cambridge, MA: Harvard University Press.

Nguyen, H. T. (2007). Rapport building in language instruction: A microanalysis of the multiple resources in teacher talk. *Language and Education, 21*(4), 284–303.

Paoletti, I., & Fele, G. (2004). Order and disorder in the classroom. *Journal of Pragmatics, 14*(1), 69–85.

Pomerantz, A. (1984). Agreeing and disagreeing with assessments: Some features of preferred/dispreferred turn shapes. In J. M. Atkinson & J. Heritage (Eds.), *Structures of social action: Studies in conversation analysis* (pp. 57–101). New York: Cambridge University Press.

Pomerantz, A. (1986). Extreme case formulations: A way of legitimizing claims. *Human Studies, 9,* 219–229.

Ramsden, P. (2003). *Learning to teach in higher education* (2nd ed.). London: Routledge and Falmer.

Sacks, H. (1987). On the preferences for agreement and contiguity in sequences in conversation. In G. Button & J. R. E. Lee (Eds.), *Talk and social organization* (pp. 54–69). Clevedon: Multilingual Matters.

Schegloff, E. A. (2007). *Sequence organization in interaction: A primer in conversation analysis* (Vol. 1). Cambridge, UK: Cambridge University Press.

Sinclair, J. M., & Coulthard, M. (1975). *Towards an analysis of discourse: The English used by teachers and pupils.* London: Oxford University Press.

Tannen, D. (1981). The machine-gun question: An example of conversational style. *Journal of Pragmatics, 5*(5), 383–397.

Tannen, D. (Ed.). (1993). *Framing in discourse.* New York: Oxford University Press.

Torff, B., & Sessions, D. (2005). Principals' perceptions of the causes of teacher ineffectiveness. *Journal of Educational Psychology, 97*(4), 530–537.

van Lier, L. (1996). *Interaction in the language curriculum.* London: Longman Group Limited.

Waring, H. Z. (2008). Using explicit positive assessment in the language classroom: IRF, feedback, and learning opportunities. *The Modern Language Journal, 92*(4), 577–594.

Waring, H. Z. (2011). Learner initiatives and learning opportunities. *Classroom Discourse, 2*(2), 201–218.

Waring, H. Z. (2012). "Any questions?": Investigating understanding-checks in the language classroom. *TESOL Quarterly, 46*(4), 722–752.

Waring, H. Z. (2014). Managing control and connection: A micro-analytic look into teacher identity in an adult ESL classroom. *Research in the Teaching of English, 49*(1), 52–74.

Waring, H. Z. (2015). Promoting self-discovery in the language classroom. *International Review of Applied Linguistics in Language Teaching (IRAL), 53*(1), 61–85.

Waring, H. Z., Reddington, E., & Tadic, N. (2015, July). *Maintaining control without undermining participation in the language classroom.* Paper presented at the 14th International Pragmatics Conference (IPrA), Antwerp, Belgium.

6 Principle of Contingency
Teaching Requires Being Responsive to the Moment

A few summers ago, I was preparing for my trip to teach in our Tokyo program. Having been told to bring an eight-foot-long string to line dry my clothes, I stood in the kitchen trying to measure eight feet from a ball of string. I pulled out a piece and asked my husband:

01 Hansun: Is this a feet? ((*shows measure*))
02 Michael: Try again.
03 Hansun: Is THIS a feet? ((*makes string longer*))
04 Michael: ((*shakes head*))
05 Hansun: Is THIS a feet? ((*makes string even longer*))
06 Michael: ((*laughs*))
07 Hansun: So tell me! ((*in exasperation*))
08 Michael: Foot.

By the time I asked *Is THIS a feet?* in line 03, it should have become clear to any eavesdropper that I was blissfully oblivious to my atrocious grammar, and a kinder, gentler Michael would have lent a helping hand, that is, offered some contingent assistance. Instead, with increasing amusement, he watched me slip deeper into confusion—comedy for him but frustration for me. What Michael did was violate what I call the *principle of contingency; that is, teaching requires being responsive to the moment* (see discussions on the theoretical underpinnings of contingency at the end of this chapter). But Michael was not teaching, and I was not the ESL student. Still, what transpired rings a bell. Years ago, when I taught pedagogical English grammar, my response to students' assignments typically included circling the problematic areas, hoping that the students would be able to look at that and come to the corrections on their own. Here is what one of them wrote on the course evaluation:

When we got the homework and quizzes back they didn't have any corrections—so if you got the answer wrong, it was hard to see how it should have been.

Clearly, the feedback I gave was not useful to the students—at least not so to this particular one. I was not offering contingent assistance. I was not being responsive.

Contingency is not a new concept. Its centrality in social interaction as well as teaching and learning has been explicated or implicated in foundational writings such as Schegloff (1996), van Lier (1996), and Vygotsky (1978). In this chapter, we first consider some cases where responsiveness may be lacking. We then work through a series of exhibits that showcase what being responsive may look like in actual pedagogical interactions. As we dissect each case, our goal is to discover the essence of responsiveness in hopes that an empirically grounded understanding may be translated into usable pedagogical knowledge and, ultimately, replicable practices. The chapter concludes with a further discussion of the theoretical paradigms that are congruent with the principle of contingency.

BEING MICHAEL

Many of us have done or experienced teaching exactly the same way as it plays out in the Michael-Hansun scenario above, with no comedy intended or perceived. Consider an episode from an adult ESL classroom (see Extract 1 below). The class is doing a fill-in-the-blank grammar exercise on the present perfect (*have done*) versus present perfect progressive (*have been doing*). For the particular item in the transcript, the correct answer as envisioned by the teacher is *have seen* instead of Marie's answer *have been seeing*. Here is a very familiar moment, and I believe we are observing a very familiar response to that moment (T=teacher; BB=board):

1. have seen

01	Marie:	hav- h̲ave been {(0.6)-((*looks tentatively up at T*))}
02		[seeing.]
03	T:	→ [have been] seeing?
04		(1.8)-((*walks back to BB*))
05		→ Are you su̲::re?
06	LL:	((*mumbling various things*))
07	Marta:	° h̲ave see:n. ° ( )
08	T:	→ Let's write this down. ((*writes on BB "Since*
09		*they started playing in 1926, more than 100 million*
10		*people in over ninety different*
11		*countries _____ them."*))
12		→ ((*turns around*)) Okay, what's the correct answer.
13		(0.8)
14	T:	→ ((*reads from BB*)) >since they started
15		playing in 1926, more than 100 million

```
16                    people in over ninety different countrie::::::s
17 Kevin:     °haveh s[een.°]
18 T:                [We  ] 're TA:LKING about SO:: FAR.
```

In a classroom, especially during a form-focused exercise such as this, what is expected after a learner response is typically teacher acceptance or rejection, and the absence of acceptance is inferable as potential or incipient rejection. In line 03, upon hearing *have been*, the teacher in overlap repeats this problematic response verbatim and packages the repetition in a rising intonation, thereby casting initial doubt on its status as an acceptable answer. She then walks back to the board during the (1.8) second-long gap, where Marie offers no uptake. As the board is the symbolic center of the teacher's epistemic and institutional authority (where lectures are anchored), approaching the board may be an indication that that authority is about to be exercised for the benefit of elucidating Marie's less-than-acceptable understanding. In line 05, the teacher launches a yes-or-no question with hearable stress on and lengthening of *su:re*, which casts doubt on Marie's state of certainty and amounts to a reverse-polarity assertion—a critical stance: "you're not sure, thereby your answer may be wrong." (Koshik, 2002a; Waring, 2012). Immediately thereafter, Marta utters the only other option in this case *have see:n* but does so in *sotto voce*, perhaps indicating uncertainty of understanding. In lines 08 through 12, the teacher proceeds to display the textbook item on the board, and by asking for the *correct answer*, she again indicates that Marie's answer earlier was incorrect without attending to Marta's now corrected answer. Having received no response from that elicitation (see [0.8] second gap in line 13), she then reads the item up to the point where the answer is due, and by lengthening *countries*, enacts what Koshik (2002b) calls a "designedly incomplete utterance" (DIU) in an effort to elicit self-correction from the students. We again hear the only other alternative *have seen* in *sotto voce*, from Kevin this time (line 17). Finally, in line 18, the teacher offers a clue for why *have seen* is the correct answer, invoking what seems to be the rule the class has been learning—*so far* for the present perfect. Thus, at each arrowed turn, the teacher provides a form of implicit negative assessment, suggesting that the correct answer is still out of reach, very much like Michael's *Try again*. (Waring, 2015).

We will consider what being responsive entails in greater detail in the next section, but for now, suffice it to say that in this particular case, given the choices for the blank between *have seen* and *have been seeing*, what the students do not need much help with is guessing the correct answer (i.e., if it's not one, it must be the other), and accordingly, eliciting the correct answer is perhaps not the most strategic way of expending pedagogical energy. The correct answer is what Marie or the others could have perhaps offered as early as line 04. Why did they not go for it then? Perhaps something else is going on. And when we do hear *have seen* twice later, in both cases, they are given in *sotto voce*. Again, something else may be going on. Maybe what they are having trouble with is not guessing, but *understanding*, what the correct choice is in this situation, and being responsive means addressing that difficulty.

Consider another scene from an after-school literacy program for kindergarten through second grade ESOL (English to speakers of other languages) students. The tutor was an undergraduate elementary education major. As a monolingual native English speaker in her early 20s, she had no previous formal teaching experience or training. Nora, the tutee, was a first grade (six-year-old) native Spanish speaker from Mexico with strong oral English proficiency. Prior to the segment, tutor and child have read a green-colored book on the table that contains the words *tree* and *bee*. They are now in the midst of spelling the word *manatee* on a small whiteboard they each have. Nora has written *m-a-n-a-t* so far and is having trouble figuring out what comes next. The tutor (Tr) suggests that it is the same two ending letters in the words *tree* and *bee* and has asked Nora to write down *tree* and *bee* to the right of the unfinished *manatee*. As the segment begins, the tutor is trying to get Nora to notice the similar double *ee*s in *tree* and *bee*:

2. underline it

```
01  Nora:          ((writes)) o↓:::h ((erases and finishes writing 'tree' and 'bee'))
02  Tr:            [Okay so underline the  ] [similarities.-((pen over words))]
03  Nora:          [((looks to the green book))]  [((moves to 'manat' on board))   ]
04  Tr:            [          What's the same      ] =
05  Nora:          [((turns to what Tr is pointing to))]
06  Tr:            = [ in the word          ] [ "tree:" and "bee."]
07  Nora:            [((back to manatee again))] [((turns to tree and bee))   ]
08                 (0.2)
09  Tr:      →     Un[derline it.
10  Nora:              [((draws one long line under everything she wrote))- (°the
11                    le::tters? °)
12  Tr:      →     What letters. ((points successively to 'tree' and 'bee'))-what
13                    letters are the same in each word.
14  Nora:          u:h
15  Tr:      →     ((draws line between "manatee" and the other words))
16  Nora:          t:, t:, ((points to t in 'manat' and then in 'tree' with pen))
17                 ((continues))
```

In response to the tutor's question, we observe a slight (0.2) second gap in line 08—this along with Nora's wandering gaze provides an initial clue that she is probably not following and that the approach to identifying similarities to figure out the final two letters of *manatee* is perhaps not a fruitful one. Still, in line 09, the tutor goes on and directs Nora to *Underline it*, without specifying what *it* refers to. Nora in line 10 draws one long line under everything she wrote and at the same time mutters *the letters?* as a possible response to what the tutor is after. Since they have been working with letters, this is essentially a non-response, perhaps showing that Nora is doing the best she could. We now have further evidence that Nora has no clue what the tutor is after. Under such circumstances, the tutor's next question *what letters?* in line 12 may not be the most responsive move vis-à-vis where Nora is at. If *the letters?* is a wild guess to begin with, chances are *what letters* will not lead to any pertinent response from Nora. Indeed, no immediate response is forthcoming, and the tutor proceeds to add *what letters are the same in each word*, pointing to *tree* and *bee*—a directive replete with its own ambiguities (Waring & Hruska, 2012). Not surprisingly, we hear a hesitating *u:h* from Nora next. Again, we see evidence of Nora's attempt but failure at keeping up. She appears to have no understanding of why they are doing what they are doing. Faced with such developing confusion, the tutor does not budge. She persists further on the trajectory she has initiated. By drawing a line to separate *manatee* from *tree* and *bee*, she presumably facilitates the letter-identifying task, preventing Nora from including *manatee* in this task. Nora does exactly the opposite, however: rather than pointing to *ee* in both *tree* and *bee*, she picks out one *t* each from *manatee* and *tree*. Seventeen lines later, the tutor is nowhere near getting Nora to conclude that the final two letters of *manatee* are *ee*.

I have acted exactly like this tutor from time to time in teaching or even parenting. There are moments when it seems that the harder we work, the wider the chasm develops between us and the child or student. Maybe we are straining in the wrong direction. Maybe if we just start tuning into the intricate clues that inhabit every interactional moment, our energy could flow in greater harmony with the emerging demands of those moments. After all, "[t]he responsive teacher must be able to recognize the child's inability to understand, and know how to reframe questions when a child fails to respond or gives a 'wrong' or unrelated response" (Stremmel & Fu, 1993, pp. 346–347). Engaging in CA work of pedagogical interactions can give us tools to hear, to see, and to become more responsive. What we have sampled so far is cases where responsiveness is lacking, but what does *being responsive to the moment* look like? What is the essence of such responsiveness? How is the principle of contingency lived in action?

BEING RESPONSIVE

What we will consider in this section is a set of real-life cases that incarnate being responsive in pedagogical encounters. Through these exhibits I highlight three facets of being responsive:

- address the simultaneity of the moment;
- adjust to the shifting demands of the moment;

- preserve the integrity of the moment.

It is important to bear in mind that in the reality of pedagogical interaction, these facets are deeply entwined and sometimes impossible to tease apart. Each facet simply foregrounds a particular element, or ingredient if you will, of being responsive, and the following exhibits are meant as an illustrative, not exhaustive, account of what being responsive entails. Without a doubt, the quest for locating the essence of pedagogical responsiveness is an open-ended one.

Address the Simultaneity of the Moment

The discerning reader might question whether the simultaneity I refer to here is in any way tangled up with the multivocality dealt with in the previous chapter. Recall that multivocality can feature conflicting messages (as an impediment) or maneuvers addressed to the competing demands, such as control and connection (as a resource). The simultaneity being highlighted here, however, entails neither conflicts nor competition. If we were to hit the pause button at any time during the playback of a classroom scene, what gets frozen onto the screen is a moment, and that moment is rarely a unidimensional one: something is said and something else unsaid; a hand is up and another on its way down; an overzealous look emerges on the left and a stone face on the right. Every single moment is fraught with such simultaneous happenings that are not in conflict or competition with each other (as are control and connection), and teachers are routinely confronted with these moments successively and incessantly. Being responsive to the moment in part means tuning into the simultaneous happenings of that moment and attending to such simultaneity to the best of one's abilities.

The following scene is taken from an adult ESL classroom, where the students are taking turns reporting on a world record each has read. In line 24, Maria completes her report of a bungee jumping record with what in the CA literature would be referred to as an assessment *It's amazing.* (line 03):

3. amazing

((*Maria reports on bungee jumping record*))
```
01 Maria:      ( ) ta::llest buildings. (.) Fifty (.) five hundred
02             and ninety eight fee:t. In, (0.6) i:n ( ) in eight
03             seconds. ((gaze shift to T))-It's ama:zing.
04 T:       →  Wo:w. Did you hear that? ((gets up and points to BB))
05 LL:         ((loud laughter))
06 T:          That's ama:zing. [hh hh hh hh hh hh hh ]
07 Maria:                       [(That's)/(It's) ama:zing.]
08             [I don't- ]
09 T:          [That's a]ma:zing.
```

10 Maria:	I don't belie:ve it. hh hh
11 T:	I don't believe it, okay goo:d.

Note that as she produces the assessment (line 03), Maria also shifts her gaze to the teacher, addressing the latter as her intended recipient. There is a reason for this. Earlier in the class, the teacher has written a list of expressions of awe on the board as part of the pedagogical goals for the class (e.g., *I don't believe it. That's amazing. I would never do that.*), and Maria's *It's amazing.* is nearly identical to one of the items. By turning to the teacher in her delivery then, Maria is specifically showcasing her competence of using the expression in context. This display quality is further highlighted via the stress on both words and the syllable lengthening in *amazing*. Thus, Maria's *It's amazing.* is simultaneously ending the presentation sequence with an assessment on the bungee jumping record and playfully initiating a language practice sequence (see ensuing repetitions of the phrase) that foregrounds her competence (see "sequence pivot" in Reddington & Waring, 2015), and she is clearly prioritizing the latter function as evidenced in her prosody, gaze, as well as bodily orientation. The simultaneity of the moment then comprises two concurrent messages conveyed by a single utterance as well as the subtle clues of what is taken to be the primary one.

That the teacher has remained utterly in tune with such simultaneity may be observed in his response immediately thereafter. As seen, without missing a beat, he orients to Maria's competence display by marveling at not the bungee jumping record but her deftness in applying a newly learned item. He does so by calling attention to the use (*did you hear that?*) and by pointing to the board, thereby effectively highlighting what exactly is noteworthy in what Maria just said. The sequence has now pivoted from oral presentation to language practice, which the class immediately registers as humorous via the loud laughter in the very next turn.

Aside from concurrent but differentially prioritized messages, simultaneity of the moment also may involve the presence of an implicit message underneath the explicit one. Consider a case from a post-observation conference. The mentor (M) is talking to Ava, whose ESL class he has just observed (Waring, 2014). Prior to the segment, the mentor noted that Ava's students may have had trouble understanding the word *metabolism*. As the segment begins, he elicits Ava's thoughts on the solution to a more generalized version of the problem, that is, dealing with difficult vocabulary in listening:

4. from listening to reading

01 M:	[h↑ow do] you deal with difficult
02	((*gaze to A*))-vocabulary in listening.
03 Ava:	(0.5)
04	u::hm, (0.2) th↑is was, (0.2) honestly this
05	was my first, (.) CD listening activity.=

```
06 M:              =>>mhm,<<
07 Ava:            that I've ever done.
((lines omitted))
08 Ava:            so:: uh- (0.2)
09 M:        →     .tch >w' l↑et's< [(    ) let's (    ) just-]
10 Ava:                             [I::, haven't gotten any]
11                 opport↑unity yet. [heh hhh]
12 M:                               [  l e t' s] brainstorm.
13 Ava:            ((nods))
14 M:              so:, let's imagine that we're doing r↑eading.
15 Ava:            m[hm ].
16 M:               >[read]ing and listening are usually the types
17           →     of activities that hang and go together .hh< if
18                 ↑you: know that you have a reading that has
19                 a lo::t of difficult vocabulary in that.
20 Ava:            mhm.
21 M:        →     what would you do.
22                 (.)
23                 with that.
24                 (0.8)
25 Ava:            u:hm you can take the potentially
26                 difficult vocabu[lary and make a prereading]=
27 M:                             [            ((nods))       ]
28 Ava:            =ac- u::h activity out of it.=
29 M:              =bingo.
30                 (.)
31                 >stop right there.<
32                 (.)
33                 °m↓ake listening.°-((gestures 'switch'))
34 Ava:            ((smiles and nods))-right.=
((lines omitted))
```

Note the (0.5) second gap in line 03 immediately preceding Ava's verbal response. Clearly, this is not a question she can easily and quickly answer. Further delays emerge as we hear *u:hm* followed by another (0.2) second pause. Next comes an explanation for her inability to answer the question (i.e., her lack of experience). Notice how this explanation is packaged: the raised pitch on *this* typically signals the beginning of a new sequence (Couper-Kuhlen, 2001), which in this case, seems to indicate a shift in trajectory—from answering the mentor's quest for solution to sharing a personal experience that explains the non-answering (Hayano, 2013, p. 404). Soon after launching her turn, Ava also quickly comes to a halt with a self-repair (Schegloff, 1979), inserting the adverb *honestly*, which upgrades the veracity of her account. Note also that after the mentor's continuer *mhm* in line 06, Ava adds an increment to further emphasize her lack of experience to her already completed turn in line 05: *that I've ever done.*

So what are all these detailed observations telling us about where Ava is at this particular moment? First, the mentor's question is not one that is easily answerable for Ava. Second, Ava is not taking her inability to answer lightly. She is certainly not wearing it as a badge of honor. We would have heard otherwise a quick and unhedged *I have no idea*. Third, Ava is working hard to attribute this momentary inability to her lack of experience rather than her inherent ability. Put otherwise, Ava is treating not knowing the answer as some sort of deficiency that warrants an explanation. With this information in hand, the mentor could have done a number of things. He could have questioned that lack of experience. He could have insisted on her answering even without the experience (e.g., *Just guess.*). He could have accepted that inexperience and offered an answer on her behalf. What he ends up doing is creating a scenario that allows Ava to respond competently with a solution that is transferrable to the problem of dealing with difficult vocabulary in listening. As it turns out, Ava is indeed capable of solving the problem after all. Thus, the mentor is able to provide a form of assistance that delicately attends to Ava's competence concerns that have become visible in her carefully designed response to his initial question. Being responsive in this case then entails devising useful guidance that addresses not just the obvious fact of Ava not having a solution to offer at the moment but also the implicit issue of her desire to meet the expectation of having a solution. Each moment has its layers. What constitutes the simultaneity of the moment in this case is the melding of the explicit and the implicit. What the teacher does specifically in this case is not unlike what politicians do to manage "unanswerable" questions—by operating on the question (Clayman, 2001, p. 428). In a memorable example in Clayman's study, when the presidential candidate Gary Hart was asked whether he had an affair with Donna Rice, he reformulates the question before answering:

> .hhhh *Mister Koppel (1.1) if the question: (.) is in the twenty nine y:ear:s of my marriage, including two public separations have I been absolutely and totally faithful: to my wife. hhh I regret to say the answer is no:. . . .*

With remarkable maneuvering, Gary Hart has made the question more "answerable" to the extent that it incurs less damage to his political image. After all, a single instance of infidelity, when situated against the backdrop of 29 years of marriage (including years of separation), can all of a sudden appear less offensive. The mentor in our case utilizes a similar tactic of operating on the question, except that what he operates on is his own question—making it more answerable for Ava by creating a scenario where the previously unanswerable question has now successfully become answerable.

Simultaneity of the moment may be a matter of scope as well—one that involves not the multiple layers of a single response but the simultaneous conduct of multiple participants in the classroom. A scene of great familiarity that manifests such simultaneous occurrences is turn allocation in the classroom. As Schegloff (1996) notes, turn taking in multiparty interaction is a key locus for interactional contingency. Much of managing contingency in the classroom then involves managing multiparty turn-taking. Observe this from an adult ESL classroom: the teacher is eliciting the understanding of the noun *produce*. He selects Ana to answer in line 05, and that selection is sustained with a nonverbal gesture in line 07. In partial overlap with the teacher's nonverbal gesture, however, Kara, who has not been selected to respond, offers an answer (lines 08–09):

5. produce the produce

```
01  T:           I can tell y- every single person in this class
02               does know this word.=°you've all seen this wo:rd,
03               in supermarkets.°
04               (0.5)
05               Ana?-((leans forward))
06               (0.8)
07               [(((left hand extends to Ana))]
08  Kara:        [It's agricultural?          ]
09               [Products?                                              ]
10  T:      →    [Ah- -((turns to K with finger up and then {((points))-°ye[ah.°}]
11  Ana:                                                                  [vege ]
12               [t a b l e:::::::s,            ]
13  T:      →    [(((gaze and arm swerved to A))]
14  Ana:         [a:::        n          [d ]
15  T:      →    [((pivots to inducing gesture))-  [A::]ND?
16  Ana:         °frui:t.°=
17  T:           =Yes-((nods and retrieves arm))
18               (2.0)-((T nods))
19               ((underlines 'produce'))
20               (1.0)-((T nods))
```

Upon hearing Kara's *agriculture*, the teacher immediately lifts his right index finger up to an "on-hold" position, which pivots to a pointing gesture to Kara along with the *sotto voce yeah* as the latter comes to a completion with *products* (line 09). Meanwhile, the teacher's *yeah* overlaps with the onset of Ana's turn, where she offers *vegetables* as an example of agricultural products, at which point he quickly swings his extended right arm toward Ana, and the extended arm pivots into an inducing gesture as Ana continues with *and*. The teacher repeats the *and* as he continues the inducing gesture, and finally, we hear Ana's *fruit* in line 16, which is accepted by the teacher in the next line.

Thus, Kara's self-selection intrudes into the space of the selected student Ana, who seems to need a bit more time and assistance to come to a response. On the one hand, shushing Kara would compromise the culture of participation in the classroom; on the other hand, abandoning Ana would be a gesture of injustice as it violates the legitimacy of her speaking right and, more crucially, deprive her of an opportunity to stretch her linguistic competence with necessary assistance. Here is what the teacher does in a nutshell: he quickly acknowledges Kara's response before returning his focus back to Ana and supports the latter in completing the phrase *vegetables and fruit*. Importantly, the *yeah* uptake extended to Kara is designed in such a way that clearly renders her voice as secondary to the teacher's primary attention to Ana: it is prefaced with an incipient but abandoned on-hold gesture and done with brevity and in *sotto voce*. In so doing, the teacher is able to protect the space of a struggling student without discouraging the enthusiasm of her fellow classmate (Waring, 2013a). In addressing the simultaneity of the moment then, the teacher also engages an ensemble of resources: lexical, prosodic, sequential, and gestural.

A similar situation transpires in the segment below. In another adult ESL classroom, the teacher is eliciting the completion of *New York is so multicultural that* . . . and has selected Hiromi as the next speaker, but Evelina starts talking:

6. so multicultural

```
01 T:              Tha:t, (.) what, Hiromi. (.) Ima:gine a sentence. New
02                 York is so multicultural tha:t, ((gestures out toward her))
03                 (1.6)
04 Evelina:        (        )
05 T:        →     ((holds up hand/nods/smiles to Evelina))
06                 $ °>Just a second, just a second.<°$
07                 (1.2)
08 T:        →     Tha::t,
09 Sato:           You never miss [your (homeland).=
10 T:        →                    [((holds hand up toward Sato/nods/smiles))
11 Sato:           = (                          )]
12 T:        →     =$Just a second, let- let her try:$]
13 Sato:           Sorry: hheh.
14 T:        →     I know, y- we have so many wonderful people who
15                 wanna [ta:lk.]
16 Hiromi:               [So:  ] multicultural that (.) uh we have many
17                 (   ) restaura:nts,
18 T:        →     Perfect, perfect. Evelina. So multicultural tha:t,
19 Evelina:        °(         )°
20 T:        →     O::kay, Sato, go,
21                 (0.4)
22 T:              So multi[cultural tha:t,]
23 Sato:                   [That you::   ] uh, (.) you never mi:ss (.)
24                 your home.
25 T:              Aa:h. Oka:y. Okay.
```

After a (1.6) second gap with no response from Hiromi, Evelina makes an unintelligible attempt, which is immediately put on hold by the teacher with nods and smiles in line 05 along with a hand gesture as well as the repeated and quickly paced *Just a second* in smiley voice. Another (1.2) second passes, and the teacher repeats the elicitation with a lengthened *tha:t* in continuing intonation in line 08, which receives Sato's volunteered completion *You never miss your homeland*. Again, the teacher extends to Sato the same on-hold gesture with nods and smiles and does so in terminal overlap (Jefferson, 1983), followed by the directive *just a second* delivered in smiley voice as well as the account *let her try*. (lines 10 and 12). After Sato's apology in the next line, the teacher proceeds to characterize the competing voices as *so many wonderful people who want to talk* (lines 14–15). In so doing, he manages to mitigate the "policing" he has "inflicted" upon the unselected and cast their conduct in a positive light. Finally, in lines 16 and 17, after much persistence on the teacher's part to give Hiromi the space to try, the latter produces a sentence completion that receives two consecutive *perfect* in line 18. Immediately thereafter, the teacher returns the floor to the unselected, first to Evelina (line 18) and then to Sato (line 20). Again, in this case, the teacher engages in a great deal of interactional work to maintain the order of the turn allocation that also protects the space of the struggling. In the meantime, he ensures that the volunteers are treated with appreciation and invited into the conversation as legitimate respondents later on (Waring, 2013a).

What we have seen here may remind one of John Dewey's observations of the experienced teacher, who "has acquired the requisite skill of doing two or three distinct things simultaneously—skill to see the room as a whole while hearing one individual in one class recite, of keeping the program of the day and, yes, of the week, and of the month in the fringe of consciousness while the work of the hour is in its center" (in van Lier, 2004, p. 149). Nowadays, few would quarrel with the assertion that teaching is multitasking, and some might even be able to enumerate with much eloquence what such multitasking entails, but demonstrating how the management of such multitasking plays out in the milliseconds of interaction is an entirely different matter. What we have witnessed above is the interactional manifestations of Dewey's "requisite skill" in action. As shown, this in-flight management necessarily engages an ensemble of linguistic and nonlinguistic resources dispensed with impeccable timing; for example, the teacher's *Did you hear that?* works in conjunction with the pointing gesture that directs attention to the list of expressions on the board to ratify Maria's competence display; an on-hold gesture along with smiles and nods does both accepting and deterring without disrupting the ongoing effort of another.

Adjust to the Shifting Demands of the Moment

While simultaneity resides in a single moment, shifting demands spread across moments. Being responsive during this moment-to-moment progression takes constant adjusting rather than persisting. Consider an example from math tutoring with young children (Creider, 2013). Here, the tutor (Tr) has initiated a game with the child Chloe (three and a half years old), where one player closes her eyes while the other puts a simple pattern of chips down on the paper. The first player then opens her eyes and tries to duplicate the pattern:

7. Chole wants red

01	Tr:		Okay now close your eyes ((*sing song voice*))
02			it's <u>my</u> turn. Close your eyes. ((*puts one blue chip on board*))
03			Your turn.
04	Chloe:		((*opens eyes and picks up a red chip from pile*))
05	Tr:	→	Oops but look what I put. I put a <u>blue</u>! ((*points to blue chip*))
06	Chloe:		((*puts a red chip under a blue chip*))
07	Tr:	→	You don't wanna put a blue, you wanna put
08			another red, huh?
09	Chloe:		Yeah.-((*places another red chip on board*))
10	Tr:	→	Is that all you wanna do? Okay now <u>I</u>'m gonna
11			put two reds then. °Everything you do I'm gonna
12			do the same.°
13	Chloe:		((*picks up a blue chip and places it on board*))
14	Tr:		Now you put a blue. Alright. Then it's my turn
15			then >I'm gonna put a blue.<

As you can see, instead of following the rules of the game that requires copying the pattern on the floor, Chloe in line 04, upon opening her eyes, puts down a different color chip. The tutor calls out her "transgression" in line 05. Still, rather than insisting on following the rule of the game as it was originally laid out, she acknowledges what Chloe wants (i.e., *You don't want X. You want Y.*) and proceeds to modify the game to accommodate the child's initiative. At the same time, they are still copying patterns. The tutor's larger goal is kept in focus. Being responsive in this case then entails adjusting the task at hand to fit the child's interest while keeping the essence of the task intact. As Tharp and Gallimore (1988) write, responsive instruction "requires flexibility; the teacher maintains goals for the discussion, but often alters and even abandons the anticipated 'script' for a given lesson" (p. 122).

Consider another case from a graduate writing center, where the tutor (Tr) is working with Lena the tutee on her dissertation. Prior to the segment, the tutor has proposed an outline of headings that would allow Lena to reorganize the materials in the draft the tutor read before the meeting.

What this reorganization eventually amounts to is the tutor's suggestion to rephrase the research questions:

8. rephrase the question

```
01 Tr:          ((lines omitted)) Yeah you need to re(.)phrase the
02              questions.
03              (0.8)
04        →     if that's what you (.) wanna do.
05 Lena:        I'll think about it. [(((laugh)) cuz th]at-
06 Tr:                               [If- yeah yeah ]
07 Lena:        You don't know what it- [took (.) for us [to get to these=
08 Tr:                                  [Yeah           [I kno:w.
09 Lena:        = three questions. u- u- you know. Over a year of going
10              back and [forth of different things.
11 Tr:                   [O- O- O-
12              Okay.
13              (1.8)
14        →     Yeah for now, if you can just do this. If you think
15              that's ( ).=
16 Lena:        =>↓I ↑can do th↑at.<
```

The tutor's advice in lines 01 and 02 makes relevant acceptance or rejection as a response. When acceptance is absent ([0.8] second gap of silence), rejection is inferable. Note that the tutor immediately attends to that incipient rejection with an increment in line 04: *if that's what you wanna do.* By rendering her directive as ultimately a matter of choice for Lena, the tutor mitigates the force of her original directive while making evident her close monitoring of Lena's stance. Not surprisingly, Lena further delays her response in line 05 with *I'll think about it*, followed by an account that strengthens the legitimacy of those questions bolstered by not only the amount of time and effort spent but also the expertise of the parties (i.e., professor) involved. Note that Lena's big-package response is carried out in a multiunit turn, in the course of which the tutor attempts multiple times to give a good hearing to Lena's concern. In line 06, upon hearing Lena's *I'll think about it*, she abandons a possible repetition of the *if* clause and proceeds to utter an affirmative *yeah* three times before launching the explicit claim *I know* in recognitional overlap (Jefferson, 1983). Such empathetic hearing is then upgraded to a potential rejection finalizer (Davidson, 1990) *Okay*, first attempted three times during Lena's turn in progress and finally produced in the clear in line 12. After another (1.8) second-long gap during which Lena may be waiting to hear more specifics of the tutor's *okay*, and the latter may be gauging the likelihood of Lena considering rephrasing the questions despite everything, the tutor concedes in line 14: *Yeah for now, if you can just do this*, meaning reorganizing the materials according to the headings she proposed. Note that the tutor's concession is prefaced with the adverbial *for now*. As an ethnographic sidenote, Lena eventually did end up rephrasing the research questions, and reorganizing the materials was a crucial step that rendered that rephrasing self-evident. As can be seen, the tutor's concession is accepted quickly and emphatically by Lena or one might even say "happily." In short, as the tutor carefully adjusts her responses throughout the sequence during the course of Lena's developing response, she manages to sidestep a potential impasse without losing sight of her long-range goal by temporarily holding that goal at bay.

So how does this type of adjustment play out in the classroom? Observe another scene from an adult ESL classroom. In this case, the class is trying to explain the word "ceremony," and Wendy offers "a special event":

9. ceremony

```
01 T:                 Who can explain to me:: what a ↑ceremony is.
02 Wendy:             a: special event?
03 T:          →      ((looks up at Wendy))-(1.0)
04             →      ((circular [inducing hand gesture))]
05 LL:                        [( )                        ]
06 T:          →      to::::: what kind of special event.
07                    (0.3)
08 L:                 formal.
09 L:                 like a [ ( )
10 T:                        [a formal event? ((nods))
11 LL:                formal. Formal. Yeah.
12 T:          →       or religious often.
13 L:                 ritual.
14 T:                 a ritual:l.
15 Rosa:              °ritual.°
```

Like the teacher in Segment (1) above, at every arrow here, the teacher is offering a form of implicit negative assessment, suggesting that the ideal response is yet to come. Beyond the initial silence that allows for Wendy to continue, however, he is also offering implicit assistance that guides the learner toward the targeted goal (Waring, 2015). We see the gesture in line 06 that indicates more is expected to come; that is, *a special event* is not incorrect, just incomplete. The *to:::::* in line 08 also offers a syntactic resource (i.e., *to* projecting a verb phrase) with which the definition of *ceremony* may be completed. When that fails, he switches to elicit a prepositioned modifier by asking for the *kind of event*. In line 14, he adds *or religious often* to the students' *formal*. There is, in other words, a consistent effort in propelling the forward movement of the sequence toward the target. In this case then, being responsive means offering contingent assistance tailored to the student understanding at the moment—assistance constantly adjusted to accommodate the shifting assessment of what the learner knows and can do in situ. It is assistance that becomes ultimately usable.

Thus, in these three cases, quick and incremental adjustments are made toward, not away from, the long-range target. In each case, such adjustment means not persisting. In playing the game of copying patterns, the tutor does not insist on being the leader whose patterns must be copied. In eliciting the definition of *ceremony*, the teacher does not insist on obtaining a definition in the format of *a special event to::* once it has become clear that the infinitive does not offer the necessary assistance for the learners to move forward. In the case of graduate tutoring, the tutor goes beyond not persisting to conceding. In each situation, small concessions are made for the benefit of a greater victory. Adjusting is done without losing focus of the ultimate goal. Such adjusting is integral to the responsive assistance advocated by Tharp and Gallimore (1988):

> [t]his continual adjustment of the level and amount of help is *responsive to the child's level of performance and perceived need*. Assisting adults appear to keep in mind the overall goal of the activity, to stay related to what the child is trying to do. New information or suggestions are made relevant to furthering the child's current goal, and at the same time furthering the overall goals. (p. 40)

Preserve the Integrity of the Moment

If adjusting to the shifting demands of the moment emphasizes the teachers' flexibility to break out of their frames if necessary, preserving the integrity of the moment is its flip side: it highlights the importance of not disturbing the (learners') ongoing frames. Consider another example from math tutoring with young children (Creider, 2013). In this segment, the tutor and Miguel the five-year-old child have been examining and sorting different-colored dice. As the excerpt starts, the tutor comments that Miguel has put out a row of dice, all of which have the three dots on top. She then starts to count the dice (lines 01 and 03). Miguel does not seem interested in the number three. Instead, he announces that *all that this is a car* (line 04).

10. This is a car

01 Tr:		°You're making it all threes in a row.°
02		(.)
03		((*points at dice in line*))-three dots, three dots.=
04 Miguel:		=all that this is a car.
05 Tr:	→	are those cars.
06 Miguel:		((*nods*))
07 Tr:	→	>Yeah but let's see< (.) Let's count the color
08		of the cars.

```
09                        (.)
10 Miguel:                ((puts out finger)) (.)
11 Tr:          →         ((Tr guides M's finger across line of dice)) pink car,
12                        green car, red car, red car, blue car, black car,
13                        red car, with white dots, red car with black do:ts.
14 Miguel:                ((places a red dice in line))
15 Tr:          →         Another red car.
```

Rather than insisting on focusing on numbers, the tutor sustains the frame initiated by Miguel by continuing the activity that is congruent with the latter's car fantasy: *Let's count the colors of the cars* (lines 07–08). This is slightly different from what she did with Chloe in an earlier extract, where she specifically identified Chloe's transgression (i.e., not following the tutor's rule of the game), making very visible her effortful adjustment.

Observe a similar scene in the after-school literacy program between the tutor (Tr) and the six-year-old Nora, whom we have met earlier. The tutor was trying to transition Nora from reading to writing, with much resistance from Nora (Waring & Hruska, 2011). They just finished reading the book *The Tree, the Bee, and Me*—with a focus on the words ending in /iy/, in the course of which Nora expressed interest in the manatee figurine on the table, and the tutor says: *Maybe we can spell that later*. And that in itself is an example of being responsive to the moment since spelling *manatee* was not part of the tutor's original lesson plan. Toward the beginning of the segment, Nora asks a question but does so through the voice of the manatee:

11. manatee has a question

```
01 Nora:        He {had a:: m-((grabs manatee))} (0.5) ((looks to Tr))-a
02              question.=
03 Tr:    →     =>He had a question.=what's his < question.
04 Nora:        [di-di-di-di-          ] di-di-di-di, di-di-di,
05 Tr:          [>How d'y spell manatee?<]
06        →     I don't understand ma:natee tal[k.-((looks helpless))
07 Nora:                                        [He say,
08              {(0.2)-((looks down to manatee))} h↑ow (.) poh
09              mana{tee?- ((looks up at Tr))}=
10 Tr:          =How {d'y spell manatee.-((move away and down to pick up
11              eraser)) w- we're gonna- wanna see how you write
12              mana[tee?          ]
13 Nora:           [>°yeah. Yeah.<] yeah. °
```

As you can see, the tutor does not take any issue with Nora's speaking through the manatee. In fact, she sustains this play frame by keeping the manatee in the picture, asking *what's his question?* (line 03). As Nora proceeds to produce a series of nonsensical sounds, the tutor also capitalizes on this opportunity to advance her agenda, putting the question

into manatee's mouth: *How to spell manatee?* She then lets Nora finish
the series of di- sounds and expresses difficulty understanding the manatee talk rather than chastising Nora for acting disruptive in any way. In
lines 08 and 09, Nora appropriates the tutor's question and agrees that
the manatee is indeed asking: how /poh/ (to spell) manatee? Mission
accomplished. In this case then, by aligning very closely with Nora's
world without incurring any disturbance, the tutor is able to secure
Nora's compliance in accomplishing the difficult task of transitioning
from reading to writing. In both cases considered so far, being responsive means validating the child's world and advancing one's agenda from
within that world.

The integrity of the moment need not concern a child's fantasy only.
Sometimes, it simply means the organic quality of the conversation at the
time. In the following example taken from an adult ESL class, the teacher
asks how everyone's weekend was in line 01, and Kara responds with *It was
good*:

12. weekend

01	T:	Oka:y, s↑o:, how was everyone's weekend.
02		(2.0)
03	Kara:	(hh)It was goo (hh)od.
04	T: →	Kara tell me about it.
05	Kara:	I prepa:red- I bought ne:wspaper, I loo:ked through
06		it, I picked (0.2) [hh hh hh, an a:rticle,]
07	T: →	[hh hh, a::ll weekend.]
08	Kara:	No::. Hh [hh]
09	T:	[hh] hh.
10	Kara:	I sp(hh)ent it with my friends.
11	T: →	Goo:d, good good. Did [you go anywhere special.]
12	Kara:	[(because) it was]
13		Valentine's Da:y, [a:nd] despi:te of the fa:ct that (.)=
14	T:	[A::::h.]
15	Kara:	my sweetie is in my (.) home cou:ntry?

Throughout the sequence, the teacher contingently guides Kara toward an
understanding of what counts as an appropriate response to a question such
as *How was your weekend?*; that is, a "plus" response (Sacks, 1975) such as
goo:::d warrants elaboration with specific activities, and such activities are
typically fun, interesting, or special (Waring, 2013b). We may or may not
agree whether this is indeed how we should answer the question *how was
your weekend?* in American English. What we do observe is how the teacher
incrementally and seamlessly nudges Kara just a bit closer to the "target"
response at every juncture. In line 04, he asks for elaboration. Once that
elaboration turns out to be heading in the "wrong" direction, he interjects
in line 07 with the extreme case formulation (Pomerantz, 1986) *a:ll weekend* (line 07), highlighting the unlikely or perhaps undesirable nature of the

reported activity. Kara backs down immediately in the next turn (line 08) and, with laughter, continues with *I spent it with my friends*—a nonwork-related activity, which is immediately embraced by the teacher with *Good, good good* as he probes further with *Did you go anywhere special* (line 11).

It is true that much of what we have observed so far is in fact the teacher adjusting to the shifting demands of the moment. By remaining very responsive to each bit of the language that Kara is producing, the teacher finds a way to ease the development of that language. But what we would like to highlight here is that he does so without breaking out of the ongoing conversational frame.

In line 04, the teacher could have simply moved on to the next person. In line 07, he could have said *No, this is not how we usually respond in American English. You're supposed to do fun things on weekends.* Put otherwise, he could have resorted to an explicit lesson of how to answer *How was your weekend?* type of questions, which would have afforded an entirely different kind of learning opportunity—one that does not allow for learning by doing, where Kara is learning to answer *how was your weekend?* by answering, with contingent assistance, *how was your weekend?* In short, preserving the integrity of the moment in part entails sustaining, not disturbing, the organic flow of conversation that facilitates learning by doing at that moment.

Of the three facets demonstrated so far, preserving the integrity of the moment is the least spoken of in discussions of pedagogy and yet perhaps the most difficult to achieve. It requires the patience and ingenuity to work within the "illusion" of the moment and get the job done, and the benefits are myriad. In the "car" case, it allowed the tutor to weave the child's interest into the ongoing lesson without invalidating the latter. In the "manatee" case, it avoided a potentially prolonged power struggle and secured a smooth transition. In the "weekend" case, it afforded a learning experience that was organically integrated with the student's personal life. In each case, a more expedient choice would have been to "burst the bubble" and get the lesson delivered, but something would have been lost on the way: a child's sense of validation, an opportunity to create authentic engagement, and an experience of learning that would leave a longer-lasting imprint than its alternative. By taking the road less traveled, the teachers manage to accomplish their agendas within, rather than imposing their agendas upon, the learners' worlds. This is done, as shown, by accepting the props, playing the characters, and sustaining the conversations in these worlds.

CONTINGENCY AS PRACTICE AND THEORY

We can never fully plan spontaneous interaction, not our own articulations nor the contributions of others; this, along with the multiple signaling systems we employ, constitutes the contingency of talk-in-interaction.

(Ford, 2004, p. 30)

Each moment in a pedagogical encounter can present simultaneous happenings, point to an unexpected direction, or propose an illusion worth sustaining. Being responsive to the moment requires fine sensitivity for detecting its rich nuances and great acrobatic agility for amassing and deploying the available resources on time so that the demands of that moment can be met. As I have demonstrated in this chapter, while teaching without being responsive can incur great frustration for all parties, being responsive to the moment lies at the heart of the principle of contingency, and such responsiveness becomes manifest in pedagogical encounters as one addresses the simultaneity of the moment, adjusts to the shifting demand of the moment, and preserves the integrity of the moment. Being responsive, in other words, involves "soft-assembling" (Thelen & Smith, 1994) the various resources to manage "the communicative pressures at hand" (Larsen-Freeman & Cameron, 2008, pp. 6–7) and being adaptable to the "organic nature of change" (Larsen-Freeman & Cameron, 2008, p. 11). It requires the kind of intelligence that is "not something possessed once for all," but "its retention requires constant alertness in observing consequences, an open-minded will to learn and courage in re-adjustment" (Dewey, 1920/2004, pp. 96–97). In a sense, one might argue that the principle of contingency is about tuning in and being sensitive to the multivocality of learner voices.

Calling "contingency" a major challenge for computational linguists, Schegloff (1996) anchors the concept in *action, interaction,* and *multiparty interaction*: a participant's action at any moment shapes the trajectory of subsequent talk; a co-participant's absence of action has the same consequence; and in multiparty interaction, orientations to turn taking, non-addressed parties, and schisms also can affect the production and understanding of talk. He writes, "[a]lthough the organization of talk-in-interaction is orderly (else it would be opaque to its participants), it is characterized by contingency at virtually every point" (Schegloff, 1996, p. 21). In other words, everything depends on everything else; nothing comes prepackaged. The concept of contingency undergirds conversation analysts' understanding of and approach to social interaction. As Schegloff (1996) so forcefully claims:

Contingency—interactional contingency—is not a blemish on the smooth surface of discourse, or of talk-in-interaction more generally. It is endemic to it. It is its glory. It is what allows talk-in-interaction the flexibility and robustness to serve as the enabling mechanism for the institutions of social life.

(p. 22)

It is this utter and unabashed acceptance of contingency as an intrinsic quality of social interaction that makes conversation analysts' work so central to our understanding of the type of pedagogical interaction that has been exemplified in this chapter. After all, it is through conversational interaction that "the work of the constitutive institutions of societies gets done" (Schegloff, 1996, p. 4). In fact, the contingency that permeates ordinary conversation seems precisely what progressive education scholars crave and seek in the classroom. The push for using conversation as a vehicle for teaching has been articulated in various proposals such as instructional conversation, responsive teaching, and conversational teaching (e.g., Shuy, 1991; Tharp & Gallimore, 1988; van Lier, 1996). According to van Lier (1996), conversation or "any language use which plays with contingencies" creates "the most stimulating environment of learning," and "[c]ontingency is the quality of language use that can most directly be associated with engagement and learning" (p. 171). In what seems to me is his signature style of whimsical writing, van Lier (1996) explains contingency as follows:

> Contingency can be seen as a web of connecting threads between an utterance and other utterances, and between utterances and the world. This web can be sparse and flimsy, as in the case of recitation, or it can be thick and strong, as in the case of conversation. Contingencies draw upon what we know and connect this to what is new. It is thus part of the essence of learning.
>
> (p. 174)

He goes on to specify the benefits of increasing contingency in classroom interaction as increased learning opportunities and increased depth of learning (van Lier, 1996, p. 184).

For van Lier (1996), the key elements of contingency are symmetry and equality (p. 148): while equality is determined by factors outside the talk such as age or status, symmetry is by talk-internal qualities such as equal distributions of rights and duties in talk (p. 175), and "[c]onversational teaching, or pedagogical interaction characterized by contingency . . . depends on the possibility of achieving interactional symmetry among unequal participants" (p. 176). He also specifies the functions of contingent utterances as relating new material to known material, setting up expectancies for what may come next, validating both preceding and next utterance, featuring neither entire predictability nor entire unpredictability, promoting intersubjectivity, and ensuring continued attention (van Lier, 1996, p. 184).

Both Tharp and Gallimore's (1988) instructional conversation and van Lier's (1996) conversational teaching can be traced back to Vygotskyan (1978) sociocultural theory of learning and development, a central concept of which is the zone of proximal development (ZPD), defined as "the distance between the actual developmental level as determined by independent problem solving and the level of potential development as determined through problem solving under adult guidance or in collaboration with more capable peers" (p. 86). Although Vygostky's original work is addressed to the assessment of children's mental development, it is not difficult to surmise that the teacher's work lies precisely within the ZPD, which contains "functions that have not yet matured but are in the process of maturation, functions that will mature tomorrow but are currently in an embryonic state" (p. 86). In fact, Tharp and Gallimore (1988) define teaching as *"assisting performance through the ZPD. Teaching can be said to occur when assistance is offered at points in the ZPD at which performance requires assistance"* (p. 31). In a similar vein, responsive teaching is typically thought of as teaching within the zone (Stremmel & Fu, 1993, p. 341). Such teaching within the ZPD has later been condensed into a concept now widely popular among educators—that of scaffolding (Wood, Bruner, & Ross, 1976). Equating scaffolding with contingent teaching that "takes place of necessity in proximal context" (p. 147), van Lier (2004) considers contingency as one of the conditions for scaffolding and stresses the "improvisational, dialogic side" of the latter (p. 15).

The principle of contingency, as has been dealt with in this chapter, is a synthesis of CA and sociocultural theory. For conversation analysts, contingency is what we experience and manage on a daily basis. It is what we assume and explore in our work. In sociocultural theory, contingency takes on a more specific meaning—with particular reference to the nature of assistance vis-à-vis learners' level of understanding and performance. While conversation analysis offers both the visions and tools to appreciate the nature of contingency in great interactional details, sociocultural theory directs our attention to what that means for learning. By bringing together a theory of social interaction on the one hand and one of learning and development on the other, as such, we are empowered to discover and create with greater efficacy moments where "the teacher plays off, and builds on, the children's responses" (Tharp & Gallimore, 1988, p. 122). "Such moment-to-moment pedagogical action," as van Lier (2004) reminds us, "requires 'just-right' and 'just-in-time' responses and interventions, and must be seen as among the most complex and demanding decisions experienced teachers make" (p. 149).

Picture this in the classroom: the teacher has asked a question, and a student has just offered a response that is somewhat off the mark. Two easy reactions come to mind: provide space (e.g., *There's a problem. You figure it out.*) and tell (e.g., *Let me explain.*). Typically, space is provided at the expense of closely tailoring the teacher's each next move to the learner's emerging understanding, and telling is done without engaging the learner in the journey of discovering that explanation. There is a vast chasm in between—the period of liminality (Turner, 1967), where the work of teaching lies. More than two decades ago, Tharp and Gallimore (1988) wrote with great urgency:

Students cannot be left to learn on their own; teachers cannot be content to provide opportunities to learn and then assess outcomes; recitation must be deemphasized; responsive, assisting interactions must become common-place in the class. Minds must be roused to life. *Teaching must be rede-fined as assisted performance. Teaching consists in assisting performance. Teaching is occurring when performance is achieved with assistance.*

(p. 21)

Indeed, the mandate to be responsive is easy to proclaim but difficult to implement. As we have observed, in actual practice, this entails being sensi-tive to the simultaneity of the moment, continually adjusting to the shifting demands of the moment, and preserving the integrity of the moment, each of which places a tremendous pressure on the practicing teacher's in-flight thinking and conduct. Truly gifted teachers are able to exercise the principle of contingency with great ease. For most of us, it takes years of practice and reflection, but that learning curve need not be as steep as its seems—if we start paying attention now, with an informed eye: if we begin with the assumption that each moment contains simultaneity, that adjusting is more productive than persisting, and that there is a possibility to make progress without compromising the frame of the moment.

REFERENCES

Clayman, S. E. (2001). Answers and evasions. *Language in Society, 30*, 403–442.

Couper-Kuhlen, E. (2001). Intonation and discourse: Current views from within. In D. Schiffrin, D. Tannen, & H. Hamilton (Eds.), *The handbook of discourse analysis* (pp. 13–34). Malden, MA: Blackwell.

Creider, S. (2013). The integration sequence: Responding to child initiations in a tu-toring session. Unpublished manuscript, Teachers College, Columbia University, New York.

Davidson, J. (1990). Modifications of invitations, offers and rejections. In G. Psathas (Ed.), *Interaction competence* (pp. 149–179). Washington, DC: University Press of America.

Dewey, J. (1920/2004). *Reconstruction in philosophy.* Mineola, NY: Dover.

Ford, C. E. (2004). Contingency and units in interaction. *Discourse Studies, 6*(1), 27–52.

Hayano, K. (2013). Question design in conversation. In J. Sidnell & T. Stivers (Eds.), *The handbook of conversation analysis* (pp. 395–414). Malden, MA: Wiley-Blackwell.

Jefferson, G. (1983). Notes on some orderliness of overlap onset. *Tilburg Papers in Language and Literature, 28*, 1–28.

Koshik, I. (2002a). A conversation analytic study of yes/no questions which convey reversed polarity assertions. *Journal of Pragmatics, 34*(12), 1851–1877.

Koshik, I. (2002b). Designedly incomplete utterances: A pedagogical practice for eliciting knowledge displays in error correction sequences. *Research on Language and Social Interaction, 35*(3): 277–310.

Larsen-Freeman, D., & Cameron, L. (2008). *Complex systems and applied linguis-tics.* Oxford, UK: Oxford University Press.

Pomerantz, A. (1986). Extreme case formulations: A way of legitimizing claims. *Human Studies*, 9, 219–229.

Reddington, E., & Waring, H.Z. (2015). Understanding the sequential resources for doing humor in the language classroom. *Humor: International Journal of Humor Research*, 28(1), 1–23.

Sacks, H. (1975). Everyone has to lie. In M. Sanches & B. Blount (Eds.), *Sociocultural dimensions of language use* (pp. 57–80). New York: Academic Press.

Schegloff, E.A. (1979). The relevance of repair to syntax-for-conversation. In T. Givon (Ed.), *Syntax and semantics 12: Discourse and syntax* (pp. 261–288). New York: Academic Press.

Schegloff, E.A. (1996). Issues of relevance for discourse analysis: Contingency in action, interaction and co-participant context. In E.H. Hovy & D. Scott (Eds.), *Computational and conversational discourse: Burning issues—an interdisciplinary account* (pp. 3–38). Heidelberg: Springer Verlag.

Shuy, R. (1991). Secretary Bennett's teaching: An argument for responsive teaching. In E. Eisner (Ed.), *The enlightened eye: Qualitative inquiry and the enhancement of educational practice* (pp. 135–149). New York: Macmillan.

Stremmel, A.J., & Fu, V.R. (1993). Teaching in the zone of proximal development: Implications for responsive teaching practice. *Child and Youth Care Forum*, 22(5), 337–350.

Tharp, R.G., & Gallimore, R. (1988). *Rousing minds to life: Teaching, learning, and schooling in social context*. New York: Cambridge University Press.

Thelen, E., & Smith, L.B. (1994). *A dynamic systems approach to the development of cognition and action*. Cambridge, MA: MIT Press.

Turner, V. (1967). *The forest of symbols: Aspects of Ndembu ritual*. Ithaca, NY: Cornell University Press.

van Lier, L. (1996). *Interaction in the language curriculum*. London: Longman Group Limited.

van Lier, L. (2004). *The ecology and semiotics of language learning: A sociocultural perspective*. Norwell, MA: Kluwer Academic Publishers.

Vygotsky, L.S. (1978). *Mind in society: The development of higher psychological processes*. Cambridge, MA: Harvard University Press.

Waring, H.Z. (2012). Yes-no questions that convey a critical stance in the language classroom. *Language and Education*, 26(5), 451–469.

Waring, H.Z. (2013a). Managing competing voices in the language classroom. *Discourse Processes*, 50(5), 316–338.

Waring, H.Z. (2013b). 'How was your weekend?': Developing the interactional competence in managing routine inquiries. *Language Awareness*, 22(1), 1–16.

Waring, H.Z. (2014). Mentor invitation for reflection in post-observation conferences. *Applied Linguistics Review*, 5(1), 99–123.

Waring, H.Z. (2015). Promoting self-discovery in the language classroom. *International Review of Applied Linguistics in Language Teaching (IRAL)*, 53(1), 61–85.

Waring, H.Z., & Hruska, B. (2011). Getting and keeping Nora on board: A novice elementary ESOL student teacher's practices for lesson engagement. *Linguistics and Education*, 22, 441–455.

Waring, H.Z., & Hruska, B. (2012). Problematic directives in pedagogical interaction. *Linguistics and Education*, 23, 289–300.

Wood, D., Bruner, J.S., & Ross, G. (1976). The role of tutoring in problem solving. *Journal of Child Psychology and Psychiatry*, 17, 89–100.

7 Competence, Complexity, and Contingency
An Embodied Theory

In their book *How to Build Social Science Theories*, Shoemaker, Tankard, and Lasorsa (2004) write, "[a] theory is simply one's understanding of how things work" (p. 6). In the preceding chapters, I have offered my understanding of how things work in pedagogical interaction, and in particular, what it means to be doing teaching. This understanding is my theory of teaching and, more precisely, my *embodied theory of teaching*. As an embodied theory, it unites the generalities and the particularities. While its generalities are sustained by realities across a broad range of pedagogical contexts, its particularities are rendered manifest in the situated undertakings made accessible by the CA microscope. By presenting this theory then, I am offering not just what pedagogical interaction entails for the teacher at an abstract level but also what it looks like to engage in such interaction in real time.

Notably, I have not offered a theory built around variables and hypotheses (e.g., teacher responsiveness leads to student learning). My understanding of how the pedagogical world works is a theory of a different kind—one that concerns itself more with building or transforming understanding (with or without specifying causal relationships). Indeed, one might find an implicit causal relationship in statements such as *achieving competence entails assuming competence*, but the robustness of the statement does not rest on the constant testing and revising that define scientific theory (Shoemaker, Tankard, & Lasorsa, 2004) in their traditional sense. The testing and revising are, instead, embedded in the microanalyses of each case that accumulatively and collectively render the statement tenable. As such, the three principles of pedagogical interaction have been tested, revised, and remain revisable with further analytical endeavors.

1. COMPETENCE: ACHIEVING COMPETENCE ENTAILS ASSUMING COMPETENCE

The principle of competence describes, paradoxically, an overall ethos or an important stance the teacher must take to establish the foundation for learner development. In Bakhurst's (1991) words, "treating children as if they had abilities they do not yet possess is a necessary condition of the development of those abilities" (p. 67). As demonstrated in Chapter 4, looking competence is indeed a participant concern whether it is in the ESL classrooms, writing center, graduate seminar, or post-observation conference. Learners across contexts defend their competence as they resist critique, foreground success, and project the image of hardworking, independent, and knowledgeable co-participants. Such learner behavior can be dismissed easily as irrelevant, subversive, presumptuous, or even delusional. Yet, the tutor, the teacher, the mentor, and the professor in my data recognize the centrality of competence in learner development and embody such recognition as they validate learner contributions, favor learner potentials, and neutralize asymmetries. They do so by referencing learner talk and ratifying diverging or playful learner initiatives, highlighting the success of learner performance, giving voice to the less vocal, claiming co-membership, and positioning the learner as professional. With great care and skill, they convey the messages of *I see you, I hear you, and I'm not better than you.* In so doing, they treat the learners as valuable contributors, discerning consumers, and equal partners. Although taking such a stance is not a direct path to learning, it can, for example, facilitate open reflections during a post-observation conference, where such reflection is key to teacher development. Upholding the principle of competence, in other words, is integral to enabling the possibility of learning. It builds the playground where learning can potentially flourish.

2.   COMPLEXITY: TEACHER TALK IS MULTIVOCALIC

While the principle of competence lays down the foundation for profitable pedagogical interaction, the principle of complexity draws attention to the potential tensions inhabiting that interaction—a tension best expressed in the notion of multivocality, a quality of teacher talk that has not yet, to my knowledge, been adequately attended to by scholars and practitioners alike. As detailed in Chapter 5, teacher talk is a locus for multiple voices. These voices can work against each other to frustrate the learning process when explicit positive assessments convey case closed, when UC questions invite consent to move on, and when elicitations breed confusion and reek of assessment. The voices also can be carefully calibrated to balance such competing demands as maintaining the necessary control on the one hand and building rapport, promoting participation, and respecting learner voices on the other. The teachers and tutors in my exhibits neutralize such centripetal and centrifugal forces by tweaking the sequential structure of classroom talk to accommodate conversational matters, by appropriating potentially derailing or subversive learner talk in such a way that preserves their agendas, and by exercising control implicitly and lightheartedly. *May, you have many voices,* for example, serves as a reminder of the turn-taking rule while preserving a friendly stance through humor. Insofar as these conflicting or competing voices are dialogically interrelated, multivocality becomes a resource when the dialectical tensions are neutralized (as in *May, you have many voices.*) and an impediment when the balance is tipped in the direction of control (as in *Any questions?*). Multivocality is, therefore, both a liability and an asset of teacher talk, and this understanding is a crucial one. It opens up a space for reexamining our routine practices and their potential pitfalls. At the same time, it awakens us to the remarkable resourcefulness of teacher talk fueled by the very glory of multivocality. That resourcefulness may, after all, be multiplied. By bringing to the forefront of our consciousness the precarious terrains of pedagogical interaction, the principle of complexity cautions us to tread lightly and, at the same time, inspires us to improvise boldly.

3.   CONTINGENCY: TEACHING REQUIRES BEING RESPONSIVE TO THE MOMENT

While the principle of complexity unveils an aspect of teacher talk that features conflicts and competition, the principle of contingency directs our attention to an ideal quality of teacher talk—its responsiveness to an unfolding moment in pedagogical interaction, whether it is a moment of simultaneous happenings, unexpected directions, or spontaneous illusions. As portrayed in Chapter 6, the absence of responsiveness is not an unfamiliar scene in our pedagogical experiences, and such absence, as in the case of the unwavering deployment of the same question despite the lack of any uptake, can be draining, frustrating, and counterproductive. Being responsive, on the other hand, is no small feat, although expert teachers exercise such responsiveness with great ease as they deftly address the simultaneity of the moment, adjust to the shifting demands of the moment, and preserve the integrity of the moment. The mentor, the teacher, and the tutors in my exhibits know how, and precisely when, to protect the space of a struggling answerer without dismissing an enthusiastic volunteer, to yield to a child's initiative without abandoning the larger pedagogical focus, and to move the lesson forward without disturbing the organic world of the moment. To a certain extent then, being responsive to the moment also involves maneuvering the delicate balance between the centripetal and centrifugal forces of control and connection. One might even argue that it simply highlights an alternative view angle of the same phenomenon, hence the inevitable overlap between complexity and contingency. What the principle of contingency brings into relief, however, is a potentially infinite number of emerging moments in pedagogical encounters that are outside the bounds of planning and prediction and the teacher's in-flight navigation of such moments with multitasking, constant adjusting, and minimal disturbance. Insofar as no pedagogical agenda can be carried out unilaterally, attending to the contingencies of these moments is not ancillary but integral to completing the very task of teaching.

Shoemaker, Tankard, and Lasorsa (2004) put forth three criteria for assessing the usefulness of a theory. For these scholars, a useful theory summarizes knowledge, informs practice, and guides research. The three principles of pedagogical interaction clearly crystallize the knowledge gained from years of extensive analytical work on pedagogical interaction. Can such knowledge also inform practice and guide research? I believe they can. By offering a version of pedagogical interaction from my particular viewfinder, I also have offered a guide to look or a way of seeing: practitioners are invited to notice and appreciate the specific relevancies of competence, complexity, and contingency. Recognizing the importance of learners' competence displays may encourage a tendency to recruit competence as a resource rather than reject it as a nuisance. Understanding the multivocalic pitfalls and potentials of teacher talk may promote a sense of mindfulness about the routine choices one makes and inspire greater creativity to neutralize the dialectical tensions that pervade teaching and learning. Accepting the reality of teaching as responding to a series of emerging moments rather than implementing a prepackaged plan may foster a readiness to listen and the acumen to adapt—a pathway to dialogic teaching that ultimately enables the possibility of learning.

Aside from offering a guide to look or a way of seeing that has the potential to transform behavior, the body of evidence that begets the three principles of pedagogical interaction constitutes a treasure trove of a guide of a different sort—of how precisely behavior may be transformed. Such evidence make it possible to view these principles not merely as academic ideals but as actionable undertakings as well. In lieu of receiving a bullet-point list of how-to advice in the abstract, we are invited to a viewing of how the principles of competence, complexity, and contingency are incarnated in the precise conduct of expert teachers—millisecond by millisecond and frame by frame in the lively contexts of actual interaction. It is one thing, for example, to recognize the importance of assuming competence or even to be told that such assuming can be done via validating learner contributions, favoring learning potentials, and neutralizing asymmetries but quite another to observe how the mentor carefully builds his/her noticing on the preservice teacher's own attention to an issue, allows for a second to pass, and launches a yes-or-no question that positions the latter as a professional with a game plan to observe how he/she then adds an increment to allow for an extra opportunity for the teacher to respond when his/her response is not immediately forthcoming and, finally, to observe how he/she admits to being "a little bit" "off his/her game" and proceeds to produce an account *as* a professional. The CA detailing of how competence is assumed, how complexity is exploited, and how contingency is coped with makes available some much-needed authentic modeling for meeting the manifold challenges of teaching. Because the numerous exhibits are presented as entirely native to, rather than removed from, their local sequential contexts, we are afforded a type of modeling that is richly textured and, by extension, of greater use as the more information one has of the specific context in which a specific practice is deployed, the better prepared one would be to assess whether and to what extent that same practice may be viably translated into one's own pedagogical context and, further, to think creatively about what adaptations may be in store to render such translation possible. Ultimately, I hope that this embodied theory of pedagogical interaction can usefully enter the national conversation on strengthening professional development and promoting clinically rich teacher preparation.

In addition to informing practice, the three principles of pedagogical interaction also can guide research as they invite fortification and falsification. Confined by my individual world as a researcher, I have by no means exhausted the repertoire of practices that embody each principle. I imagine the terrain for further expeditions is vast and unending; numerous practices await discovering and elucidating—with different theoretical lenses, analytical tools, and empirical settings. Continuing investigations will no doubt further substantiate these principles—or not. After all, such principles may be falsified as well. It remains to be seen, for example, whether assuming competence can in fact obviate its development or whether disregarding the moment can in fact create a more expedient path to learning.

I am acutely aware of my limitation of having captured only a slice of reality in the world of pedagogical interaction, constrained by the particular data sets within my access as well as my particular investigative tool—the lens of CA. On a different level, however, in a profoundly Bakhtinian sense, my voice is filled with echoes and reverberations of those of my intellectual predecessors: Vygotsky, Tharp and Gallimore, van Lier, Larsen-Freeman and Cameron, and unescapably, Bakhtin. As noted in earlier chapters, assuming competence is akin to allowing children to behave as if they were a head taller in the Vygotskyan (1978) sense of play, and it is not unlike assuming something to be the case before it has been encountered in van Lier's (2004) interpretation of prolepsis as he draws upon Bakhtin, Rommetveit, and others. For these thinkers, the importance of play and prolepsis is unmistakable: play creates the zone of proximal development (ZPD), and prolepsis allows for greater contingency that benefits language learning. The complexity of teacher talk as embodied in its dialectical multivocality, on the other hand, evokes instant allusions to the Bakhtinian concepts of "heteroglossia," "hybridation," and "double-voiced discourse," as well as the nonlinear interrelatedness so prominently featured in the ecology of language learning (van Lier, 2004) and complexity theory (Larsen-Freeman & Cameron, 2008). Finally, managing the contingencies of pedagogical interaction is analogous to the soft assembling required for adapting to an open and emerging system as elucidated in complexity theory. It also harkens back to the central task of offering tailored assistance within the ZPD in sociocultural theory along with its various incarnations such as responsive teaching (Shuy, 1986), instructional conversation (Tharp & Gallimore, 1988), and conversational teaching (van Lier, 2004). In a sense then, I simply have joined the chorus of thinkers whose refrain has always revolved around the profoundly social and dynamic nature of teaching and learning.

Despite these myriad echoes and reverberations, I hope that my voice still matters—because of its very origin in the raw and messy particulars of pedagogical interaction, because of the specificity and analyzability it brings to such important concepts as prolepsis and assistance, because of its illumination of previously unattended to dimensions of pedagogical interaction such as multivocality or heteroglossia, and last but not least, because it makes evident, unequivocally, that what great thinkers hold in high regard (as in the case of play and prolepsis) lies at the heart of participant concerns as well. In short, what I have offered or have intended to offer in the preceding pages comes directly from the front lines of pedagogical interaction—with all of its chaos, intensity, and liveliness, amid which I have found great inspirations, and I hope the reader will, too.

REFERENCES

Bakhurst, D. (1991). *Consciousness and revolution in Soviet philosophy*. Cambridge, UK: Cambridge University Press.

Larsen-Freeman, D., & Cameron, L. (2008). *Complex systems and applied linguistics*. Oxford, UK: Oxford University Press.

Shoemaker, P.J., Tankard, J.W., & Lasorsa, D.L. (2004). *How to build social science theories*. Thousand Oaks, CA: Sage.

Shuy, R.W. (1986). Secretary Bennett's teaching: An argument for responsive teaching. *Teaching and Teacher Education*, 2(4), 315–323.

Tharp, R.G., & Gallimore, R. (1988). *Rousing minds to life: Teaching, learning, and schooling in social context*. New York: Cambridge University Press.

van Lier, L. (2004). *The ecology and semiotics of language learning: A sociocultural perspective*. Norwell, MA: Kluwer Academic Publishers.

Vygotsky, L.S. (1978). *Mind in society: The development of higher psychological processes*. Cambridge, MA: Harvard University Press.

Appendix
Conversation Analysis Transcription Notations

(.)	untimed perceptible silence
(number)	length of silence in seconds
<u>underline</u>	stress
CAPS	very emphatic stress
↑	high pitch on word
↓	low pitch on word
.	sentence-final falling intonation
?	yes-or-no question rising intonation
,	phrase-final intonation (more to come)
-	a glottal stop or abrupt cutting off of sound
:	lengthened vowel sound (extra colons indicate greater lengthening)
=	latch
◊	highlights point of analysis
[]	overlapped talk
°soft°	spoken softly or decreased volume
> <	increased speed
(words)	uncertain transcription
(syl syl)	number of syllables in uncertain transcription
.hhh	inbreath
$words$	spoken in a smiley voice
((*words*))	comments on background, skipped talk, or nonverbal behavior
{((*words*))-words}	dash to indicate co-occurrence of nonverbal behavior and verbal elements; curly brackets to mark the beginning and ending of such co-occurrence if necessary
T	teacher
L	unidentified learner
LL	learners

Index

dialogic teaching 38–9, 40, 149; *see also* responsiveness
dispreferred action 62
Duff, P. 35–6

educational psychology 32–4
Edwards, D. 5, 18–19, 107
EFL classroom 27, 32, 35–6, 38; *see also* L2 classroom interaction
elicitations 15–6; pitfalls of 104–10, 147; *see also* IRF, questions
embedding conversation in IRF 111–3
Erickson, F. 33
ethnomethodology 2, 45, 46, 47
exploratory talk 4, 18, 19; presentational talk versus 18, 40
extreme case formulation 114, 139

Faneslow, J. F. 25
favoring learner potentials 79–80
feedback 26, 27, 39, 53; *see also* assessments, IRF
Foster, M. 33–4

Gallimore, R. 5–6, 134, 137, 142–4, 151
Garfinkel, H. 2, 45
giving voice to the less vocal 82–5; *see also* favoring learner potentials
Goffman, E. 2, 45
Goodwin, C. 3
Goodwin, M. H. 51
graduate seminar interaction 62–5, 74–7, 80
grounded theory 47
Gumperz, J. J. 33
Gutiérrez, A. G. 39
Gutiérrez, K. 29–30, 32

Hall, J. K. 37, 52
Hanrahan, M. U. 31
Have, P. ten 47, 54
He, A. 36
Heath, S. B. 20–1, 33
Hellermann, J. 3
Heritage, J. 102
heteroglossia 95, 118–19, 150–1
highlighting success 80–2; *see also* favoring learner potentials
humor: teacher use of 116–7, 118; student use of 79; *see also* play

institutional frame: alluding to 116–7
instructional conversation 24, 142, 151; *see also* conversational teaching

interactional competence 45; in a second language 3
IRF sequence 14–15, 19, 24, 26, 27, 29, 31, 35, 38, 53, 111–13

Jarvis, J. 38–9
Jefferson, G. 45, 46, 52

Kasper, G. 2, 3, 54
Kleifgen, J. 25–6
Koole, T. 53
Koschmann, T. 52, 53
Koshik, I. 124
Kumaravadivelu, B. 29

L2 classroom interaction 27, 51, 52, 53–4; *see also* EFL classroom
language socialization 20; study of classroom discourse 35–8
Larsen-Freeman, D. 2, 119, 141, 150
learner initiatives 54, 55: teacher responses to 77–9, 91, 113–17, 128, 137–9
Lee, Y.-A. 53
Lemke, J. 16–17, 33
Lier, L. van 24–5, 33, 92, 110, 123, 142–3, 150, 151

Macbeth, D. 51, 52, 54
Markee, N. 2, 3, 53–4
McCarty, T. L. 34
McHoul, A. W. 46–7, 51–2
Mehan, H. 10, 15–16, 48, 54, 110
Mercer, N. 5, 18–19, 107
Michaels, S. 32–3
Morita, N. 36, 37
multiple-*yeahs* 63–5
multivocality of teacher talk 8–9, 147–8; as impediment 96–110; as resource 110–17

neutralizing asymmetry 85–91

Ochs, E. 20, 35, 38
Ohta, A. S. 39
ordinary conversation 2, 15, 118, 142
Oyler, C. 34

participant orientation: as analytic focus 2, 16, 45, 46, 50–1, 54–5; to learning 54–5
play 91–2, 138–9, 150; language 28; *see also* humor
Pomerantz, A. 48–9
Poole, D. 35

CPSIA information can be obtained
at www.ICGtesting.com
Printed in the USA
FSHW01n1514080818
51194FS